TRANSATLANTIC MIGRATION

TRANSATLANTIC MIGRATION

The Contemporary American Novel in France

by Thelma M. Smith and
Ward L. Miner

DUKE UNIVERSITY PRESS | 1955

To
the Memory of
T. R. M.

PREFACE

IN THIS BOOK we have undertaken a study of the reception of the contemporary American novel in France. Both of us are students of American literature, not French, and inevitably certain limitations result from this, though there are advantages, too. The chief limitation will no doubt be found in our treatment of the problem of influence on French writers. Saying that one author has influenced another is frequently dubious, and so we have included in Chapter V only what we have found said by French critics or by the writers themselves. This chapter is therefore quantitative, not qualitative. We hope that what we have written will be of some use to those who make the individual qualitative studies. Our aim has been to tell the interested reader something of the extent of this influence and no more.

A word of warning on the sales figures which we have included. Any agent or almost any author, either French or American, can tell much about the difficulties involved in trying to get accurate sales figures from French publishers. Some of these difficulties result from a certain tradition: the relation between writers and publishers is that of gentlemen fostering the creative arts—financial discussions are to be avoided. Such a tradition dies hard in France. Another cause for the hesitancy of publishers to furnish exact figures is poor bookkeeping. All too frequently the French publisher is not too sure himself what exact sales have been. A final cause lies in the problem of income tax. The sales figures given may therefore be what the publisher wants the government to know. All this results in the probability that sales figures are low. We are presenting representative sales when we have secured them, but they should be taken with some scepticism.

Certain comparative figures may prove helpful to the reader. We were told that except for *The Grapes of Wrath* (120,000) and *For Whom the Bell Tolls* (200,-000) none of the books by any of our five men has sold more than 30,000 copies. Also we were told that 3,000 to 4,000 copies of a first novel by an unknown author is a usual printing. The average Prix Goncourt novel sells between 80,000 and 120,000.

A study such as this inevitably results from the willing co-operation of many people. To the French writers, critics, agents, and editors whose conversations have helped us so much we say a warm thank you. We remember the patience of the staff of the Bibliothèque nationale faced with our problems day after day for a year and a half. Particular appreciation goes to the staff of the office of the cultural attaché at the American Embassy in Paris for assistance and suggestions. It is a pleasure to express our gratitude to Mme Felicia Andersen, who patiently strove to make adequate our knowledge of the French language and answered our many questions concerning French literature and life. For help in verifying translations we wish to thank Mrs. Patricia Bennett, research assistant in the Mutual Security Agency in Paris. Miss Ruth McBirney, librarian of the American Library in Paris, freely gave us information concerning that institution. Professor Gaston Berger, the general secretary of the Commission Franco-Américaine d'Echanges Universitaires, kindly verified what we wrote on French universities and the Fulbright program. Finally, we are indeed grateful to the American Council of Learned Societies for the grant which made possible this study.

THELMA M. SMITH
WARD L. MINER

November, 1953

CONTENTS

	PREFACE	vii
I.	FRANCE	3
II.	DISCOVERIES	15
III.	ENTHUSIASMS	27
IV.	REACTIONS	45
V.	INFLUENCES	61
VI.	STYLE AMERICAIN	69
VII.	DOS PASSOS	87
VIII.	HEMINGWAY	99
IX.	FAULKNER	122
X.	CALDWELL	146
XI.	STEINBECK	161
XII.	FRANCE-AMERICA	179
	CHECK LIST	193
	INDEX	247

TRANSATLANTIC MIGRATION

1. FRANCE

FRANCE—for some people it is the land where the food talks only to the chef and the chef talks only to God. For others it is the land blessed by the vineyards of Chambertin, Montrachet, and Romanée-Conti. For some it is the land of the chateaux along the Loire, along the Dordogne, or nights on the beaches of the Riviera. Yet for every American there is some aspect of Paris which is part of his France—perhaps the *Grands Boulevards* and the Champs-Elysées, the shops along the Rue du Faubourg St. Honoré, perhaps the Latin Quarter, or the galleries and art museums, or perhaps even the Bibliothèque nationale.

Not only is there the France of the tourist, but there is the France of the Frenchman. He bothers little about either Montmartre or Montparnasse, though he probably knows the Impressionist painters. The cafés of St. Germain-des-Prés are for him frequently a source of jokes, not of ideas. Like most of us, no matter what our country, he spends his day earning a living. Unlike the average American, he will have relaxed for two hours over his noon meal and another two over his evening meal. For the French, eating is an important sensual entertainment. The epicure finds another sensual pleasure in the great French wines, but the average worker is content with his liter bottle of *vin ordinaire,* and that is drunk, not sipped.

Similarities, differences—we could go on listing and counterlisting. Each thing named brings back memories for us of play, of work; of delights, of drudgery. It takes all these, and much more, to make France. Yet we keep remembering the tide at Biarritz, the prehistoric cave of Lascaux, the vine-covered slopes of the Hermitage vineyards, the trimmed trees along canals, the flamboyant splendor of the roof of Chambord, the voluptuousness of the fountains at Versailles, the gemlike beauty of Sainte-Chapelle, and the play of lights on the fountain of the Place de la Concorde. Our memories return to Paris, because Paris is part and parcel of our France, too.

And so it is for the French. The American thinks of Broadway and plays, of Hollywood and movies, of Chicago and wheat, of New Orleans and cotton, of Philadelphia and its symphony orchestra, of Rochester and its clinics, of Washington and politics. In France, Broadway, Hollywood, Chicago, New Orleans, Philadelphia, Rochester, Washington are all rolled into one—Paris. To Paris the Frenchman comes to work, play, study, think, drink, eat, and make love. Is this strength, or is it weakness? Both. The intellectual and aesthetic stimulus of Paris is a strength. The intellectual and aesthetic dependence of the provinces upon Paris is a weakness. There are exceptions, of course. Alsace, Brittany, the Basque country—each struggles to keep its cultural entity. Yet Paris also enchants these sturdy independents.

What is this thing called Paris? It is the "city of light," and it is the city of streets deserted by eleven o'clock in the evening. It is the most feminine city in the world, boldly flaunting its eternal love affair with the Seine, whose waters continually caress the twin breasts of Paris—the Ile de la Cité and the Ile St. Louis. Yet the physical beauty of Paris is gray, cold, and rather forbidding on first glance, because Paris is first masculine and then becomes feminine as the onlooker steeps himself into the city. It is a city whose suburbs are downright ugly, whose parks delight even the maids pushing the baby carriages. It is a city where drivers drive as though the hounds of hell were howling against their spines; yet it is the city of leisurely strolling on a Sunday afternoon or of visiting a museum or the latest exposition in the Grand Palais.

Paris is also a work-a-day world. Frenchmen labor with their bottle of wine nearby. The housewife must shop three times a day since refrigeration is a dreamed-of luxury. Only 17 per cent of the apartments and houses of Paris have bathtubs. Within the city 500,000 people live in hotels because there are no apartments to be found. Priorities are granted to newlyweds and couples with large families. For 100,000 families these priorities cannot be claimed; there are no available apartments. And 186,000 people live in flats long since condemned as unsanitary. Even where they exist, French plumbing and heating are never to be depended on. Paris—the city of light.

The money of France goes to Paris and so do the writers. We in America say that New York is our financial capital; but is it our literary capital? Not all our writers live in New York, nor even in Hollywood for that matter. There are a good many places in-between. And something of the same thing is true for publishers. Most of the general trade publishers have New York as their headquarters, but there are Little, Brown and Houghton Mifflin in Boston, Lippincott in Philadelphia, Bobbs-Merrill in Indianapolis, and the various university presses scattered all over. Paris—all the leading publishers operate out of the metropolis and just about all the writers live and work in Paris, even those who write regional books. What goes on in Parisian intellectual circles is what goes on in France.

About a week before Christmas, 1952, we were at the annual book sale of the Paris PEN Club held in the Hôtel Rothschild, one of those beautiful eighteenth-century *hôtels* seemingly numberless in Paris. The sale, for charity, occupied three enormous rooms. Along the walls were tables where were seated some fifty or sixty of the best-known writers of France. Above each writer's head was a placard with his name. On the tables were copies of his books to be autographed for the buyers. What caught our attention was the contrast. We in the United States have the custom of individual authors signing copies of their books in book stores, but never have we gotten together most of our well-known writers in one room to have them autograph their books. At great expense and trouble it could be done, of course, but we were intrigued by the relative ease with which it was done in Paris. The recent winners of the four leading literary prizes were there, so was François Mauriac, fresh from receiving the Nobel Prize, and so were such people as Jules Romains and André Maurois. And there are several of these sales each year, particularly in the pre-Christmas season.

Because writers can see each other every day or so in Paris, they have frequent opportunities to talk over their literary problems. Coteries, cliques are inevitably formed. The literary historian often calls these coteries of writers literary schools and discusses at great length the influences of one writer of the group upon another. And French literary historians love to do this. Part of the intangible quality called Gallic is a love of categorizing. French writers and French life may lend themselves to more-or-less neat pigeonholes, but the rub comes when the French mind, limited by its own logicality, is faced with the sprawling fact of America.

The problem of this book is the impact of the contemporary American novel upon the French mind. Before we can begin to discuss the American novel in France, we must delve a bit into the preconceptions, the prejudices, understandable enough, of the French mind. The human mind meets a new situation by evaluating the new in terms of previously known situations and old ideas. Like amoebas we seek to engulf the new by sticking out the pseudopodia of our old ideas and prejudices. Education tries to enlarge our reservoir of ideas and thereby reduce the strangeness of new situations. Imagination, in its ultimate sense, is the ability to grasp the new in terms of new principles, new modes of conduct, and so on. This ultimate imagination is an ideal one, and no human beings are ideal. And the French critic shares with the rest of the world the limitations of being human. But he is also French, and his limitations are going to result from a set of Baconian idols of the mind different from those of his American colleague. The experience of the French critic has been that writers fit into literary schools. That is one of the pseudopodia he is going to stick out in trying to comprehend a new literature or a foreign literature.

This tendency of the French to categorize has been called part of their Cartesian heritage. But Descartes started his method by doubting before he said to himself, "Cogito ergo sum." The doubting preceded the categorizing. Today the French tend to categorize and then look around to see if it is necessary to doubt. In a way Descartes the mathematician is more typically French than Descartes the doubter. Though it may well be a matter of analogy, not origin, we can understand

French logicality and love of categorizing better if we think of the totality of the seventeenth and eighteenth centuries instead of the individual Descartes. As indicative symbols from the *grand siècle,* picture the harmony of a garden designed by Le Nôtre, the balancing of details in the façade of the Hôtel des Invalides, the satire of Molière against personalities discordant in his society. From the eighteenth century think of the efforts of Diderot to engulf within one encyclopedia all of human knowledge, the attempts by the Académie Française to standardize and purify the French language. The French mind is much more the child of the Enlightenment than it is the child of Descartes. (It would be possible to say that the Enlightenment was the child of Descartes, but one could also say that Descartes was the child of medieval scholasticism, and then there is Aristotle. One must stop somewhere, and here we have stopped with the Enlightenment.) The milieu of the seventeenth and eighteenth centuries did more to produce the French mind of today than did the ideas themselves of that period. Comprehend Pascal and we understand Pascal; comprehend the Port Royal milieu and we understand something that is France.

An obvious statement, and yet so obvious that its importance may be overlooked, is that the French are primarily reading American novels in translation. This is not the place for a detailed study of the relation of translations to the originals or the weaknesses inevitable in depending upon translations for knowledge. But the existence of the problem demands that we discuss it. The first thing that the observer is faced with is the differences between the American (and with the contemporary American novel it is particularly American, not

English) and French literary languages. An easy generalization is that French prose (with relief we avoid all discussion of poetry) translates into American more easily than vice versa. Why? One reason is the size of the French vocabulary compared with the American. Another and more important reason is the difference in kind of vocabulary. Though there are many exceptions, particularly since World War II, most French novels are written in rather formal French. Contrast this kind of vocabulary with that used by most American novelists since 1900. Almost all have written a quite colloquial language frequently including slang, street argot, and whatnot. Such intensely idiomatic words and phrases do not translate well into any other language, especially into such a precise language as literary French.

Yet another difficulty is the translator himself. France is not unique in regarding translation as a kind of hackwork. Certain big-name translators are paid well, but the run-of-the-mill translator in France averages a little less than fifty cents a page for his work. Since this chore is so poorly paid, not always is the publisher going to get the right man for the right book. Many of the translators working with highly colloquial American have never been to the United States, and their knowledge of the language is pretty well dependent upon what they learned in the lycée and what they can con out of a dictionary. As a result ludicrous errors—ludicrous from the point of view of an American—occur. Two examples will illustrate this. In a recent novel the *I* of CIO was translated *internationale*. And in the posthumous novel by Sinclair Lewis there is the following sentence: "Roxanna Eldritch—Roxy—had been a friend of Caprice, as fond as she of gin-rummy. . . ." The translator had her addicted to gin and rum: "Roxanna Eldritch—Roxy—

avait été une amie de Caprice, aussi férue qu'elle de rhum au gin. . . ."

The translator of American into French is faced not only with the problem of the constant changes in American speech, but also with the changes that are occurring in French itself, particularly since the war. Even the French Academy has accepted such a word as *cocktail* into its listings. The older translators who grew up under Gide and Proust omit such new expressions from their work, and the result is inevitably weaker because of the omission.

All this is not to say that there are not many good translations. Faulkner's *Le Bruit et la Fureur* is one. Professor Maurice E. Coindreau, who did the translation, is the source for the following story, which brings out some of the difficulties in going from one language to another, and also well illustrates Faulkner's rigid control over his material and his precise awareness of what he is attempting to do. Coindreau talked with Faulkner about the problems involved several times during the summer of 1937. One trouble was the pronouns. The English language has no grammatical gender and therefore an *it* may have a very vague reference. Every time the translator asked the novelist what his reference was Faulkner answered the question specifically. The result of this collaboration is a good translation of one of Faulkner's novels most difficult to render into another language.

Because American novels must be translated, there is an inevitable time lag between the appearance of a book in America and in France. Some of this lag is easily explainable by the time involved in arranging for a translation, making the translation, and getting it in print. But there is also a cultural lag. For how many Americans is the picture of the court of Louis XIV more vivid than that of France today? A statement by a Frenchman, Pierre de Lanux, gives the other side of the coin:

In my childhood, we believed the United States still peopled with redskins (it was a little the fault of Buffalo Bill). In 1917, we believed it a nation of vulgar merchants, incapable of idealism, and pro-German (it was a little the fault of Hearst). In 1940, we hoped no more for its intervention in Europe (it was a little the fault of Coolidge and Hoover). In 1946, we discovered its immaturity, at the same moment in which the United States begins finally to emerge from it. Each time we adopt an image at the moment when it becomes false.

In other words, there is always between two countries a cultural lag of several years, particularly when there are three thousand miles of ocean and a McCarran-Walter Act in between.

What one country conceives of another as like may be determined by little things more than big ones. An all too familiar story shows how impressions are formed. One day we were in the Baccarat sales and display rooms. On raised platforms above the tables are masterpieces of glass made by Baccarat over its history and here displayed. None, of course, are for sale. Suddenly we heard a strident American female voice, "How much is that setting?" The woman was pointing to an array of crystal wine glasses, goblets—a complete service made in the nineteenth century for a foreign embassy in Paris. The casual conversational hubbub of a sales room died down enough that we could hear the quiet voice of the clerk reply, "I'm sorry, madame, but that is not for sale as you can see from the placard." Several Americans in the room cringed when the loud voice burst out with, "Oh, come now, I know anything can be bought if I offer enough. What's the price here?" The woman did not get her crystal, but several Frenchmen got their impression of Americans. Many, if not most, Europeans think of

Americans as loud-mouthed and interested only in money. Because this clamorous voice so well fitted into these preconceptions, a hundred other Americans will have a hard time to remove the impression created by this one.

Preconceptions, prejudices—all are mixed up in the following newspaper story. In December, 1947, Caldwell and Steinbeck, both visiting France, were interviewed by Paris journalists. Julien Sans, in *Climats,* reported that he and his confreres were horrified when Caldwell replied to the question, "What would you like to see in Paris?" with the query, "Is there a good boxing match tonight?" And what was even less understandable, Caldwell refused, very politely, but refused to talk about his books. The same paper reported:

Steinbeck fut proprement ivre-mort de son arrivée à son départ. Alcools, guitares, braillements et ronflements, il joua avec quelques amis une scène vécue de Tortilla Flat; les quelques visiteurs horrifiés n'eurent d'autre consolation que d'entendre, dans la chambre voisine, les hurlements de Madame, folle de whiskey.

It is necessary to say a little about the French novel since 1900 so that the events narrated in the chapters which follow can be placed in their context. Though it is an oversimplification, it can be said that the dominant type of French novel between 1900 and 1939 was the novel of psychological analysis as exemplified by Proust and Gide. The naturalists of the latter nineteenth century had been most interested in the external world about them. Then the inevitable reaction occurred, and the external world was almost ignored. The most frequent standard of literary judgment was how well something was said. What was said was nearly neglected.

Foreign novels had some influence during this period. Between 1900 and 1914 there was a great deal of French interest in the Russian novel, and no doubt the interest in Dostoevski helped push the then young novelists away from the exterior world of the naturalists into the interior world of Proust. And because England and France are so close to each other, there has always been considerable cultural interchange. After World War I the dominant foreign literary influence was from England. James Joyce and Virginia Woolf were widely read and talked about in French intellectual circles. Their influence served to abet the already present tendency toward the novel of psychological analysis.

Much of the story that is to be unraveled in this book is the supplanting of the English novel by the American. Why this took place only in the novel and not with other literary forms is an open question, but the fact remains. That American poetry would have had little influence in France is not surprising because of the difficulty of translation, although it must be admitted that Poe and Whitman have had some influence, particularly Poe, sometimes regarded as more French than American. In drama only O'Neill has had an extensive presentation on the Paris stage. Since the war Tennessee Williams and Arthur Miller have attracted considerable attention, but nothing comparable to that given dozens of American novelists.

The story we are attempting to unfold in this book is the vogue in France of the contemporary American novel. We hope we can help the reader to see when, how, and why this vogue grew. We cannot answer all the questions but we can make suggestions, and the reader will draw some of his own conclusions. Though the fundamental purpose has been to see what has happened to the contemporary American novel in France, we have let the French define for us the Americans they were and are most interested in: Faulkner, Hemingway, Steinbeck, Dos Passos, and Caldwell. And so we have concentrated our story on them.

2. DISCOVERIES

WHERE BEGIN the story of the growth of the vogue for reading American novels in France? At the end of World War I perhaps. Then the cultivated Frenchman would have known Emerson, Poe, Whitman, and Twain, to a certain extent Thoreau and Hawthorne, something of the philosophy of William James. He was beginning to hear the names of Jack London, Theodore Dreiser. But the great public still held fast to its notions about America. America—country of the eccentric millionaire, of the cowboy, of Uncle Sam whose pockets were lined with gold.

However, even this great public would soon have its picture of America influenced by reading at least a few American novels. Between 1918 and 1929 an amazing total of twenty books by Jack London were translated. Dreiser's only book to appear in French in this decade was *Twelve Men*, 1923. Sherwood Anderson fared better —in 1924 *The Triumph of the Egg*, 1925 *Winesburg, Ohio*, 1926 *Horses and Men*, 1928 *The Story Teller's Story*, 1929 *Notebook, 1926*. Four books by Upton Sinclair appeared. In 1925 *One Man's Initiation*, Dos Passos, was translated by Marc Freeman and sold perhaps 3,000 copies but made seemingly little impression. Three years later, however, *Manhattan Transfer* was published and picked up at least nine reviews—and excited ones. The young Ernest Hemingway in 1923 had seen published in English in Paris 300 copies of *Three Stories and Ten Poems* and the following year *in our time* in an edition of 170 copies. Of much more importance to the French reading public was his volume of six short stories entitled *Cinquante mille Dollars* which appeared in 1928 and called forth nine enthusiastic notices.

Straws in the wind, perhaps. Louis Bromfield in March of 1927 could still write for the *Bibliothèque Universelle* with truth that Americans know European letters much better than Europeans know the American literary scene. He summarized the European interest: Jack London, whom he called third-rate; Upton Sinclair, a propagator of eccentric ideas; and James Oliver Curwood. Only a handful of American books have been translated—one Willa Cather, one Scott Fitzgerald, one or two Sinclair Lewis, three or four Edith Wharton, one Sherwood Anderson and perhaps two or three others which he had not managed to discover in his vagabonding. And Bromfield went on to complain, somewhat justly, that Europe was getting its entire idea of America from the movies and the newspapers.

A month later an *enquête* in *Cahiers du Sud* confirmed Bromfield's criticisms. This special issue of the magazine was entitled "L'Enquête sur les littératures étrangères en France." Two questions were asked of critics, translators, and writers; and thirty-eight replies were printed. The questions were: "Do you think that the literatures familiar to you are exactly and sufficiently known, in their content and form, by their translations in French? If not, what are, in your opinion, the works or the authors, old or modern, we ignore, we translate insufficiently or badly, but we should know?" Among those replying was Fernand Baldensperger, who complained that the French had not gone beyond Selma Lagerlöf in Swedish literature or Jack London in American. Louis Fabulet, a translator of Thoreau and Whitman, replied by asking, "Who knows anything in France of transcendentalism? Still untranslated is *Moby Dick,* one of the greatest books ever conceived by the human mind." Eugene Jolas, of *transition* fame, said that France knew Stewart Edward White and James Oliver Curwood, neither of whom represents the intelligence of the "psychic impulsion of modern America." Anderson was known a little but Dreiser only for a book of sketches, *Douzes Hommes.* Cather, Frank, Westcott, Hemingway, and Fitzgerald were all only superficially revealed to the French. Victor Llona wanted the French to learn more about Dreiser, particularly his *American Tragedy,* "which I am sure would take its place beside *War and Peace* and *Crime and Punishment.*" Frank Schoell also thought the French should know Dreiser and he added William Carlos Williams' *In the American Grain* as a book needing translation. Pointing up these remarks is the special issue of *La Revue Nouvelle* published in 1928 on "La Littérature étrangère contemporaine." The only American author—Sherwood Anderson.

But the decade of the thirties presents a different pattern. Now there are more than just straws in the wind. Sinclair Lewis's *Babbitt* appeared in March, 1930, and within a few months sold 80,000 copies. Lewis was awarded the Nobel Prize that same year, and between then and the outbreak of war no fewer than fourteen of his books were translated into French. He far outstripped in popularity any other American novelist except Jack London, whose translations for this ten-year period numbered fifteen. (London still sells well in the bookshops in working-class neighborhoods.) Pearl Buck was a slow second with nine translations to her credit. Bromfield and Upton Sinclair tied for third place—each had seven. Faulkner followed with six. Dreiser in the first four years of the decade had three translations and Anderson two, but interest in these men was supplanted by (among the critics certainly if not with the wide reading public) a growing taste for the new. In 1945 one critic, André Molitor, looking back upon the period between the two wars, wrote:

The young American literature was carving a way for itself. We read Lewis, Dreiser, who were criticizing on a somewhat superficial level life in the United States, using the traditional technique of the realistic novel. Then began to appear in the windows of our bookshops translations of new writers: Faulkner, Steinbeck, Caldwell. And these men astonished us. Strange, upsetting novels written in a new manner, considering American life in a new way. We decided that certain American novelists had reached the age of reflection and were recognizing a profound spiritual and moral crisis. This crisis they were expressing with an unequaled brutality, rawness, and vigor.

Of *les cinq grands,* as the French have come to consider Faulkner, Dos Passos, Hemingway, Steinbeck, and Caldwell, Hemingway continued to be translated: *A Farewell to Arms* 1932, *The Sun Also Rises* 1933, *The Green Hills of Africa* 1937, and *Death in the Afternoon* 1938. Dos Passos also: *The 42nd Parallel* 1933, *In All Countries* 1936, and *1919* 1937. But Faulkner's rapid rise to fame in France is perhaps the most interesting story of all. By 1933 Coindreau had translated *As I Lay Dying* and Valery Larbaud had written a preface. Raimbault and Delgove were working on *Sanctuary.* André Malraux's enthusiasm for the American writer made him decide to write a preface for the first Faulkner novel to appear in France. He wrote it for *Sanctuary.* So that was the first to come out—the year was 1933—and in 1934 *As I Lay Dying* appeared, 1935 *Light in August,* 1937 *Sartoris,* 1938 *The Sound and the Fury,* and 1939 *These 13.* Erskine Caldwell was first printed in 1936, *God's*

Little Acre. Tobacco Road followed the next year and *We Are the Living* the year after that. Steinbeck appeared with *Of Mice and Men* in 1939 and Gallimard managed to get *In Dubious Battle* out April 7, 1940, a few weeks before the German occupation of Paris.

And obviously a growing number of Frenchmen were reading American novels in English—buying the American editions occasionally, more often the cheaper English editions, or the paper-bound Crosby Continental Editions. This series began in 1932 in Paris, selling for twelve francs a volume, sixteen francs for a double volume. It was a new collection of English and American books complementing Tauchnitz and Albatross. A critic writing in the *Revue Anglo-Américaine* welcomed the new venture, pointing out the boldness in choice of titles, the good quality of the paper and printing. The first two volumes reviewed were *Sanctuary* and Hemingway's *In Our Time.*

Most French critics agree that there was decided confusion concerning the American novel during all this period. In the preface to his book, *Le Roman américain au XXe Siècle,* Jean Simon summarizes: "We can't ignore these American writers, we said to ourselves, and then read with an almost complete lack of critical judgment and discernment. We made best sellers of such books as *Gentlemen Prefer Blondes* and *Show Boat.* We attributed genius to Bromfield, and mixed up Melville, Upton Sinclair, Sinclair Lewis, Tarkington, Hawthorne, London, Hemingway in a frightful 'Irish stew.' "

To a certain extent the confusion, and clearly the growth in general interest, are illustrated in the *Nouvelles Littéraires,* a literary weekly of prestige and popularity. A search through the issues published in 1931 revealed only two articles on American literature, one on Whitman and the other on American novelists. In 1933 we found an article on Alfred Kreymborg, a biographical sketch of Upton Sinclair, a short story by O. Henry, and reviews of the following books: *Expression in America* (Lewisohn), *Americans Abroad* (anthology of expatriate writers), *A Hoosier Holiday* and *An American Tragedy* (Dreiser), two books by Vicki Baum, *Operas and Plays* and *Autobiography of Alice B. Toklas* (Stein). By 1937 considerably more space was given to American literature. There were short stories by Saroyan, Hemingway, O'Hara (2), Tom Kromer, Kay Boyle (2), Bromfield; reviews of books by Kay Boyle, Melville, Bromfield, and of Brodin's *Le Roman régionaliste américain*; articles on Hemingway, Dos Passos (2), Pearl Buck; and, finally, excerpts from *1919* and *Green Hills of Africa*.

Among the intellectuals there was no doubt of the importance of this writing coming from across the sea. Léon Lemonnier bluntly avowed in a special edition of *Cahiers de Paris* (1939), "Le Roman contemporain aux Etats-Unis," that American literature "est actuellement l'une des grandes littératures mondiales." Looking back, Thierry Maulnier wrote: "Faulkner, Hemingway, Steinbeck, the tragic naturalism of the American novelists had started to awaken powerful echoes in France before 1939." And Jean Paul Sartre:

The greatest literary development in France between 1929 and 1939 was the discovery of Faulkner, Dos Passos, Hemingway, Caldwell, Steinbeck. . . . [T]hese authors have not had in France a popular success comparable to that of Sinclair Lewis. Their influence was far more restricted, but infinitely more profound. . . . To writers of my generation, the publication of *The 42nd Parallel, Light in August, A Farewell to Arms* evoked a revolution similar to the one produced fifteen years earlier in Europe by the *Ulysses* of James Joyce. . . . At once for thousands of young intellectuals, the American novel took its place, together with jazz and the movies, among the best of the importations from the United States. The large frescoes of Vidor joined with the passion and violence of *The Sound and the Fury* and *Sanctuary* to compose for us the face of the United States—a face tragic, cruel, sublime.

And the great old man, master of them all, Gide, spoke his approval from Algiers in 1943. "There is no contemporary literature which excites my interest more than that of young America." Malraux had insisted that he read Faulkner:

It took me some time, I admit, to get used to him whom I consider today as one of the most important, the most important perhaps, of that new constellation. But the one who has given me the greatest satisfaction is Steinbeck. As for Dos Passos, I have more admiration for him than delight in him. I feel that the framework shows through; his pointillism wearies me, even when most successful; and I see in his intrepid modernism the forecast of an early dating.

After reading through Dos Passos, Gide finds himself unable to group together his impressions, but he is dominated by the book while he is reading it. Speaking again of Steinbeck, he admits he prefers *In Dubious Battle* to *The Grapes of Wrath,* for he feels that the former presents in a clear light one of the most urgent and agonizing of social questions. "But Steinbeck, to my mind, has written nothing more perfect, more accomplished, than certain of the short stories gathered together under the title *The Long Valley.* They are equal to or surpass the most moving stories of Chekhov." Hemingway, especially in *A Farewell to Arms,* shows a sensitivity penetrated with intelligence. When asked about Caldwell, Gide replied, "He bothers me. He escapes from the classifications and theories I make for myself; what I have said of the others does not apply very well to him, and I praise him for this. But where Caldwell rejoins the others is in the interest that he takes in life." And again, in writing of the novelist most French critics place at the top, he said, "Of puritan heritage, Faulkner in particular is essentially and powerfully, in the plain sense of the word, a 'protestant.'" Then Gide concluded: "These new American authors are all, like children, drawn by the present instant, by the now, far from books, exempt from the ratiocinations, from the preoccupations, from the remorse which dull our old world; and that is why going to them can be for us very profitable, for us who are weighed down by a too rich past."

Other American novelists besides these five came in for their share of praise also. One critic asked his readers, "Qu'est-ce qu'un roman? une histoire, ou bien des histoires. Et un grand roman? l'Histoire. Parce qu'ils ont fait revivre à jamais une époque, leurs spectateurs et leurs acteurs, Erich Maria Remarque, Barbusse, Sinclair Lewis, Pearl Buck sont de grands romanciers." Another writer reviewing the years before the war declaimed:

The years of the thirties were in fact an American decade and it was surprising to see the same works appreciated simultaneously in Moscow, in Paris, in Berlin, and in Buenos Aires. The greatest successes in the book stores were *The Good Earth, Anthony Adverse, Northwest Passage, Gone with the Wind,* and *Grapes of Wrath.* Americans had the occasion once more to be astonished at how a literature such as *Gone with the Wind* or the works of James Cain which they considered chiefly commercial was winning the respect of intellectual Europeans.

Margaret Mitchell and Steinbeck bring us to the war years. *Gone with the Wind* had been published by Gallimard in 1939 and had sold 100,000 copies before the occupation. (Since 1945 sales have topped the million mark and this book remains the twentieth-century best seller in France. Even today it sells and widely—in the expensive de luxe binding as well as paper covered.) In 1940 the Germans passed a law prohibiting the sale or translation of any books from the Allied countries. That meant all books in the English language published after 1870, though America was at the moment still neutral. Immediately a black market in American and English books sprang up. *Gone with the Wind* had been priced at 55 francs. On the black market it sold for as much as 2500 francs. Many explanations have been given for the overwhelming popularity of this particular novel. Jean Simon has suggested that the French who read it during the somber days of enemy occupation recognized in the calamities of Georgia at war an astonishing prefiguration of the miseries of their own country. Contributing also to the book's popularity was the strong nostalgia for the United States, that paradise of liberty. Reading *Gone with the Wind* gave some a sense of belonging to a secret society. And it was an act of protest as well.

The reading of any American novel became a symbol of resistance. Certain French, although bored and perplexed by Faulkner, persisted in hunting for all his translations and confused this snobbism with more active resistance. One man recalled that on a day in 1943 a friend of his showed him five or six shelves filled with detective stories. "All are American," he confided triumphantly. "If the Germans knew that!"

The Germans tried to use pessimistic American books for propaganda purposes, Sartre recalled. They permitted publication of *In Dubious Battle,* he said (sales, more likely, since publication date for this book was April 7, 1940). The occupation forces offered Gallimard permission to print *The Grapes of Wrath,* but Gallimard refused. However, the book was later translated and published by a Belgian collaborator under the title *Grappes d' Amertume,* and the offices of the Franco-Germanic Institute were ready to flood the French market with this edition but were prevented by the American breakthrough in Normandy.

The enthusiasm in France for Steinbeck ran high. *Of Mice and Men* had come out in 1939, *In Dubious Battle* the next year. English and American editions of *The Grapes of Wrath* had some circulation during the war years. Then in February, 1944, during the occupation, *The Moon Is Down* was published clandestinely by Editions de Minuit under the title *Nuits Noires.* The translator was Mlle Y. Desvignes. About 1,000 copies were distributed, passed from hand to hand quietly and often fearfully, each copy read till it fell to pieces. It "seemed to us all like a message from fighting America to the European underground."

The year before, Editions Jean Marguerat in Lausanne had published a French translation of this book done by Marvède Fischer, slightly cut and altered, under the title *Nuits sans Lune.* After the liberation of Paris in August, 1944, Editions de Minuit reprinted *Nuits Noires* and within fifteen days sold out the entire printing of 5,000 copies. Realizing that here was a probable best seller, they prepared 60,000 copies to be sold at 50 francs apiece. Before these had been sewn or bound, Editions Marguerat objected, saying this publication was a violation of their translation rights. Attempts were made between the two publishers to come to some sort of understanding, but no agreement could be reached.

After the liberation *Nuits sans Lune* sold perhaps 1,000 copies in France. It was priced at 320 francs—too expensive for the Frenchman—and its unfamiliar title was a strong handicap. Editions de Minuit had made known *Nuits Noires,* and because of its clandestine publishing the prestige of this courageous press was naturally high. This prestige was signalized towards the end of 1944, when one of the literary prizes, Prix Femina, ordinarily given a single novel was awarded to Editions de Minuit for its clandestine activities in publishing 24 French books and *Nuits Noires* during the occupation. But in the end the 60,000 copies of Steinbeck's book had to be sold for scrap paper.

In 1944 also appeared Steinbeck's *Lâchez les Bombes!* published in the Overseas Editions and *Tortilla Flat,* brought out by Marguerat at Lausanne. It is hard to judge how widely any of these various translations of Steinbeck were read, but the evidence seems clear that though he was the latest of the "five greats" to appear on the French scene, he engendered a quick and lasting enthusiasm. Indication of this is found in the following story. Coindreau had begun his translation of *The Grapes of Wrath* before the war and had chosen to call it "Le Ciel en sa Fureur" from a line of *Animaux malades de la peste*: "Mal que le ciel en sa fureur." But during the long months of the war the French people had used the literal translation in speaking of the book and had fastened it so firmly that Coindreau and Marcel Duhamel (cotranslator) submitted. And we do know that as quickly as possible this new translation was made available to French readers. From May to December, 1946, it appeared serially in *Les Lettres Françaises,* a literary weekly, and was published in book form in early 1947. It sold 120,000 copies.

These are the facts and the figures. This is the history of the *entre-deux-guerres.* But what is behind this bare skeleton? Why did the French gradually but surely translate and read more and more the American novel?

Intangible and difficult though the answer is, there are certain possibilities. Curiosity first. The American soldier had been in France. Wilson and his ideals were warmly welcomed by the man in the street. American tourists arrived in ever-growing numbers. American movies, American jazz—the creative artistry of the Negro. Europe began to interest itself in the out-of-doors—a healthy mind in a healthy body—let us go camping, walking, bicycling. From Jack London and Curwood to Hemingway was not too difficult. And then the novel of satire appealed to the French who saw and disliked our sensational extravagances—the fortunes of the movie stars, the gangsters, the divorces, the flappers. Waldo Frank, Dreiser, Bromfield, and above all Sinclair Lewis denounced the emptiness and the mediocrity of American life. Came the depression. Men everywhere yearned for answers, for understanding, for knowledge about other men everywhere. And so we find a kind of preparation for the impact of Dos Passos, Hemingway, Faulkner, Caldwell, and Steinbeck as one after another they became known, and for the dozens, perhaps hundreds, of American novelists whose novels are in all the bookstores now.

3. ENTHUSIASMS

THE LIBERATION of Paris in August, 1944, determines the beginning of the postwar period in France. With Paris free, France felt free. And the collaborators began to seek ways of hiding their occupation activities. From Algiers the various little magazines that had been published there during the war quickly moved to Paris. Also from Algiers returned André Gide. From England and America other writers slowly came back. Life in Paris was still difficult but it did become French again.

Confusion was inevitable—France had to put up with both de Gaulle and the American soldiers. And the publishing situation was as confused as everything else. The pro-German publishing houses immediately disappeared. The magazine *NRF,* which had been collaborationist during the war under the editorship of Drieu la Rochèlle, was an unlamented casualty of the liberation. (It reappeared finally in January, 1953, as *La Nouvelle Nouvelle Revue Française.*) The *beurre-oeufs-fromage* men, as the Parisians called the wartime black marketeers, wanted to move from the neighborhood where they had lived and out of the trade where they were known. Some of them picked publishing as a respectable business to go into, and one in which they could quietly invest their newly won gains without attracting attention. What better way to establish their political respectability in the immediate postwar months than to publish American books, no matter by whom or how well translated. What was important was to have that phrase, "Traduit de l'Américain," on the cover. Paper was scarce and rationed by the government on a bonus system based on prewar sales. The b-o-f men had money to buy it on the black market.

But the paper situation was difficult for the courageous clandestine publishers, who now hoped that they might ride their prestige on to commercial success. All told there were enough new publishers to increase the number from five hundred (before the war) to fifteen hundred within a year after the liberation. And all these publishers seemed to want to publish American books. No wonder the small bookseller in the provinces, as well as his confrere in Paris, was confused and did not know what to make of the deluge, nor did the townspeople, who had always depended on him for advice.

Another part of the postwar story finds its origins in the actions of American publishers and literary agents during the war. Apparently assuming that the French were out of the picture indefinitely, they sold French translation rights helter-skelter to whoever came along. Swiss publishers—French, German, and Italian language —secured many of these rights. But before long the Swiss government passed a law saying that French-language publishers could publish only books in French, German in German, and Italian in Italian. Some of these French translation rights on American books were held by Swiss German-language publishers who now had something they could not use. They sold these rights to the Swiss French-language presses for little or nothing. The net result of this mix-up was that certain American books and authors got lost in the shuffle or never got the attention they would have gotten if published in France. The story of Steinbeck's *The Moon Is Down* illustrates this.

Much the same sort of thing happened to his *Tortilla Flat* published in Lausanne in 1944. There were few reviewers and few readers among the general public even though the clandestine press had made Steinbeck's name known all through France.

In many ways the story of the postwar vogue for the American novel starts in 1943 in Algiers. Here several magazines were being printed, some for the use of the French underground. In August, 1943, one of these, *Fontaine,* got out a special issue on American literature, "Ecrivains et Poètes des Etats-Unis." It was an anthology containing selections from the works of Hemingway, Steinbeck, Faulkner, and Caldwell, among others, and included remarks by Gide on the American novel. The magazine *Confluences* also got out a special issue, devoted this time to "Problèmes du Roman." Though the theme of the issue was the French novel, many of the contributors discussed the possible influence of the American novelists on the French. Typical of these remarks was that by Georges Simenon, who described the Americans as "perhaps the most authentic novelists of the moment." He went so far as to say that the American novels have been made into a literary school among the French.

As soon as Paris was liberated, these special issues, book size, were on the French market; the *Fontaine* was reprinted in 1945. And there were other special numbers of magazines. *L'Arbalète*—glossy, avant-garde—made of its autumn 1944 issue an anthology of selections from American novelists. During 1946 special numbers devoted to American literature and life were done by *Cahiers des Langues Modernes, Esprit, Renaissances,* and *Les Temps Modernes.*

And American books were pouring from the presses. Many of the books already translated were reissued. In London, Heinemann and Zsolnay had published a hastily done French translation of Hemingway's *For Whom the Bell Tolls* in early 1944 with a printing of 5,000 copies. This book, ready when it was for French distribution, hit the jackpot. Here are some figures on the printings: February 1945, 6,533 copies; May 1945, 8,146; July 1945, 10,105; February 1946, 7,964; June 1946, 8,103; October 1946, 9,734. By 1948 over 100,000 copies had been sold. In this year a new translation was made, and the new edition has sold over 60,000 copies (including 10,000 distributed by a book club) through the end of 1951.

So vast was the deluge that we have frequently seen and heard the statement made that in this immediate postwar era eight out of ten books sold in France were translated from the American. The total number of translations jumped from 190 in 1945 to 421 in 1946. The literary weekly *Carrefour* in January, 1947, canvassed the bookstores to determine the best sellers of the previous year. Leading the list of fiction was Koestler's *Darkness at Noon,* followed by Kathleen Winsor's *Forever Amber.* Fourth on the list was *Gone with the Wind.* The only French book among the first six was Vercors's *Le Silence de la Mer,* and that was sixth. The comment on the list was, "This inquiry leads to a certain number of reflections, notably on the disfavor of the public for the French novel; it is true that certain great French authors such as Mauriac, Collette, Montherlant, Aragon, etc. have not published novels in 1946." In this same year, nine different editions of the books of our five Americans were published in France, including the de luxe editions of *Tobacco Road* and *As I Lay Dying.*

Part of this postwar boom in the American novel is the winning of what we Americans call the lending-library trade, not that France has many lending libraries, but there does exist this type of book buyer and reader. The million-copy sales of *Gone with the Wind* has already been mentioned. There is no doubt but that the average man in the street in France has formed his picture of the American Civil War from either this book or its movie version, which as late as January, 1953, was running in four Paris theaters. In the nineteenth century *Uncle Tom's Cabin* was the most popular American book in Europe; for the twentieth it is Margaret Mitchell's novel. Similarly, *Forever Amber* has sold in the hundreds of thousands. Wallace Stegner's *The Big Rock Candy Mountain* is another big seller. Other authors still selling widely are Bromfield, Vicki Baum, Pearl Buck, and Frank G. Slaughter. Whether we think of it as a compliment or not, American books, and particularly those of the low-bosom school of historical fiction, have won an important place in the French market. Typical are the novels by Frank Yerby, and it should not be surprising to the American visitor to find the latest book by him featured in the windows of many French bookstores.

So far in this chapter we have been talking about the general publishing scene and sales. What of the French critics? Were they as excited as the average reader over the American novels? The answer is yes, beyond any doubt. The critics were raving over Faulkner, Caldwell, Steinbeck, Dos Passos, Hemingway, and they found space also for enthusiastic discussion of Wright, Saroyan, Henry Miller, and a score of others. Full-length studies on the American novel appeared, in 1946 those

31 | ENTHUSIASMS

by Maurice E. Coindreau and Pierre Brodin. Jean Pouillon's *Temps et Roman* devoted twenty pages each to Dos Passos and Faulkner. Anthologies of contemporary American prose appeared in 1947 and 1948. Claude Edmonde Magny in 1948 entitled her book on the contemporary American novel *L'Age du Roman américain*. And for France the period 1945 to 1948 was beyond any question the age of the American novel.

This postwar phenomenon, of course, must be thought of as a continuation and intensification of already existing trends. That the critics recognized this is clear:

The success of American literature, which could be easily seen before the war, has taken, since the liberation, an intensity nearly frenetic. The new novels of Faulkner, of Hemingway, of Caldwell are awaited with feverish impatience far beyond the crossroads of St. Germain-des-Près. The public is not alone in being swept off its feet. A whole school of young writers copy Dos Passos. Monsieur Jean Paul Sartre, while smoking his pipe, has given them his benediction, and all the adolescents who formerly looked to Gide, Montherlant or Malraux now turn their eyes towards Texas and Oklahoma.

St. Germain-des-Près raises that familiar problem, literary snobbism. What authors had the greatest snob value in postwar France? The answer is Sartre and *les cinq grands* Americans. Faulkner was deified by certain literary *chapelles*. And the difficulties inherent in his novels have helped maintain his snob appeal. But it may be a shock to American readers to find that Caldwell was and in a certain measure continues to be one of the prides and joys of the French avant-garde. Dos Passos has never gained the popular reading public and remains primarily a writer's writer for the French. The other two, Hemingway and Steinbeck, soon lost much of their snob appeal because they sold so well. But on the same high level the French critics at first placed many other American writers. Dashiell Hammett and James Cain were treated as Faulkner's equals. Armand Hoog called Henry Miller one of America's greatest writers, bracketing him with Steinbeck and Cain. He justified this judgment by a discussion of Miller's "global vision." Placing everyone who wrote American on the same high pedestal added to the confusion of the booksellers.

Henry Miller's name brings us to a *cause célèbre* in 1946 and 1947. Miller had been living in Paris during the 1930's and writing his *Tropics,* which he could not get published in the States, but did finally get printed in English in Paris. The French paid little attention to Miller until after the war. In 1946 *Black Spring* and both *Tropics* appeared in French editions. Many of the reviews were ecstatic in their praise, and frequently the Americans were taken over the coals for banning these works: "I believe the Americans most obtuse. They exert themselves to silence Henry Miller, not for rational reasons, but through horror and great fear before a picture of their manners which goes to the roots of the tragedy of humanity." Other critics just as violently reacted against his books. All would have remained a literary debate had it not been for the activities of M. Daniel Parker of the Cartel d'Action Sociale et Morale. He announced that he was going to bring suit against the publishers of Miller's books, Editions du Chêne and Gallimard, for publishing pornography. Quickly, in April, 1947, a committee for the defense of Henry Miller was formed by Mme Magny and Maurice Nadeau. Remembering the difficulties of Baudelaire and Flaubert, many prominent writers joined the committee, some confessing that they did so not because they liked Miller's works but because of the principle involved. The affair became a *succès de scandale*. No legal action was finally taken against Miller's books, but the name of Miller became familiar to French readers. Miller himself added to the discussion by writing an article in *Fontaine* on obscenity. French critics wrote on the lyricism of Miller. Many words went down the drain, but the conclusion of the "case of Henry Miller" was that his books continued to be printed and read.

It is pertinent to point out the omissions as well as the excesses of French enthusiasm. Strangely enough, Thomas Wolfe has been almost completely ignored. Except for the little read and critically unmentioned Swiss edition of *The Web and the Rock* in 1946, it was not until 1951 that a Wolfe novel was translated into French —*Of Time and the River*. Three years earlier a collection of short stories had appeared, but except for an infrequent article in the academic journals, the critics seem unaware of him. A partial explanation of this is Wolfe's expressed dislike of the French; Miller likes France and says so vociferously. James T. Farrell is another writer surprisingly little known in France. The Studs Lonigan trilogy is all that has been translated, with an eighteen-year lapse between the first and the third volumes and little enough critical comment. Other writers more understandably ignored are Willa Cather and Ellen Glasgow. In general, the realistic novel without the overtones of either naturalism or symbolism does not interest the present-day French reader.

The peak of the enthusiasm for the American novel was perhaps the year 1946. For in 1947 the inquiry in *Carrefour* showed that a French novel, Camus's *La Peste*, led the best sellers while Steinbeck's *The Grapes of Wrath* was sixth on the list. Of the first five, four were by French authors. And what is more important, the

French critics began to sort out in the American novel
the wheat from the chaff. Faulkner took his place as the
best of the Americans, in fact, frequently as the best in
the world. The publishers started to print early works
by the well-received Americans. In 1948 Faulkner's
Soldiers' Pay and *Mosquitoes* were published. Steinbeck's *The Pastures of Heaven* and Dos Passos's *Three
Soldiers* were released in the same year. Almost all of
Hemingway's short stories had been published with the
appearance in 1949 of *Paradis perdu,* his third collection in French. Caldwell's *Poor Fool* had come out as
early as 1945. These translations enabled the French
critics to see more clearly the work of these writers as a
whole. Their evaluations will be dealt with when our
five men are discussed separately, but we should recognize now what was going on in 1947 and 1948. The
books by Coindreau, Brodin, Magny, and Guyot and the
special numbers of various magazines all contributed
their share in this process of evaluation. Also there were
anthologies of American short stories. Particularly important was the one edited by the young Albert J.
Guérard in 1947, *Ecrit aux U.S.A.* Guérard stated in
the preface that he had specifically in mind to show the
French that there were other American writers besides
the hard-boiled, pessimistic ones. Also he wanted to
show the French that there was no "American school"
of writing, that the diversity of the country was reflected
in the diversity of the writing. Unfortunately the anthology seems not to have had a wide circulation. Robert Laffont, the publisher, told us that of 7,000 copies
printed only 3,300 were sold. The other 3,700 were re-
maindered to a Belgian book club.

Guérard was not the only one to inveigh against the
French critics and readers for their ignorance of the

American scene. Others were John Brown, Gilbert Sigaux, Raymond Las Vergnas, Coindreau. As early as
1945 Guérard described a conversation with Marcel Duhamel, whom he was trying to persuade to publish an
American novel outside the cult of violence. Duhamel's
reply was, "Not interested! But if you were to show me
something truly American, a new story of lynching."
Another kind of confusion is shown by Maurice Carisey's
reference to "le grand succès du livre de T. S. Elliot
[sic] 'mon dernier séjour à Paris.' "

This ignorance of America took many forms. One
was the kind already talked about—the lumping of all
American novelists into an *école américaine* and the believing that the writers of this "school" (Faulkner, Hemingway, Dos Passos, Steinbeck, and Caldwell) are American literature. Related to this was the idea held by
many that literature in America did not become American until Hemingway and Dos Passos broke away in the
1920's from the old traditions of writing. Raymond
Hauger insisted: "In 1924 the Americans had no *style*,
they did not even have an original language. Both were
borrowed from works grandiose and elegant, indeed gra-
cious, of certain English novelists. It is Hemingway who
taught the United States its own tongue." Even Coindreau in his book, *Aperçus de Littérature américaine*
1946, pushed back the beginnings of the American novel
only to 1900 and Dreiser.

The emphasis upon the novels of violence is seen
most dramatically in the story of the *Série Noire*. In 1946
Marcel Duhamel started the series under the banner of
the publishing house Gallimard, where it has continued
ever since. This series is devoted exclusively to the detective story, exclusively to the hard-boiled detective
story. Each month the publication schedule of *Série*

Noire calls for three books. By now over 150 have been published. The selling price today is 220 francs, about half to one-third the price of the ordinary novel. According to Monsieur Duhamel, still the director of the series, 90 per cent of the books are translated from the American. The English authors Peter Cheyney and James Hadley Chase are to be found here, but the French consider them Americans or at least writers in the *style américain*. Sales of these books is spectacular—40,000 up to 130,000 a title, the latter figure for a Cheyney volume. A Raymond Chandler novel will average about 50,000 copies. Besides those already mentioned, popular authors are W. H. Burnett, Horace MacCoy, James Cain, Dashiell Hammett, Raoul Whitfield, Don Tracy, P. J. Wolfson. So successful has this series been that other publishers have copied the formula. Between Duhamel's *Série Noire* and the other series, about twelve hard-boiled American detective stories are released each month to the French reading public.

The literary events of 1947 well illustrate the process of evaluation by the critics, in spite of the deluge of books in the *Série Noire* and its imitators. In February the club *Maintenant* held a series of lecture-debates on the subject, "For or against the American Novel." During January and February the newspaper *Combat* ran a series of interviews with prominent French writers, asking, "What do you think of American Literature?" A literary weekly, *Les Nouvelles Littéraires,* over the last three months of the year ran another series of interviews with various writers on the subject, "Is there a crisis in the French Novel?" And most of the replies were framed in terms of the American novel. As Albert Guérard has put it, what was most talked about in Paris in the years right after the war was the American novel and the philosophy of Sartre.

By 1948 the vogue had passed its peak. But the number of separate book publications of our five men since the war shows the high level of continued interest: 1945 —2; 1946—8; 1947—6; 1948—9; 1949—8; 1950—5; 1951 —4; 1952—7. Another full-length study, this one by Jean Simon, of *Le Roman américain au XXᵉ Siècle* appeared in 1950. And in this same year Gilbert Gadoffre gathered together a group of critics and writers at Royaumont for a series of talks and discussions on the American novel. Professor Jean Jacques Mayoux spoke on the concept of time in the novels of Stein, Hemingway, and Faulkner. One critic in commenting on the conference as a whole said, "Faulkner was put in the hall of fame beside Balzac and Dostoevski."

The persistence of the vogue is seen too in the articles, "Les traductions," which appear in the annual *Almanach des Lettres*. These volumes are published in December and give a résumé of the preceding year from September to September. Concerning 1949 we find, "Anglo-Saxon literature, and in particular American literature, remains, this year still, the center of interest." For 1950, "American literature, if it has lost its preponderant and even exclusive influence, has not yet ceased to astonish us by its richness and its diversity." A year later, "American literature occupies always the first place [among translations] in numbers, and it offers us the opportunity of tasting its immense possibilities, but it is equally certain that it astonishes us less than it did about fifteen years ago, and that we are accustomed to its technical prowess, to its *dépaysement* and to its violence." And for 1952, "From the point of view of number, American translations always occupy the first place."

Why this tremendous interest in the American novel? A ground swell, hardly noticeable from the shore, began at the end of World War I. Slowly the wave built up through the thirties. It crashed with huge force, flying spray, and loud noise immediately after World War II. The war itself with its ban on American novels was obviously the first reason for the force. The French were hungry for what had been forbidden them. They were insatiably curious over what had been occurring in those long bitter years cut off as they were from the rest of the world. "Before the war," one writer admitted, "a Frenchman could forget America and the Americans and live as if Christopher Columbus had never sailed. But the war has narrowed the Atlantic. Today it is necessary to know this immense country *qui coiffe le monde,* and those millions of people who inhabit it." And indeed the French were in love with the liberators. They felt a respect for the enormous and powerful nation across the sea and a warmth and devotion for the man who symbolized it—Franklin Delano Roosevelt. They were seeking—the young especially—a new message, and there was a *cristallisation New-York* as there was a *cristallisation Moscou.* They felt a relation must exist between the economic and political power of the United States and its *rayonnement artistique.* And they admitted bitterly that France, the heart of the universe, held now a less important role in the world scene, going so far as to say, "There is a sort of inferiority complex of the French intelligence faced with the all-powerful American."

A second group of reasons for the vogue belongs under the general heading of escape. Just as the cultivated bourgeoisie and marquises of the eighteenth century had read of the noble savage and oriental idyls, the postwar French reader turned to the American novel as a source of *dépaysement*. He expressed in this reading a sort of distaste for his world, for his miserable corner, a desire for literary escape which corresponded to a real desire for emigration frequently. Or perhaps the American novel astonished him without delighting or pleasing him, thereby reinforcing his long-held feeling of superiority. He felt a most natural sense of pleasure when he discovered from his reading that America was not all a land flowing with milk and honey. Every American did not live in a penthouse as he had been led to believe by American movies. Both the elite and the great public thus were won over—those who searched through novels for the most pointed and complete *conscience de leur époque* and those who merely wished to be amused and distracted. If both essential functions of the novelist's art had been assumed in France, generally speaking, between 1918 and 1939 by books such as Pierre Benoit's *L'Atlantide* or Malraux's *La Condition humaine,* after the war they were taken over by *Gone with the Wind* or Bromfield's *Monsoon* on the one hand and by Faulkner's *Sanctuary* or Kafka's *The Castle* on the other.

Third, the French critics and the novelists themselves agreed that the French novel had become too much concerned with a bloodless, overrefined psychological analysis. The great French tradition had been a moralistic literature. Balzac and Zola belong in this tradition, as do the between-the-wars writers—even Gide and Montherlant. But now this seemed insufficient to the young French writer. "In France the author takes his subject from on high and judges. Christian moralist, naturalistic moralist, immoralist, the point of view changes, the approach is the same. But there are dangers in this when the world is upset. Who would deny the sublime beauty of Pascal's message? But how can one use it in a time which has produced Buchenwald and the atom bomb?" questioned Charles de Peyret-Chappuis. "For a long time we have been denouncing the excess of intellectualism in our novels—a too mechanical play of passions. Our writers analyze, explain, define—descending into a labyrinth which exists only under their pens," Alexandre Astruc wrote. And Simone de Beauvoir felt that the French language was becoming an end in itself, entirely academic, and that French literature as written by Gide, Valery, Giraudoux was far too abstract. Nadeau added, "Our present literature, it is necessary to admit it without pleasure but as a matter of fact, has ceased to interest."

France had lost the revolutionary, the violent, the critical in her literature. Sartre insisted, "The success of Faulkner, Hemingway, Dos Passos was the defensive reflex of a literature which, feeling itself menaced because its techniques and its myths no longer permitted it to face the actual situation, grafted on itself foreign methods in order to fulfil its function in dealing with the problems placed before it." Many French novelists agreed with Sartre that the simultaneity of Dos Passos, which tried to get at the American reality, was valuable for them too. They sensed that no longer was it the individual who was the essential, as he had been for Flaubert, Proust. Now it was much more important to express the social interactions rather than indulge in psychological analyses. Or perhaps better, the writer should place these analyses in a much larger cadre, since all men are *hommes-dans-le-monde*.

The *enquête* in *Nouvelles Littéraires* brought replies from some thirty French novelists, mostly the young generation. To the question, "Is there a crisis in the French novel?" they replied emphatically, "Yes." Each gave his reasons—stressing what has already here been suggested, adding occasionally a complaint. Robert Morel said perhaps the crisis is the fault of the bookseller who does not push the new French novelists. The booksellers "sont avec le public bien pensant de droite et de gauche. Ils préfèrent le chewing-gum." Jeanine Delpech suggested the French novel needs enriching from foreign and exotic sources. Jean Jacques Gautier, though far from wanting to model the French novel on the American (he said the malady the French novel is suffering from comes from journalism and the adoption of *des tics américains*), also complained that the French novel lacks something. It no longer does what it used to do— tell a story. Françoise d'Eaubonne said that the French novelist is writing for himself alone, turning away from the public. While the French reader throws himself upon translations, the novelist turns his back "and continues to measure to the millimeter his navel and the parts adjacent to it. . . . The most authoritative French writers chant on two immutable notes—eroticism and philosophic despair." Half a dozen agreed that today too many French novelists are professors. They are too intellectual. There are too many thesis novels and philosophic, social, moral essays. Marcel Aymé said of his fellow writers, "They believe they can replace thinking by logic, observation by theory, action by moralizing." French novels are too often unsupportably pretentious, Marc Blancpain protested. Young writers write only for the critics, for certain critics. Joseph Delteil was more violent still. "Le roman français m'a bien l'air d'être la peau de chagrin . . . Ça file à l'anguille, ça f. . . . le camp."

The fourth category of reasons for the vogue of the American novel is attested to by an overwhelming number of writers who in dozens of articles puzzled over the influence of American literature, particularly the novel, in France. Granted all the foregoing explanations, to a greater or less degree, the final answer, they wrote, rests in qualities of the American novel itself. With some amazement the Old World learned that from the other side of the sea a "healthy and strong" literature was establishing itself. The reader found a full, rich content, a dynamism of thought and action. He called the American novel objective, impersonal. He found in it a hidden allegory and a nearness to Greek tragedy. He discovered it working with fresh, new material which had hardly been exploited. He sensed an atmosphere of freedom, a new method of recognizing and of feeling. Sartre wrote, "What fascinated us all really—petty bourgeois that we were, sons of peasants securely attached to the earth of our farms, intellectuals entrenched in Paris for life—was the constant flow of men across a whole continent, the exodus of an entire village to the orchards of California, the hopeless wanderings of the hero in *Light in August,* and of the uprooted people who drifted along at the mercy of the storms in *The 42nd Parallel,* the dark murderous fury which sometimes swept through an entire city, the blind and criminal love in the novels of James Cain."

And Sartre's name brings us to the existentialists, who found the world of the American novel to be the "absurd" world of their philosophy—to the extreme of calling even Steinbeck "un des pères de l'Eglise existentialiste." They believed that no one knew better than the

Americans how to make use of the novel to represent the modern condition of mankind—to express more forcefully, more sincerely, and more brutally the despair of our time.

The American novel, then, which has made the widest appeal in France is the pessimistic novel because that is the prevailing European mood. The French have found in our novel the sound and fury which characterize the absurd world in which they live.

4. REACTIONS

WHAT HAS JUST BEEN said about the vogue of the American novel in France in the immediate postwar years is not, of course, the whole story. It did not take long for the debate on the value of the contemporary novel to start. The translation of Caldwell's *Poor Fool* occasioned several adverse reviews. After calling the book bad, Jean Vagne asked if it were wise to continue without reflection to give to the American novel the highest place. Jeanine Delpech questioned the claims being made for symbolism in the American novel. Indirectly referring to Malraux's preface to *Sanctuary*, she said, "I doubt that certain authors of detective stories know the Greek myths that the enthusiastic critics discover in their works."

The debate over the merits of the American novel was full-blown by 1946. It was pointed out that the influx of American books represented the writing output of several years. So France inevitably looked bad in comparison. If the same period of time were taken for each country, France could oppose to the American books an equal number of valuable works. Various adverse criticisms were summed up by Blanchot:

Many good critics begin to complain about American literature; they judge it less original than it appeared at first; they esteem it of mediocre interest to a culture which has gone beyond naturalism for more than half a century; they mock the young writers who believe to be modern in imitating Faulkner, Dos Passos, or Steinbeck, since for the Americans themselves these novelists represent yesterday rather than tomorrow and, having become official glories, have lost the prestige of independent creators. To these remarks are added others: the technique of the American novel does not accord with our novelistic tradition; the American novel supposes the decline of art; it renders useless the variety of works and the diversity of artists since it loses itself in a brutal and dull monotony.

One of the most frequent charges placed against the enthusiasts for the Americans was that of snobbery. This was particularly directed against the existentialists. René Lalou in the midst of a review of Steinbeck's *The Long Valley* (which he liked) had this to say:

Frogs in the pond, watch out! Brave esthetes of Café de Flore, you who imagine yourselves to be off the last transatlantic boat by praising pell-mell the "young American novelists"—you must sing another tune. The most important literary movement in the United States today is the return to Henry James. But console yourselves, dear star-gazing snobs; you are no more ridiculous than certain editors.

Another complaint was that the new techniques of the Americans had come originally from the French themselves anyway. Therefore all the young French writer had to do was to read his own literature more carefully and he would find there what he needed. These techniques and their French antecedents were summarized by Gabriel d'Aubarède: (1) simultaneity of Dos Passos—from Jules Romains [ignoring Dos Passos's ten-year precedence]; (2) interior monologue—from Honoré d'Urfé, Chrétien de Troyes, and Valery Larbaud [usually French critics say that Edmond Dujardin invented the interior monologue]; (3) use of time in Faulkner—from Proust; (4) attacks against puritanism—from the influence of Flaubert, Maupassant, Zola.

Hoping to combat the influx of foreign novels, *Les Nouvelles Littéraires* in July, 1947, announced a prize of a million francs for the best French novel. This weekly newspaper said it wanted to re-establish the rightful pre-eminence of French writers. And in the same issue the paper asked its readers what fictional character they would most like to be and why. The character most frequently named—20 per cent of the votes—was Robinson Crusoe, not exactly a happy choice from the point of view of the editors.

Of more importance was the *enquête* conducted in *Combat* in January and February, 1947. The question asked was, "What do you think of American literature?" As would be expected the replies were mixed—dislike, indifference, approval. But a careful reading reveals the various attitudes of a number of established French writers. Many of them had by 1947 written a novel or two strongly influenced by the Americans. Already they were beginning to react against their earlier enthusiasm.

The series started on January 3; Jean Paul Sartre was interviewed. He contrasted France and the United States saying that the average American reads only the daily paper and the technical books of his trade. In France people read current books. The American influence on the French is not as important as it is said to be.

The next day's issue featured Louis René des Forêts. According to him, the American novel can perhaps deliver the French from a certain form of analysis which they have abused. But while profiting from the lesson, they should remain moralists. Much is said of the pernicious weight of the American novel on the French novel. But why fear the influence? It little matters that the technique is imported if the artist can subordinate it to his personal vision.

Georges Charensol compared Hemingway's *For Whom the Bell Tolls* with Stendhal's *The Red and the Black*. What Stendhal did for his decade Hemingway has done for his. Each novelist takes for his theme the problem of the relation of man and society, and this theme is the great theme of the novel. In Faulkner, Charensol continued, there is an integration of the universe and a cosmic anguish. He found it curious that the French "know only an anti-American literature, a literature of rebellion, coming from a people who appear to us, at a distance, to have a passive acceptance."

Jacques Lemarchand called American literature a blow of the fist, though asserting that he is French and writes French, and American novels seem foreign to him, even in translation. His somewhat random comments included: Stendhal said the same things Faulkner has, but under a more accessible form. Hemingway and Steinbeck I appreciate, but as phenomena exterior to my life. Because England is nearer, English literature can have a greater influence on French writers. The naïve admiration of the Americans for Zola is puerile. Henry Miller's books have no construction or cohesion. The public reads American novels, but is it going to understand America?

Alfred Rosmer talked mainly about the influence of the left-wing writers in America. He found that they have less influence there than in Europe. The average American, he said, reads only magazines and best sellers. Works purely literary will have a printing of only 5,000 copies. Even in Holland the corresponding figure is 10,000. Proletarian writers in America are likely to be Greenwich-village bohemians.

On January 17 Albert Camus, then on the staff of *Combat,* had his say. He suggested that Americans are surprised at the success of certain writers in France. Caldwell, for example, sells ten times as well in Paris as in New York. If Steinbeck is compared with Melville,

Camus continued, we can see that the universal
of nineteenth-century American literature has
placed by a magazine literature. There are two
tions for the success of contemporary Ameri
ture. One is a general taste for the efficacious and the
quick, now introduced into narrative technique. But the
real subject of literature is the interior life of man. Today man is described, not explained or interpreted. The
second explanation is the elementary nature of Steinbeck
and other Americans except Faulkner. They are universal at the level of the elementary. The American technique is excellent to describe a man without an interior
life, otherwise no. It has only distant rapports with art.
To understand why Americans write as they do, we must
comprehend commercialization, publicity techniques,
and best sellers. Just as Melville and Poe were unknown
to nineteenth-century America, so other good writers
may be lost in today's America. Hemingway's *For Whom
the Bell Tolls* is the book of a child beside Malraux's
L'Espoir. It is the introduction of a Metro-Goldwyn-
Mayer style into a prodigious Spanish adventure. Hollywood and Guernica do not go together. But Camus admits he is not completely hostile to American literature
because he finds evidence that America will go beyond
such things. The French must see the greatness of Melville and Hawthorne over Steinbeck and Caldwell; they
must remain calm.

Roger Caillois spoke of the American novel in France
as a fashion. Authors before Dos Passos have known that
people exist simultaneously. When Caillois reads works
using this technique, he wants to skip and follow the
story of each character. He feels in the American novel
a kind of anarchy coming perhaps from the convention
of violence. Only Steinbeck has a social sense. The

American novelists "de la 'N.R.F.' sont, certes très améri-cains, mais aussi très 'N.R.F.' "

André Bay called the American a man searching for his soul. Behind each great name in American literature can be placed the name of a great European: Dostoevski and Joyce behind Wolfe, Zola behind Frank Norris, Proust behind Henry James [sic]. Intellectually the message of the Americans remains poor. The morality of Faulkner is exactly that of Alfred de Vigny. The dominant virtue of the Americans is pathos. But the French are paralyzed by their past, and the American novel can help renew them. Modern French literature is one of abortion; modern American, one of rape.

For François Mauriac American literature is particularly Hemingway. His greatest book is *Death in the Afternoon*. *A Farewell to Arms*—a denuded art, the eloquence of simplicity. Hemingway makes him think of Tolstoi. *For Whom the Bell Tolls* has more of the novel in it than Malraux's *L'Espoir*. Sartre's novels present no characters; Caldwell makes his characters live. However, American writers lack grace. They have suppressed God but cannot replace Him. Their only tradition is the puritan.

Henri Parisot found that American literature (he has read Faulkner, Caldwell, Steinbeck, Hemingway, Miller) interests him very little. Too often the French reader is enchanted by the platitudes of an easy naturalism. America has no Kafka, Michaux, or Raymond Rousset. However if we consider that it took Poe fifty years to become known and Melville a hundred, perhaps we can hope for genius in America today. We cannot despair of art in a country that produces the prodigious gags of the Marx brothers.

Emile Henriot saw the contemporary American novel

as stemming from nineteenth-century naturalism, particularly Maupassant. Maupassant has influenced Hemingway especially. *For Whom the Bell Tolls* does not compare with Stendhal or Malraux. Hemingway writes in an American style no matter what his setting is. Before 1920 America was only an annex of Anglo-Saxon literature. The interest of today's Frenchman in the American novel is to be explained by his interest in the American man because of present world conditions. France has had a slow evolution in its literature. America, being a land of puritans, hurries and tries to force this development overnight. It is true that the French novel is too often weakened by abstractions acting as characters and that in the American novel the characters are seen directly. But once the novelty of Dos Passos's technique wears off, will he be remembered? What really matters is the individual writer facing his world.

Pierre François Caillé saw the success in America of *Gone with the Wind* and *Northwest Passage* as indicating a search for a past, since America has very little history. Dumas and Maupassant are the French writers most read in America. The desire of the Americans to treat only the exterior world deprives them of much. Their literature is basically amoral; for a literature to be great it must have a moral basis.

On February 17 Mme Claude Edmonde Magny said that Faulkner dominates the present period. His best three books are *Sanctuary, Light in August,* and *These 13.* Until 1917 American literature was provincial, quasi folkloric. The true beginning of American literature dates from 1920. The American novel is more metaphysical than social. It is a combination of *reportage* and poetry. Perhaps this *reportage* marks the great American influence on French writers.

Thierry Maulnier found Faulkner a pessimistic writer among a people in general optimistic. American writers express their opposition to the current optimism by a pessimism. There is the danger in France that the American novel will be the basis for a new conventionalism, a new academism.

Henry Poulaille, the last of the writers interviewed, called Whitman, Jack London, Upton Sinclair, and Dos Passos American literature. Except for these men Americans merely write for the movies. What Céline was to World War I, Miller is to World War II. Poulaille enjoys Upton Sinclair. Even if his style is poor, he has something to say. He is less boring than Dreiser. As for the rest, if the French want books well written, then they should stop all translations of American books.

Since 1947 there have continued to be reactions against the American novel. These criticisms hardly balance the eulogies, but they have appeared. For example, Robert Kanters in 1948 spoke of a "return to the novel in the French tradition." Over a year later Maulnier said, "The influence of the American novel appears today to decrease." Another critic talked about the fatigue and satiety of the French reader caused by the tremendous numbers of American novels which had appeared in the years since the liberation. Blanc-Dufour found three reasons for wanting fewer translations of American books. One, these translations deprive French authors of paper. Two, most of the American novels lack merit. Three, the invasion of the publishing scene by American books is only a prolongation on a cultural level of dollar imperialism. Looking back over 1951, Kanters again said hopefully that the French novel had returned to its older tradition of classicism. And in an article in the *Partisan Review*, May-June, 1952, Albert Camus reiterated in expanded form his original statement in the *Combat enquête*.

Though the critics during these recent years have made no particular point of it, no doubt one of the reasons for the leveling-off of the vogue is that the hard-boiled novels of the Americans have lost most of their shock value. By now the average French reader is familiar with the brutal subject matter of many American books and is no longer reading for sheer novelty. All considerations of literary merit aside, the exotic flavor of *God's Little Acre* had an impact not felt fifteen years later by the readers of *Episode in Palmetto*. The hard-boiled formula has been accepted in the *Série Noire,* but that does not prevent its lessened appeal outside the rigid conventions of the detective story.

Interesting commentary on the swing of the pendulum occurred in Jean Guehenno's review of the French translation of Hemingway's *The Old Man and the Sea*. Here the young French writers are criticized for not going beyond the American techniques—as Hemingway has done.

This book, justly speaking, rises above these hastily done novels, these "slices of life" which seize us only through their brutality, and those other novels, too clever, that are fabricated so often today, laden with artificial techniques, in which there is no more *time* under the pretext of making us feel time better, in which the characters ramble endlessly neither in dawn nor in twilight, in which the simultaneity struggles with the interior monologue, in which the scaffolding prevents us from seeing the building, in which chattering puppets, dressed in cast-off ideologies, "economically strong or feeble," take the place of what in the old language we called the rich and the poor. This technical and pretentious nonsense has misguided young novelists for the last ten years.

A kind of cycle has been completed when we find the French novelists criticized for their "American" techniques and an American writer praised for having gone beyond them.

Part of the French scene is the activities of the French Communist party, and this holds true for the literary scene as well. To understand the path of Communist criticism of American novels since the war, it is necessary to keep in mind constantly the political events of the period—the gradual separation of East and West, the cold war, the Korean war, and so on. We all know that today "Americanism" is the *bête noire* of Communist writers. How has the literary criticism of the French Communists reflected the changing political attitudes of the party?

The first thing to be said is that in the immediate postwar years there was no distinction between the criticism by the Communists and by the non-Communists. We have not separated one from the other. For example, Claude Roy writing in *Europe* in July, 1946, called Dos Passos the Balzac of the twentieth century, *U.S.A.* the most considerable novelistic work produced in America; Dos Passos perhaps the greatest Marxist novelist of the era, and his novel the American epic of dialectical materialism. The terminology varied but the praise was equally high.

In 1947 Ilya Ehrenburg, the Russian journalist, published his book on the United States, *Retour des Etats-Unis*. He bluntly said, "I place very high the American writers: Hemingway, Faulkner, Steinbeck, Caldwell, and others." The Americans are organic, he continued, while French writers suffer from too much abstraction. He has known several American writers, and in life as in their books they resemble immense trees with strong roots.

Late in 1947 the party line shifted. *L'Humanité* on October 24 published a lengthy article attacking American literature. Three themes were developed. First, American literature itself denounces America. Each book is a boomerang which returns to its source. Second, this literature is the exact reflection of the pessimism of the American man. Third, this pessimism is both a literary merchandise and a political weapon lowering the morale of the Europeans. French readers should not buy American books, but instead should read the healthy writings of Rabelais, Montaigne, Voltaire, Rimbaud, Eluard, and Aragon.

The attack on American writers was extended and amplified in a long article by Jean Kanapa in *Les Lettres Françaises*, February 5, 1948. Kanapa, whose writing mannerisms and blindnesses resemble Westbrook Pegler's, is frequently a hatchet boy for the Communists. His article deserves notice if only for its ludicrousness. He distinguished two American literatures—one represented by Howard Fast, the other by Henry Miller. Where is America? In the defecations of Miller or in the joys and struggles of the democratic America Fast writes about? Kanapa continued by attacking the publishing house Gallimard and its correspondent in the United States, Maurice Coindreau. These two have made a certain American literature important in France—the literature of Hemingway, Faulkner, Gertrude Stein, Caldwell, and Steinbeck. The works of Fast, Maltz, Sillen, and Langston Hughes have been ignored through devices of commercial dishonesty. Has not Gallimard made known in France American authors—even those unknown in America—who best serve the plans of reactionary French ideologies? The advocates of the literature of American rottenness say that the *Tropics* of Miller are published in Paris and forbidden in America and that their success in France is therefore not owing to American publishers or publication.

Miller est interdict aux U.S.A.? Bien sûr! Il est destiné à la consommation externe. Comme la bombe atomique. Article d'exportation. Pas besoin de Miller aux U.S.A.; il ne toucherait pas le "grand publique"; mieux vaut, là-bas, des recits d'espionnage sovietique ou des romans érotiques sans prétentions métaphysiques.

But in France Miller helps reinforce the morbid literature that the French reactionaries today think the best soporific for the French intellectuals. Miller's eroticism turns readers away from concrete and progressive action. This is how the diffusion in France serves American imperialism.

Kanapa went on knocking down straw men: another argument of the defenders in France of *la littérature de pourriture américaine* is that the works of Caldwell, Hemingway, and Faulkner are progressive, even revolutionary, since they describe the rottenness of American capitalistic society. The answer—what is revolutionary in America is not necessarily so in France. The French are today constructive revolutionaires; they no longer need despair. Despair, in fact, works against them. These writers perhaps play a useful role as negative critics in the United States; in France they play a cursed role as blockers of democratic action. And have these writers ever spoken for the American worker? In France there is a silence about Dreiser (the true pioneer of the American novel), Upton Sinclair, Sinclair Lewis, Whitman. Articles are written on Kenneth Patchen (the

Miller of poetry) but not on Carl Sandburg. In fact, it is nothing more or less than a literary assassination.

And Kanapa still: French publishers print Richard Wright, since under the pretext of defending the Negroes he today sabotages their cause. And renegades are always welcome. If you ask the Negro leaders in the U.S.A. what they think of Wright, they will reply that he is not one of them because in his works he seeks actually to stir up racial hatred between Negroes and whites. He represents Negroes as beasts, barbarians, and children. A little further on in this diatribe the critic complains that Clement Greenburg of the *Partisan Review,* an aggressively fascist magazine, wrote on American art in a recent issue of *Les Temps Modernes.* And, finally, Kanapa's peroration: Where or when in America could such a congress be held as was held in Russia in June, 1947? There philosophers from all countries discussed the *History of Western Philosophy* by Alexandrov. Where is freedom of discussion in America? What person in America could say what he thought of the banning of Fast's *Citizen Tom Paine?* The balance between America and Russia is *not* equal.

With the party line now determined we find in 1949 many attacks on the American novel. Hemingway was taken over the coals by Daix in *Les Lettres Françaises* of January 20 for his lies and deliberate falsification of the Spanish Civil War in *For Whom the Bell Tolls.* Claude Roy in *Action,* January 11, contrasted the decadent American novel with the healthy works written by young European progressives. *Les Lettres Françaises,* February 10, carried an article by Ehrenburg, who defined the attitude to be taken on Faulkner. He called the novelist a witness of the injustices in America. No more can be expected from him since his life has been limited to Mississippi. Faulkner's pessimism is the result not of a literary mode but of his having lived in that society and having known no other. *Nouvelle Critique* for July featured an exchange of student letters concerning Faulkner. One remarked that in France Faulkner is considered by the progressives as the "principal rampart of reactionary philosophy." Another criticized the novelist for his deformation of history and his calumnies on the carpetbaggers.

Renaud de Jouvenel, in *Europe* of March, 1949, stated that the real problems of American democracy had been touched on by Steinbeck and Caldwell but without real awareness. Richard Wright is more guilty still, for, far from being an accusation, his books seem to justify the contempt of the whites for the blacks. The writers of the twenties—Lewis, Sinclair, Dos Passos, Dreiser, and Anderson—had more truth and closeness to reality than is found in the drunks and degenerates of Steinbeck, Caldwell, and Wright. De Jouvenel gave for the benefit of his readers a bibliography on America:

On the birth of the American republic—
    Fast: *Citizen Tom Paine*
On the life of Negroes—
    Fast: *Freedom Road*
    Langston Hughes: *The Big Sea*
                       Sandy
On the Indian question—
    Fast: *The Last Frontier* (not translated into French)
On the birth of capitalism—
    Jack London: *The Iron Heel*
    Dreiser: *An American Tragedy*
    Lewis: *Babbitt*
    Bromfield: *A Modern Hero*
    Fast: *The American*
On the contemporary period—
    Fast: *Clarkton* (not translated into French)

Maltz: *The Subterranean Current*
Steinbeck: *The Grapes of Wrath*
Tom Kromer: *Waiting for Nothing*
William Floyd: *People versus Wall Street: A Mock Trial*
Sayers and Kahn: *The Plot against the Peace* (not translated into French)
Vladimir Pozner: *Les Etats-Désunis* (written in French)
Georges Magnane: *Le bon Lait d'Amérique* (written in French)
Horace MacCoy: *Shrouds Have No Pockets*
Budd Schulberg: *What Makes Sammy Run?*

Various statements in this same article by de Jouvenel, though not on literature, are interesting.

New Yorkers speak the most bastard language in America; it is deformed each day by Italianisms, Germanisms, Slavisms, etc. . . . San Francisco is another city of gangsters. . . . The American press is less independent than any other in the world. . . . America is racist, anti-Semitic. . . . In no democratic country is brutality as current, as natural. It is enough to see a football game to convince oneself of this.

Beginning in 1950 the omission of almost all reference to American literature in the Communist press is noticeable. Reviews were still given to new books by Fast and Maltz and occasionally to Frederick Prokosch, however. And Faulkner's winning the Nobel Prize caused *Les Lettres Françaises*, November 16, to continue the attack on him. The article referred to the one by Ehrenburg published almost two years before. This had shown Faulkner's "true significance." The critic added that Faulkner is a writer who in America was treated as a regionalist dealing only with Mississippi and almost ignored until Malraux and Drieu la Rochèlle and later the existentialists made of him a glory. Faulkner has peopled his works with degenerates, idiots, weaklings, and has caricatured Negroes.

The attack on Faulkner (that the Communists should

think it so necessary to continue to flay him is a tribute to the high esteem he is held in France) was pushed by Michel Denoreaz in the January, 1951, *Nouvelle Critique*. For him Faulkner is the novelist who represents and defends as a class the feudal bourgeoisie of the South. The recent decline in the works of Faulkner parallels the intellectual situation in Nazi Germany, from which not one work of merit remains. Thus, in this America which is the successor to Hitlerian Germany, Faulkner is silent. Or, if he speaks, it is to say a good word for fascism. On rereading his novels, Denoreaz discovers that *all* lead to fascism; they propagate the myth of the inferiority of the Negroes. By taking this position, "Faulkner helps powerfully to justify the colonial wars of the Yankee imperialists and to separate— especially this!—the American working class from its most useful allies in the struggle against war, misery, and fascism—the black Americans." It is only logical that "after the apologist for pederasty, André Gide, the academicians of the Nobel Prize have crowned William Faulkner, the prince of death and putrefaction."

The present-day attitude is revealed by Samuel Sillen in the November, 1952, *Démocratie Nouvelle*. Sillen treated Mickey Spillane as a typical American writer and discussed American characteristics as presented in Spillane's novels. Also he berated General Eisenhower for his alleged comment (when he became President of Columbia University) that he hadn't read a book for nine years. Sillen concluded that few books are read in America because only a standardized product can be published. And the American novel is thereby dismissed for all faithful Communists.

5. INFLUENCES

THE AMERICAN novel of the *entre-deux-guerres* has had influence in France—that much is clear. It has specifically influenced the technique and content of the contemporary French novel—that, too, is evident but the evidence here is as intangible as it is tangible. What follows then is a gathering together of a few of the statements French critics and French novelists themselves have made on this touchy question.

A general pattern of widespread influence emerges. In 1946 the director of one of the largest publishing houses in Paris said that seven out of ten French novelists who submitted manuscripts to him had borrowed something from Faulkner or were deliberately imitating him. At the same time Sartre said that two-thirds of the manuscripts he received for *Les Temps Modernes* were written à la Caldwell, à la Hemingway, à la Dos Passos. Even the young Communist writers assimilated the new techniques, and there was an American influence in the best books of the best Communist writers, Roy announced in January, 1949. He found this specifically in *Mal de Mer* by Roger Boussinot, in *Les Circonstances* by Pierre Courtade, and in *Comme si la Lutte entière* by Jean Kanapa. Communist or non-Communist, "A novelist would feel himself dishonored if the critic did not make a special point of his 'technique,' and did not invoke the names of Faulkner, of Hemingway, or of Joyce," wrote Claude Edmonde Magny.

There are a number of writers who name Faulkner

or have Faulkner named as an influence on them. Blanzat, writing in 1943, suggested *Les Mendiants* by Louis René des Forêts as the first novel which manifests with striking evidence the immense influence of the American novelists. From *As I Lay Dying* and *The Sound and the Fury* des Forêts has borrowed his technique, "but it is from the entire universe of Faulkner that he has inseminated his own world. . . . The impregnation is widespread and profound, . . . intelligent. It is not a question of a copy but of fertilization. . . . It represents a capable attempt to enrich our literature." Later des Forêts himself, in the *Combat* interview, said, "When I began *Les Mendiants* I had read only Faulkner's *Sanctuary*. Actually I was modeling my book on S. Hudson. Two months later I read more of Faulkner and *As I Lay Dying* especially influenced my book." *Gerbe Baude* by Georges Magnane also used the technique of *As I Lay Dying*, Sartre said. Both men "took from Faulkner the method of reflecting different aspects of the same event through the interior monologues of different sensitivities." The novels by des Forêts and Magnane raise an interesting apparent employment of the "American" technique. Both were published in Paris during the occupation (1943). Neither used America as subject matter; yet both suggested America through their imitations of Faulkner. Blanzat could point out the derivations since he was writing from Algiers, but the Parisian intellectual had to depend on his own familiarity with Faulkner in order to recognize the disguised act of resistance.

The technique of Simone de Beauvoir, also, was inspired by Faulkner. "Without him she would never," Sartre believed, "have conceived the idea, used in *Le Sang des Autres*, of cutting the chronological order of the story and substituting instead a more subtle order, half logical, half intuitive." The critic Nelly Cormeau suggested that Luc Estang in *Les Stigmates* had used the method of Faulkner's *Light in August*. Genova wrote in *Fontaine*, June, 1942, "This talent of painting on two levels at once . . . gives us reason to compare the short stories of Elsa Triolet with those of Faulkner." Marguerite Duras in *La Vie tranquille* has certainly been influenced by Faulkner, Rode insisted, but associated with the French existentialists she has been able to add to this influence an inner significance of her own. Robert Kanters objected to the technique of obscurity that Gérard Jarlot used in *Les Armes blanches*. He has managed, the critic felt, to tell his story so that the reader understands nothing—or almost nothing. This ideal of unintelligibility seems to be in the pages of *The Sound and the Fury* and has unhappily become a literary virtue, Kanters complained. And even in dramatic criticism we found Faulkner's name invoked. We were told that André Obey wrote the play *Maria* after having been struck forcefully by a Faulkner short story.

The young Mouloudji wrote "American" inevitably, his friend Sartre felt, since he had read American novels before he read the traditional French greats. His first novel, *Enrico*, written when he was seventeen, won the Prix de la Pléiade for 1944; Sartre considered it not inferior in its violence, its naïve perversity, realism, and poetry to *Tobacco Road* or *Tragic Ground*. (Interestingly enough Mouloudji played the role of Dude Lester in the theatrical production of *Tobacco Road* which opened in Paris March 15, 1947, and ran for a year.) His second novel, *En souvenir de Barbarie*, Sartre said, marked a technical progress, although another critic felt that the bold but simple *procédés* borowed from Faulkner or Caldwell did not serve to show at its best Mouloudji's subject. The young writer admitted in 1947 that the critics had found a great influence of both Faulkner and Caldwell and also Dos Passos in his novels.

Dos Passos's technique in *Manhattan Transfer* seems to have influenced the many volumes of Jules Romains's *Les Hommes de bonne Volonté* although Jean Simon, at least, suggested that Romains was not as successful as the American. For Simon, the irrepressible rapidity and the precipitate rhythm which Dos Passos kept were necessary, and these were impossible on the vast scale of the *Men of Good Will* series. Dos Passos's influence on Sartre, particularly in *Le Sursis* and *La Mort dans l'Ame*, volumes two and three of *Les Chemins de la Liberté*, is obvious. *Le Sursis* seems to combine the simultaneity of Dos Passos with the jumping from one character to another within a sentence of Faulkner. It has also been suggested that Dos Passos's use of the imperfect tense was copied by Sartre in *L'Enfance d'un Chef*. Others have indicated that David Rousset in *Les Jours de notre Mort* employed the Dos Passos technique to give an all-over view of the concentration camps and the men in them.

The world described by Albert Cossery in *Les Hommes oubliés de Dieu* was likened to the world of Caldwell. The characters are miserable, ill, evil, drunken. They can react towards one another only brutally and at the same time uselessly. Their word means nothing; their love is pure instinct. A cruel humor exists in the disproportion in power between their hopeless efforts and the fatality which dominates them. Claude Elsen in *La Table Ronde*, October, 1950, agreed with other critics that Marguerite Duras's *Un Barrage contre le Pacifique* was influenced by Caldwell, particularly by

God's Little Acre. And he continued, "It is Marguerite Duras has openly avowed this in her first book, *La Vie tranquille.*"

Jean Blanzat writing in *Poésie 44* found *rapprochement* between Marcel Aymé's *La Vouivre* and Caldwell. Both paint immobile creatures, closed within their own desires, rolling mechanically down the same slope. If the reader goes beyond the first level of such figures as the *Dévorante*, insatiable girl, tormented with perpetual carnal desires, or the *Requiem,* gravedigger, to whom has been given a love potion by a sordid old woman, then he will think of the obsessed people of *God's Little Acre* or *Tobacco Road*, of their terrible and savage primitivism.

Camus's *L'Etranger* was said to be *à la manière* of Hemingway's *The Sun Also Rises.* Because Camus wanted in his book to express the absurd, the American technique suited him perfectly. One critic called *La Peste* a work of many values which combined the story telling of Voltaire, the myth of Kafka, and the clarity of Hemingway. A recent novel, *Le Marin de Gibralter*, by Marguerite Duras (who has already been called an imitator of Faulkner and Caldwell) aroused the comment that it read like "an excellent French translation of a novel by Hemingway." Sartre made a similar comparison between Hemingway and Jean Jausion's *Un Homme marche dans la Ville*—the same short, brutal sentences, the same lack of psychological analysis, the same heroes. Another critic wrote in more general terms that in this book were perceptible influences of movie techniques and of the American novel.

This combination of influences—the movies and the American novel (and one writer went so far as to insist that saying this was saying the same thing twice)—is apparent, we are told, in Raymond Queneau's *Lion de Rueil* and in the works of Louis Aragon and Elsa Triolet. General influence from the American novelists was found in Louis Pauwels's *Saint Quelqu'un* and in *On meurt les Yeux ouverts,* a collection of three stories by Jules Monnerot. Jacques Laurent Bost's novel of a French soldier, *Le Dernier des Métiers,* was called a *roman-reportage* and a critic felt this was not a simple, easy method of writing but a new form of some importance borrowed from the American novel more than from journalism. The Prix Goncourt for 1949 was Robert Merle's *Week-end à Zuydcoote,* the story of four French soldiers trying to cling to life during the British evacuation at Dunkirk. Merle had been taken prisoner by the Germans at Dunkirk and could write his novel from personal experience. He is a professor of English at the University of Rennes and was in the United States for a year studying acting and the theater. Perhaps it is not surprising to find critics saying that the technique of his book is very close to *la technique américaine,* particularly to *A Farewell to Arms. Week-End à Zuydcoote* has been a Gallimard best seller. To date (1953) it has sold 255,000 copies. In 1946 the first novel of Yves Malartic, *New-York, Ville farouche,* appeared in a detective story collection. "It is, as the title indicates, a work *dans le gout américain* after the style of books by Peter Cheyney or *Pas d'Orchidées pour Miss Blandish* by Chase."

The prestige of the American novel was so apparent and translations which accustomed the public to this *style américain* and delighted them sold so well that not only was there an "influence" on French novelists, there were also blatant imitations. Perhaps most interesting is the story of *J'irai cracher sur vos Tombes,* published in Paris in 1946. This novel—very much in the *style américain*—was supposedly written by a young American Negro, Vernon Sullivan, who was "unpublishable" in the United States. His "translator" was Boris Vian, a young Frenchman. The book was enormously successful; at first everyone believed it *traduit de l'américain*. In *Samedi-Soir*, December 7, 1946, there was a highly enthusiastic article on the new *romancier noir américain*. After overwhelming praise for the novel and the author, the critic informed his readers that Vernon Sullivan was only one-eighth Negro but that in the United States he was, of course, forced to live the life of the blacks. The whole thing caused considerable excitement. By early 1947, however, Monsieur Vian admitted in an interview, "I suppose you will ask me questions on the subject of the famous *J'irai cracher sur vos Tombes*. I don't mind. I'm used to it. I am willing for people to say I am the author." One critic got quite angry at the fraud and finished by saying that the novelist had sought approval by flattering in the reader the instincts of the beast. "Ma foi," wrote cynically M. Vian, "c'est une façon comme une autre de vendre sa salade."

The publishers and book sellers have made it clear that anything translated from American or signed with an "American" name would sell—and would sell better than a novel signed by an unknown Frenchman. Thus in the 1953 *Almanach des Lettres* we find G. M. Dumoulin who

translates *merveilleusement* Mickey Spillane and Bill Ballinger and is himself author of a novel which yields nothing to the Americans he is in the habit of translating. The book, *Qu'est-ce qu'on risque,* was published under the pseudonym, G. Morris. . . . And similarly there is the curious novel by Jean Meckert signed with an American pseudonym. It is the story of the small village of Tignes, the whole transplanted to the U.S.A.: *Y a pas de Bon Dieu,* by "John Amila."

All this influence and imitation makes appropriate Malraux's remark: "It is undoubtedly the first time that a country [U.S.A.] has imposed its sentimental myths on the whole world—its underworld, its lovers, its thieves and murders, and its comedian. Did we know before Chaplin that the whole world would laugh at the same man?"

6. *STYLE AMERICAIN*

WHAT QUALITIES in the American novel so captivated the French readers and critics? The first French answer to this question lumps together all contemporary American novelists into what is called the *école américaine*. As a result certain Americans are either ignored because they won't fit into the "school" or else they are labeled European. For example, Poe is often claimed by the French in spite of the accident of his living in the United States. Among contemporary novelists Thornton Wilder and Frederick Prokosch have received similar critical treatment.

And an occasional non-American novelist has been mistakenly labeled American. The autumn 1944 issue of *L'Arbalète* was a special volume devoted to the *roman américain*. Primarily it was an anthology of selections from American novelists—Caldwell, Hemingway, Faulkner, and several others. Also included was a selection from the English writer Peter Cheyney. The translator, Marcel Duhamel, added a note of apology saying he was much chagrined to find that Cheyney was English but that, after all, Cheyney's style and mannerisms justified his inclusion. The selection was defended in the March, 1945, *Confluences* by Alexandre Astruc, who said of Cheyney, "An Englishman, yes, but if he writes like an American, then he is an American, because being American is first of all a style." The phrase *style américain* has become a commonplace in postwar France, and there have been innumerable articles, each one trying to describe and define the term.

A frequent approach to definition was by means of contrasts. The traditional French novel was contrasted with the contemporary American, the English with the American, and sometimes the Russian with the American. The traditional French novel followed chronological order exactly. Its characteristics were extensive psychological analyses, individualization of the characters, frequent intervention of the writer, and a limited choice of protagonists. The American novel was the complete opposite. The French novel of analysis was called a form of art; the American was only *reportage*. One was intellectual; the other not.

America was described as young, raw, crude; France as old, mature, civilized. American literature was new and in its epic stage. Malraux commented, "The essential characteristic of contemporary American writing is that it is the only literature whose creators are not intellectuals. The writers I met in the United States did not remind me of European writers, compared to whom they have neither the relative historical culture nor the love of ideas (a prerogative of professors in the United States)." The tradition of the man of letters is still strong in France and the absence of this tradition in America puzzles the Frenchman.

The contrast between English and American literatures was sketched in much the same way. English society had evolved; American was evolving. English writers accepted their society; Americans were in revolt against theirs. And quite specifically, the American novel interested the French critic only when it seemed different from the English. When an American wrote following English traditions, the French frankly said they were bored.

Between Russian and American literature the parallels were what the French most frequently talked about. Both exhibited an intense regionalism and at the same time gave the reader a sense of space that no Western European literature has ever given. A vivid human quality and sympathy were seen in both, evoking such parallels as Steinbeck and Tolstoi. And more than one American was compared with Dostoevski.

The details of the French definition of the American novel lead us back again to the lives themselves of the American writers. How did the French picture them? They were surprised that so few American novelists had studied at a college or university and therefore could not have a thoroughgoing background in the literatures of the past. As writers, they had no status in society and must earn their living by catch-as-catch-can methods. In amazement the French commented on the seemingly innumerable trades that American novelists have followed before becoming financially established in their chosen profession. Farm-hand, dishwasher, ditch-digger—the writers' necessity for such jobs shocked the French.

Many American novelists have begun as journalists. And the French have found journalism one of the strongest influences on American writing. Americans learned to write on the staffs of newspapers not on the staffs of universities. Journalism helped to teach the Americans their sense of reality, of immediacy, of concreteness. The reporter must be both explicit and exact—qualities reflected in many American novels. French critics talked at great length about the relationship between *reportage* and the ordinary American novel. Being trained in writing *reportage*, the average American writer took over into belles-lettres the techniques and mannerisms he had already learned.

Denis de Rougement in the special issue of *Fontaine* continued the discussion by calling this training one in American rhetoric. He contrasted this with French rhetoric, whose rules would demand that "an article should be introduced by some verbal precautions which would create an atmosphere or orient the mind." American rhetoric dislikes such rules and considers them a dead weight. Articles in American magazines "begin almost obligatorily by a striking anecdote, an enumeration of brutal facts, or some impressive figures." What is important for the Americans is the *catch phrase*. The article itself does not follow the logical, but the most efficacious, order. The French writer attempts to convince by his elegance or the rigor of his deductions; the American by dramatizing his material. The French style is at its best in its figures of speech and its epigrams; the American in its effect of shock or of accumulation. One is static; the other rhythmical. American magazine editors seek the *human touch* in their articles. Americans are taught in universities to avoid all intellectual expression and to cultivate the concrete. The criterion of the American is how effective, not how well written. Writings must be inspiring, stimulating.

Characteristic of American literature therefore is the short story. Its rapidity of movement, conciseness, and variety of subjects make of it, for the French, a miniature of the American novels. In short stories the French find the Americans most American. That the average citizen spends more time reading short stories in magazines than he does reading books seems somehow typical of life in America. Few European critics would question the claim that America has pushed the short story to its greatest development both quantitatively and qualitatively. For them the short story seems practically to belong to America, even though the modern story owes much to Maupassant and Chekhov—a fact the French critics are very much aware of.

Probably the commonest remark made in France about the American novel concerns its poetic quality, called often America's greatest contribution to the novel form. The French, recently interested in Melville's *Moby-Dick,* have found in this book proof that American novelists at their best have frequently had a tremendous gift for lyricism. Almost every review of a Faulkner book will at some time or other refer to Faulkner's lyric tone. Much the same thing is true for Steinbeck and Caldwell. There is even an article entitled "Le réalisme lyrique de John Steinbeck."

What do the French mean by the lyricism of the American novel? That is not an easy question to answer since the French critics assume that their readers will know what they are talking about and never try to define. Rather they discuss the poetic symbolism of Faulkner, the poetic humor of Caldwell, the poetic realism of Steinbeck. From this it can be seen that the lyric quality is not just a matter of form but of content as well. The French feel that the Americans have brought into the novel a lyricism never before present. And this is no small reason for what they regard as the aesthetic triumph of the Americans.

A stylistic device thought of as characteristic of the American novel is what we usually call stream of consciousness and the French, interior monologue. Most frequently French critics credit the French novelist Edmond Dujardin with having invented this technique, though all admit that Joyce developed it and saw its real possibilities. Valery Larbaud in his preface to Faulkner's *Tandis que j'agonise* traced the interior monologue back to the ballads of Bayard Taylor. As so frequently happens in French criticism, this remark, rather tentatively made by Larbaud, has been picked up and used as gospel truth by other critics in discussing the interior monologue. Whatever the origins, all agree that the interior monologue is a device typical of American novels. Faulkner is considered the past master of the technique, especially in *The Sound and the Fury* and *As I Lay Dying*. The French commentators do not regard the interior monologue as a tool of psychological analysis, but one of presentation of novelistic material. Psychological analysis is exposition; the interior monologue is narration. So much removed is this device, for the French, from analysis that critics comment on the overuse of the interior monologue as an indication of the psychological poverty of the American novel. Except for the master, Faulkner, American writers have found in the technique a substitute for their own lack of comprehension.

The relation of the cinema to the American novel is a much discussed problem in France, dating particularly from the series of articles Claude Edmonde Magny published in late 1944 and early 1945 in *Poèsie*. Later these articles became the first part of her book, *L'Age du Roman américain*. Mme Magny tried to show that what is most characteristic of the American novel is its dependence upon devices borrowed from the movies. She talked about such qualities as rapidity of narrative, objectivity, and sudden shifts in time and place. It is inevitable that the American author whom she treats at greatest length is Dos Passos. Her conclusion was that the American novel derives in no small part from the cinema. Therefore the influence of the American novel in France becomes a film influence. Allied with the movies is, of course, jazz music. Not all critics accepted Mme Magny's conclusions. Some objected to her finding so many similiarities between novelistic and movie techniques. The devices she was talking about originated long before the movies were ever thought of. Others accepted her basic premise that the American novel owes much to the cinema, but disagreed with her statement that the American novel was the means of spreading this influence in France. Rather they saw the influence of film and jazz as operating not only in the United States but also in Europe as well. The widespread popularity of movies and jazz made for influences just as important in Europe as in America. The American novel was not an intermediary, except as it reinforced an already present tendency. Though Mme Magny represents an extreme position, undoubtedly most French critics would agree that there is some influence of the film on the American novel. In the United States there are frequent comments on the influence of the movies in producing a well-made plot and a happy ending. In France discussion of the influence of the movies is almost always in terms of technical narrative devices.

The to them new and experimental use of colloquial American speech has aroused interest and controversy among French critics. The French literary language had become somewhat formal and stereotyped. Writers prided themselves on their knowledge of the intricacies of French grammar. The nineteenth-century naturalistic revolt in France was not against vocabulary but against subject matter. Theodore Dreiser and Frank Norris may have gotten their basic philosophy and many ideas for selection of material from their reading of Zola, but their attempts at more natural dialogue had their origins in American traditions, not French. That these traditions existed in nineteenth-century American literature few European critics are aware even today. During the early thirties the French began to see how much different was the conversation in Sinclair Lewis's novels from their own. Unfortunately the translations very inadequately represented the Lewis dialogue. As time went on and translations of our five men appeared, the French readers could see better how colloquial speech was used. And they commented. The war also played its part in disrupting French vocabulary just as it had French life. Writers, such as Sartre, exploring the possibilities of street slang, found justification in the Americans. Though agreement was by no means universal, most of the critics found what the Americans were doing a means of enriching the literary vocabulary and therefore approved.

Allied with the problem of diction is that of narrative technique. All American novels are characterized by the rapidity of narrative, commented many, done in no small part by the omission of most physical description. In the hands of some American writers the result was, for the French, a kind of nervous, jerky narrative, a *style* or *temps saccadé*. And the *style saccadé* was emphasized as a trait of the *style américain*. This rapid, nervous style was compared to the rapid, nervous life of America.

The expression *temps saccadé* leads into the problem of time in the American novel. This is not the place for an extended discussion of all the ramifications of this complicated problem, but we should point out the importance given by the French to this question and how they related it to the American novel. As a one-sentence history, think of the following sequence of writers: Bergson, Proust, Joyce, Woolf, Dos Passos, Faulkner. What is in common among these writers? Bergson gave to the young Proust a philosophic justification for the idea that time is more subjective than objective, no matter what man's physical measuring devices indicate. And, for one reason or another, we find a similar attitude towards time in the other novelists named. Vast numbers of bottles of ink have been drained by the French on time in relation to both character and plot. Faulkner has attracted more of this commentary than anyone else, except perhaps Proust. The philosophic problems involved are commented on in great detail in the book by Jean Pouillon, *Temps et Roman*. Twenty pages are devoted to Dos Passos and another twenty, the place of importance just before the concluding remarks, to Faulkner. It is only typical that Jean Paul Sartre should say that the theme of Faulkner's *The Sound and the Fury* is man's revolt against time. Nor should it be surprising to find many critics discussing Dos Passos's fragmentation of time in his attempts to show the simultaneity of human actions. Much of the influence of the Americans on younger French novelists was in terms of this intensely subjective quality given to time by Faulkner and Dos Passos.

In what is labeled *style américain* content is as important as form. Thus we find much discussion of such a question as, Is the contemporary American novel a kind of realism or romanticism? No French critic would quibble over the answer. The Americans are beyond a doubt romantic. French commentators have occasionally applied the derogatory expression *fleur bleue* to the Americans. This figure of speech is particularly used by French literary historians to suggest the sentimental idealism in the German romantics of the early nineteenth century. But, for the French, the greats of the American novel despite their romanticism have their feet solidly on the ground. Perhaps the training in journalism that so many American writers have had keeps reality constantly before them, no matter how romantic their approach.

Concrete detail is a writing device used by the Americans to stick to reality. Not only is a novel by Caldwell concrete, but the objects and events described are made immediately perceptible to the reader. This immediacy and concreteness are obtained by the Americans because of their tremendous objectivity. In part objectivity is thought of as a technique of the writer who completely effaces himself from the narrative. But more often the French critics think of the objectivity found in American novels as a problem of content instead of form. Complete psychological objectivity would be Watsonian behaviorism, and so Mme Magny in her book has pointed out how popular behavioristic psychology has been in the United States.

Although American critics have found regionalism an important feature of our contemporary writing, the French have almost ignored this critical approach. An interesting minority point of view is expressed in the book by Pierre Brodin, *Le Roman régionaliste américain, Esquisse d'une Géographie morale et pittoresque des Etats-Unis.* In the preface to this book Maurice E. Coindreau went so far as to say that essentially there are forty-eight literatures in the United States and that the story of American literature should be written for each state. On the few occasions when the French critics have recognized American regionalism, they have related it to the American novelist's attachment to reality.

More widely accepted as a distinguishing feature of the American novel is the highly developed social sense of the writers in contrast to the seeming lack of this among the French. Steinbeck, Caldwell, and Dos Passos are the ones usually mentioned as having a deep awareness of the plight of their fellowmen. This quality is usually thought of as a tradition of the American novel. This attitude is particularly understandable if it is remembered that the American novel of the nineteenth century that Europeans knew best was *Uncle Tom's Cabin*. Inevitably reviews of Steinbeck's *The Grapes of Wrath* brought in the name of Mrs. Stowe's book as showing a similar desire on the part of these two writers to ameliorate the conditions of their fellowmen. The tendency of Americans to use the novel as a means of social reform was discussed by more than one commentator.

Not entirely separate from this social sense is the attitude of the French readers that there is in the American novel a strong human quality lacking in the traditional French novel. More than one French critic spoke of his desire to have the young French novelists acquire this quality from the Americans. Frequently the term *healthy* is opposed to the so-called diseased, morbid French novel of psychological analysis. Much of the healthiness of the American novel is to be explained by the feeling of the French that the novels of Faulkner, Hemingway, Caldwell, *et al.* were a breath of fresh air in the stuffy atmosphere of the French novel. The human quality of the Americans represented an art closer to the people and to the aesthetic needs of the time.

Not all critics found that the humanity of the Americans was necessarily an aesthetic strength. Many saw the Americans as being carried away by their *fleur bleue* of idealism into a kind of sentimental primitivism. As the remarks of André Malraux (page 70) indicate, what the French criticized in the Americans was not their anti-intellectualism but their lack of intellectuality. But in spite of such criticisms by the French intellectuals, one of the very important appeals of the American novel was its—to the French—exotic primitivism. Caldwell's books well illustrate this. Malraux's criticism found support among some critics, but the public continued to be entertained by the Lennies and the Ty-Tys.

When we first came to France and started our research, we were thinking as students of American literature of the question: What has been the impact of the contemporary American primitivists on Europe? By primitivists we meant the five men now being discussed with perhaps the exception of Dos Passos. It did not take us long to realize that our concept of primitivism and, say, Faulkner is an American literary judgment, not a European. It is a minor factor in the European reception of the Americans. American critics may discuss Faulkner's going back to the Chickasaw Indians for his positive values, but we have yet to read or hear such a remark in France. The appeals of exoticism and primitivism are not the same thing, and it is exoticism that in no small part explains the tremendous popularity in France of Caldwell's *Tobacco Road*. So we had to redefine our approach because of what the French have thought about the Americans.

A kind of indirect admission of primitivism is present in the oft-repeated statement that it is typical of the American novel to have extremely simple people—Faulkner's Benjy and Steinbeck's Lennie—as characters. There are enough idiots and drunkards in the various books by our five men to make the French think of them as typifying the American novel. When the French critic tries to explain why there are so many idiots and drunkards, his explanations are apt to be twofold. One is that everybody in the United States drinks, and the other is that these characters should be thought of as symbols—aesthetic not social. Actually there is very little agreement on why there are so many such characters in the American novel. Some critics expound at great length to show that the American people lack a soul because they have neither suffered nor had a long history behind them. For these critics it is inevitable that the characters in American novels should lack a well-rounded personality since that very quality is lacking in the American people. For other critics, especially the young French novelists, the American novel presents for the first time the "totality of man," whatever that phrase might mean. They find that the American novel, from Henry Miller with his "global vision" to Faulkner, has liberated the European writer by means of this very totality. And so the confusion is compounded.

A particular word found frequently in French criticism of the American novel is *dépaysement*. The word, of course, suggests being uprooted or taken away from one's native land. *Dépaysement* reflects the European's concept of the solitariness of the average individual in America who lacks the strength of long-held traditions and is therefore immature. Man has lost his tie with the past and exists only as a solitary being in the midst of an unfriendly world. Thus *dépaysement* is a precise description of modern man in the world of the atom bomb and the cold war. This characteristic explains some of the postwar interest in the American novel, particularly among the existentialists.

The French feel that the greatness of their own literature rests in its morality. It is therefore only natural that they should judge foreign literatures in terms of morality. Some French critics call American literature moral; others disagree. The French recognized Faulkner as a moralist long before American critics did. Caldwell is usually regarded as amoral, and his amorality becomes for them a source of his naturalistic comedy. In other words, there is more agreement on individual authors than on the American novel as a whole. Perhaps this is another place where French criticism breaks down by reason of its love of categorizing.

There is, however, general agreement that American morality is puritan and that introduces one of those vague words subject to a million and one definitions. In America there is much confusion over whether the word refers to seventeenth-century Puritanism or to a kind of scarecrow creature in an ungainly tall hat and umbrella who spends his time inhibiting himself and his fellow creatures by prohibitions, book censoring, and blue laws. It is only recently that we have begun to differentiate the seventeenth-century Puritan from the Comstocks and Bishop Cannons of the twentieth century. Since we ourselves are so confused about what the word *puritan* means, it should not be surprising to find the French confused also. Our understanding of the French use of the word is helped by thinking of French history. First, the Jansenism of the Port Royal group operating within the Catholic Church. Jansenism insisted on self-denial and a rigorous rigidity in religious life. Such a modern Jansenist as the novelist François Mauriac has added his own dislike of women, but this does not seem inappropriate in the eyes of the French critics to his fundamental Jansenism. Second, French Protestants have had, and still have, a well-nigh universal tradition of

Calvinism. So, when French readers talk about the American tradition of Protestantism, they tend to be equating this tradition with Calvinism because of their own experience.

We ask the question, how universally is the term *puritan* applied to American novelists? And it is necessary to reply that almost everyone has been given the label at sometime or another.

In 1935 Coindreau prefaced his translation of *Light in August* by an extended discussion of Faulkner's puritanism. Coindreau had asked Faulkner whether or not he were a puritan. Faulkner rather cryptically admitted that he was, "in the good sense of the word." Coindreau found other support for his theory in Faulkner's heritage of puritanism, his violence, his hatred of women, and his erotic morbidity. Though later critics of Faulkner did not necessarily state their indebtedness to Coindreau, they applied his label.

In general the critics gave two reasons for insisting that Faulkner was a puritan. One was related to D. H. Lawrence's remark, "I am a puritan." Lawrence wanted to throw away the trappings and impedimenta of modern civilization and get back to original purities. He wanted to purify himself. The French critics saw a similar desire in Faulkner. The other reason was Faulkner's pessimism, a quality he shares with many other contemporary American novelists. The French consider pessimism a characteristic of puritan morality, so it seems only natural to them that the most moral of the American novelists should be the most puritan.

One other puritan characteristic of Faulkner—his passionate intensity—was pointed out occasionally. Lawrence, of course, shared this quality. The critics who know historical puritanism recognized the tradition and found the moral intensity reflected in the stylistic intensities of a Faulkner novel, one serving as cause for the other.

To the average American it comes as somewhat of a shock to find that the French have firmly fixed upon each of us the label "puritan." Julien Green's novel *Moira,* the story of a neurotic, frustrated college student who kills a girl in a moment of sexual rage brought on by his feelings of guilt, is a clever study of a certain limited facet of American life, but the French stressed the "true picture" which it presented. For them the boy's confused morbidity is typically American. Cotton Mather comes closer to the French concept of the average American than does Benjamin Franklin.

Involved in this concept is the Frenchman's awareness of the popularity in America of psychoanalysis. There was, in the early twenties, a literary vogue of psychoanalysis in France, but it failed to take deep roots, was satirized by Gide and others, and more or less faded. As any American reader knows, this is not true in the United States. The psychoanalyst is such a potent literary figure that in Eliot's *The Cocktail Party* we find him symbolizing God—an amusing symbol to the French. More fundamentally the French see the popularity of psychoanalysis in American criticism and novels as another evidence of American immaturity. This sexual immaturity is related to American puritanism with its repressions and resulting neuroses. Therefore the average American has recourse to the psychoanalyst and the novelist tries to psychoanalyze his characters instead of delving into their psychology.

While pessimism is considered by the French a part of puritan morality, it takes other forms for them also. The most spectacular present-day literary form is what they call *littérature noire,* defined by Maurice Heine as that which seeks to move the reader by terrifying him. And they name as the leading practitioners of this genre Kafka, Faulkner, Henry Miller. How important this is for the French in evaluating the contemporary American novel is demonstrated by the title of the last chapter, "La Littérature noire," of Jacques Fernand Cahen's brief general history, *La Littérature américaine.* This phrase expresses the dominant tone of American literature since World War I for Monsieur Cahen. And *Sanctuary* is most often considered the chef-d'oeuvre of the *littérature noire.* Frequently commented on was the seeming paradox of a *littérature noire* in a country noted for its blatant optimism. The usual resolution of this paradox is that literary pessimism is a form of social criticism and protest. The more prosperous the country and the more boisterous its optimism the more the writers must have recourse to the pessimism of the *roman noir.*

Beyond pessimism or optimism lies tragedy. The ultimate greatness for the French of the *style américain* stems from its kinship to Greek tragedy. In 1933 Malraux's famous preface to *Sanctuaire* ended, "Sanctuaire, c'est l'intrusion de la tragédie grecque dans le roman policier." The critics have quoted and requoted Malraux's remark and increasingly the emphasis falls on *la tragédie grecque.* Hemingway, Steinbeck, indeed the American novel in general provide, the French say, the equivalent of Greek tragedy for the modern world.

How does all this come about? The answer is found in the impersonal fate which serves to control the destiny of the characters in the novels by *les cinq grands* and by many others also. This fate may have its origins in heredity, in society, or in pure chance; but whatever the source, it is still an impersonal fate controlling man's destiny. Also, remember that the best of the novels by our five men are concerned with the problems of good and evil in today's society. Then add the French feeling that the American novel has a lyricism, a poetry—the epic writing of a youthful nation. Now ask where in the literatures of the Western world has such a combination of literary qualities appeared before, and it is hard to avoid the French answer—Greek tragedy. For the French critics American literature resembles the Greek, and the American novelists are today's heirs of Aeschylus and Sophocles. Both Greek tragedy and the modern American novel at its best share a catharsis not elsewhere found. The critics do dispute over whether or not there is the same freedom of the individual in the two literatures, but almost no one disputes the similarity of the role of fate.

This question arises: How do the American novelists stand up in comparison with the giants of Greek tragedy? And the answer given by the French is that they, particularly Faulkner, stand up very well. In both are found similar aesthetic values and much the same aesthetic worth. It is in this judgment that the French show how profoundly they have been moved by the contemporary American novel.

7. DOS PASSOS

UP TO THIS POINT we have been presenting the story of what has happened to the contemporary American novel in France in general terms. Because by far the most important novelists in this story are Dos Passos, Hemingway, Faulkner, Caldwell, and Steinbeck, we will now tell in some detail what has happened to the works of each of these five men.

The first of the five to be published in France was Dos Passos, who, strangely enough, is the least known on the popular level, though he shares with Faulkner the honor of influencing most strongly present-day French novelists. Since it has been shown that the writers themselves have been perhaps primarily interested in the American techniques, it stands to reason that they should hold Dos Passos in high esteem. Why he has not obtained the popular audience is not so clear. But there are suggestions which can be made. Nine books by Dos Passos, six of them novels, have been translated over the years from 1925 to 1952. And never the same translator twice except for Yves Malartic, who did *Tour of Duty* and the new (1952) translation of *1919*. And Dos Passos has had seven different publishers. Cause or effect? It is difficult to judge. Most important of all perhaps in attempting to understand the relatively small sales of Dos Passos is the confused publishing history of *U.S.A. The 42nd Parallel* was translated by Guterman and published by Grasset as early as 1933 but for some reason received almost no critical attention (surprising after the enthusiastic critical reception given to *Manhattan Transfer*). In 1937 Editions Sociales Internationales published Maurice Rémon's two-volume translation of *1919*. Again we found few reviews. Léon Moussinac, then editor, believes four thousand copies of the book were printed. (All records and the stock of Editions Sociales Internationales were confiscated during February and March, 1940, by the French government, and M. Moussinac was imprisoned.) Finally, thirteen years after *The 42nd Parallel* had appeared, *The Big Money* was translated by de Richter and published by Gallimard. Then in 1951 Gallimard took over the Guterman translation of *The 42nd Parallel* and republished it. And at the end of 1952 this house brought out a new translation of *1919*, entitling the book *L'An premier du Siècle*. Never has there been a one-volume edition of the trilogy. And not until 1952 were all three books in print at the same time. A final reason for the poor sales is suggested by the check list. Dos Passos has had printed notably fewer fugitive pieces than Faulkner, Steinbeck, or Hemingway. He is not a short story writer and therefore does not lend himself to the magazine and literary weekly publication (so frequently done in France) which reaches a wide reading public and quickly familiarizes a new name.

So much for the popularity of Dos Passos among average French readers. He has always ranked high with the intellectuals, with the avant-garde. The story begins in February, 1924, with the publication in *Europe* of an excerpt from *One Man's Initiation*. A year later F. Rieder, who then published *Europe*, brought out the translation of this book. According to Presses Universitaires, who absorbed the publishing business of F. Rieder, *L'Initiation d'un Homme* had a single printing of 3000 copies. Petit, writing a favorable review in the

Revue Nouvelle, admitted that the French lack precise and accurate knowledge of American literature. *L'Initiation* is excellent and should be put beside the war stories by such eminent French novelists as Georges Duhamel, Barbusse, and Dorgelès. Though perhaps not quite as effectively as these men, nevertheless Dos Passos has written a powerful, honest, and strongly colorful account. The next year in the same magazine a biographical sketch by Pazos praised *Three Soldiers* (American edition) in much the same terms, ranking it with the works of Duhamel and Barbusse and saying it would remain the chef-d'oeuvre of American war novels. This biographical account preceded eight pages of excerpts from *Manhattan Transfer* translated and commented on by Coindreau. The wide orange-colored paper band "Dans ce numéro" which encircled the magazine carried in block capitals the advertisement, "JOHN DOS PASSOS: MANHATTAN TRANSFER." Coindreau suggested that the virtuosity of Dos Passos's style would please the literati who award the Prix Goncourt. A year later Coindreau contributed to the August-September issue of this magazine a long and highly favorable review of *Orient Express* (American edition) which he considered a new form of writing. This prepared the way for his translation of excerpts from the book, which appeared in November.

Earlier in 1927 Rapin reviewed *Manhattan Transfer* (American edition) in the *Bibliothèque Universelle*. In a staccato style imitating Dos Passos, the reviewer indicated the multitude of things, places, people in the book.

All is done admirably—the eye of John Dos Passos seizes the significant trait, the relevant nuance. His ear, with the precision of a phonograph registers the vocabulary, grammar, tone appropriate to each person, to each class of people. His prose takes on the rhythm of the street, the dance, of a drunk, a train, a dream.

When Coindreau's translation appeared in 1928 the critics almost uniformly approved. *Manhattan Transfer* "is absolutely original," "an astonishing book," "a so amazing success," "a capital work," "an imposing book." It "classes Dos Passos among the best novelists of today not alone in his own country but without doubt in all contemporary literature." Dos Passos's technique was much discussed. It was compared to the movies, lauded for its objectivity, for its breaking with the old traditions of the novel. To the critics it marked a date in the evolution of the contemporary novel. It showed the way to analyze certain collective facts such as the whole of a modern city. "The technique is the soul of the book itself—cause as well as effect, source of inspiration as well as helpful device. This swarming, teeming book is nearly more than a book—it is Manhattan." A few mixed in an adverse comment or two. One said the book is not a complete success because we see New York only from the outside and not all of it at that. Another, so many scenes, so many people blur the picture. A third, Dos Passos does not always evade the pitfalls of monotony or of a too wide scattering of his forces. But the scales weighed heavily on the side of vigorous approval. To judge the sales of this book is difficult. Gallimard told us that within the first twelve months *Manhattan Transfer* sold 2,250 copies. We know that it was in at least a second printing by 1929 because we found a one-volume copy so dated. (The original printing was in two volumes.) And since the war the book has been reprinted.

An anthology, published in 1931, *Les Romanciers américains*, contained Dos Passos's "L'homme qui disait s'appeler Jones," prefaced by a three-page article by Ludmila Savitzky, who suggested that this writer tells the true secrets of life in America. Reading any of his books sweeps away our superficial notions about America. In the same year an article on the American novelist came out in *Nouvel Age*, written by Upton Sinclair and translated by Henry Muller. A few months later Muller translated Dos Passos's poem "Sacco and Vanzetti" for the same magazine.

In 1932 Coindreau wrote a long review of *1919* (American edition) in *NRF* and used this occasion for an evaluation of the author. His enthusiasm was tempered by his belief that the eye cannot take over the usual functions of the ear. All the devices cannot bring the whole together, and the complexity of the counterpoint makes the reader forget the themes. His attention wanders. But the critic concluded that *1919* and *The 42nd Parallel* mark in American literature a date of great importance. If Dos Passos has not created a perfect whole, he has at least created an original technique. In the same year *Europe* published "La grève de Harlan" and *Le Mois* a long article entitled "Les romans de John Dos Passos, ou une épopée de l'Amérique moderne." The anonymous critic placed Dos Passos beside Faulkner among the most representative writers of the young America, saying that Dos Passos perceives the individual as a person and at the same time as part of the crowd of humanity.

Manhattan Transfer is the only work in modern literature where we feel the reality of a multitude with its fluidity and its unawareness, its acknowledged bad taste and contradictory opinions, and also the reality of a certain number of individuals plunged into this multitude, contributing to form its ideologies, but clearly characterized and differentiated and made human.

Better than any other American writer, the critic felt,

Dos Passos has presented the America of today. "The result is a tableau of a human crowd adrift—tableau disparate, multi-colored, often depressing and even repugnant, but palpitating with life."

In 1933 Bernard Grasset published *The 42nd Parallel, Cahiers du Sud* printed "Meester Veelson," an excerpt from *1919*, and the Tauchnitz editions of *Three Soldiers* and *Manhattan Transfer* were both reviewed by Charles Cestre in the *Revue Anglo-Américaine*. *Three Soldiers* was characterized as a *roman de début* and as an intentionally sordid picture of the American army. "The platitudes, the bestiality, the monotonous repetition of the same ignominies produce an impression of disgust." But M. Cestre applauded *Manhattan Transfer*. Dos Passos in this book "achieves mastery of his form, of a brilliant language, of a sharp and rapid dialogue, of impressionistic description which evokes the multiform variety, the splendid and the ugly, the enormous and powerful, the feverish hate and the confusion behind the apparent order."

Philippe Soupault wrote "John Dos Passos" for *Europe* in 1934. This essay was primarily concerned with the three books already translated into French—*One Man's Initiation, Manhattan Transfer*, and *The 42nd Parallel*. In all three Soupault found Dos Passos presenting human beings—hurt, bewildered—who are given no aesthetic value, only the value of witnessing and of representing the mass. The critic emphasized the need to study this writer with great care.

We are not surprised however that many critics have neglected to do him justice. The aims of Dos Passos are beyond the understanding of most, and it is easier to keep silent than to pass judgment on a work of such power. Thus it is up to the reader . . . to comprehend one of the noblest writers of our age. The modesty, the absence of bombast, the freshness of the author of *The 42nd Parallel* are not just admirable qualities in a novelist but qualities which have never before been so needed.

In All Countries appeared in 1936 under the title *Sur toute la Terre*. The reviewer for *Cahiers du Sud* severely criticized the translation but found the *reportage* valuable in its objectivity. American authors, he concluded, as diverse as Dos Passos, Hemingway, and Faulkner have in common this ability—to put into clear focus the exterior world. Then we can ask how to modify and change the condition of human beings existing in this world. Dabit, writing for *NRF*, held that unlike many travel books *Sur toute la Terre* was a work of genuine merit. Here, as in *Manhattan Transfer*, Dos Passos reveals a sense of life itself—precise, pointed, poetic and at the same time realistic.

Four years after *The 42nd Parallel*, *1919* was available to the French reader in a two-volume edition. One excited review appeared at the end of the year, December 11, 1937, in *Nouvelles Littéraires*. "If the Prix Goncourt were not reserved exclusively for French writers, this extraordinary book should certainly receive the award." Of far more weight was the essay by Sartre which appeared in *NRF* in August, 1938, and was reprinted later in *Situations I*. Sartre analyzed with care and ingenuity the sense of time and fatality in Dos Passos. He concluded:

These people of Dos Passos in retrospect how I hate them. . . . Man for him is a hybrid being—*interne-externe*. We are with him, in him, we live in his vacillating individual *conscience* and at one stroke it plays a double game, it yields, it melts into the collective *conscience*. . . . The world of Dos Passos is impossible —as is the world of Faulkner, of Kafka, of Stendhal—because it is contradictory. But that is what makes its beauty; beauty is a veiled contradiction. I consider Dos Passos the greatest writer of our time.

Another critic, Acaste, used a completely different approach to Dos Passos in *Le Mois*, January, 1938. Dos Passos's love of Spain gives his books their essential character, he wrote. The multiplicity of characters, events, the dreamer-realist (Quixote-Panza) dualism—all this is reminiscent of that picturesque country.

Jean Simon undertook an evaluation of the American for the special issue of *Cahiers de Paris*, "Le Roman contemporain aux Etats-Unis," May, 1939. In the over-all picture Simon recognized and paid tribute to Dos Passos. But he pointed out weaknesses in individual books. *Three Soldiers* is interesting, courageous, he wrote, but it fails because it does not show the reality of an army. The three characters represent the discouragements, the atrocities of army life but not what is equally true, the moments of joviality, of camaraderie. Simon suggested that a reason for this failure was probably that war is always peculiarly difficult for the intellectual. *Manhattan Transfer*, the critic continued, produces a truly considerable impression. This enormous chaos— full of color, of noise, of smells, of movement—gives the impression of the huge city with extraordinary power. However, the book has its faults: (1) the characters are all a little gray; (2) there is only a crowd—not an ordered hierarchy of social classes; (3) the antipathies of the author are too visible. Next Simon discussed the trilogy. Here Dos Passos has used the same devices in general that he used in *Manhattan Transfer*, but here they are perfected, varied, and in the third volume particularly he is in complete mastery of them. His art has become sure. Not only has the reader before him an enormous image of America, but he feels he understands that country. But, Simon asked, does Dos Passos give the true picture of America? No. By his unwavering condemnation of America society he falsifies. Is America so uniformly grim? Others do not find it so.

Then came the silent war years. Comparing criticism before and after merely in terms of bulk, we see that twice as much has been written on Dos Passos in the seven years since the liberation as in the fourteen years before war broke out. The American edition of *Number One* was enthusiastically reviewed or commented on in such general magazines as *Paru, Confluences, Mercure de France*. Before, an American publication of Dos Passos would probably have received notice only in such academic magazines as *Etudes Anglaises*. And as many of his books have been translated since the war as were between 1925 and 1939. *The 42nd Parallel* in 1949 even made the French Book Club. The criticism at the height of the vogue featured ecstatic approval much more than careful evaluation.

Most of the reviewers of *The Big Money*, which came out in 1946, were deeply concerned with the technical innovations. Several, understandably enough, seemed not to be aware that the other two volumes of the trilogy had been, thirteen and nine years before, available to the French reader, and both Magny in *Une Semaine* and Roy in *Europe* deplored the neglect in France of Dos Passos. There was general approval of the American's techniques, though the critic writing in *Bataille* remarked that what was new in 1930 was now dated and, ignoring chronology, gave Jules Romains credit for the "paternity of this unanism." Considerable comment was made on the social, economic, and political criticism of the United States implied in this volume: "Un enfer de

600 pages," "a war machine of prodigious vigor launched against capitalism and against the blindness of the men who represent it," "a documentation of the misery of life in America." Jouve in *Etudes*, June, 1947, recapitulated the last scene in this "vision of Babel." By the side of the road a tramp, foodless for two days, tries in vain to hitch a ride. He raises his eyes to the sky where the wealthy, flying across America in a Douglas, vomit their steak and mushrooms into the airline's paper bags—"the parable of Lazarus and the evil rich, 1936." Final judgments were generally glowing: Dos Passos is capable of using magnificently every tone, every style. *U.S.A.* is the most important novelistic enterprise ever produced in America. Dos Passos is the Balzac of the twentieth century. Whoever wishes to understand America today and through America the whole universe should read these three enormous books—our Odyssey.

State of the Nation, published also in French in 1946, received considerable praise and was widely reviewed, but *Tour of Duty*, which appeared early in 1947, was seemingly ignored. *State of the Nation* was called "as living and vital as the best of novels," "a book which speaks directly to the heart and mind." It widens our horizons and brings us close to our friends across the sea. It shows us the America of the melting pot with its immense possibilities, its future limitless as its prairies, forests, and mineral wealth, its fierce pride which to tired Europe seems a bit naïve but which explains the dynamism of this new race. *State of the Nation* is not the book of a revolutionary novelist as we have known Dos Passos to be, but it is the work of an inquiring, liberal journalist, loyally patriotic, sympathetic to the worker's movement. From the literary point of view the book raises *reportage* to the level of a great literary genre. Dos Passos is extraordinarily curious but without passion or feverishness; the rhythm of the book is that of *Notes de Voyage* of Samuel Butler, prince of Anglo-Saxon voyagers.

Three Soldiers was translated in 1948 by Raimbault, well known and highly respected for his fine translations of Faulkner. The publisher told us he printed seven thousand copies of the book. Faulkner's *Soldiers' Pay* appeared this same year, and one reviewer made a careful comparison. He found Dos Passos speaking through John Andrews but Faulkner remaining objective. Dos Passos shows the machine of war rolling over mankind. Faulkner shows what remains after the machine has passed. The French in 1948 agreed with what Pazos had written in 1926 of the American edition of this book—that it would remain one of the most solid and convincing war novels, an authentic success. Certain commentators noted that *Three Soldiers* was written in the classic style with none of the experimental devices of Dos Passos's later work. But still they approved. "A nonconforming book, uneven, swarming with life, filled with magnificent passages of realistic painting." "Maturity of thought, an exactitude of observation, intensity of dramatic incident—there is a revolt in this book."

When Le Club Français du Livre chose *The 42nd Parallel*—this was in 1949—Claude Edmonde Magny was asked to write the preface. She is a critic of considerable prestige, and her *L'Age du Roman américain* had just appeared the preceding year. She reminded the French reader that *The 42nd Parallel* was the first of a trilogy begun twenty-one years before.

But its most evident originality, that of technique, has not been dulled by time. . . . It is only in appearance that the work seems disconnected. Actually the interwoven devices are joined to the personal narrative by a *thématisme rigoureux.* . . . Not one of the invented techniques but has a multiplicity of significations. . . . The trilogy is a terrible indictment against civilization which permits man to be alienated, dispossessed. . . . And so the "message" of the book goes beyond America; it concerns us all, and the introspective reader will no doubt tremble at finding in Evelyn, Eleanor, Janey, Mac the specter or the caricature of what he secretly fears himself to be. . . . *The 42nd Parallel* is not limited to a single latitude—it is *la condition humaine.*

The rest of the story of Dos Passos in France has already been indicated. Gallimard took over *The 42nd Parallel* in 1951 and came out with a new translation of *1919*, entitled *L'An premier du Siècle* in 1952. Both publications gave rise to various general evaluations of this novelist's work.

The picture in this chapter has been drawn primarily from the magazines and literary weeklies, but Dos Passos also holds an honored place in the books which are concerned with American literature. Magny devotes two lengthy chapters to him—"La trilogie de Dos Passos, *U.S.A.,* ou le roman impersonnel," and "Le temps chez Dos Passos." Pouillon in *Temps et Roman* gives considerable attention to Dos Passos under the section on "Les modes de la compréhension." The chapter in Brodin's *Les Ecrivains américains de l'entre-deux-guerres* opens with the statement that Dos Passos of all the writers between the wars is the most ambitious in the scope of his work and the contemporary writer most justly to be compared with Balzac. Guyot, Simon, Coindreau in briefer space, and several others have analyzed the novels both for style and content, have presented the writer to the French reading public.

But when all is said, Dos Passos is most important and influential in France as an innovator, as a writer's writer; and it is in the imitations of his style that his imprint is heaviest.

8. HEMINGWAY

HEMINGWAY'S first French publication was the short story "L'Invincible" in *Navire d'Argent* for March, 1926. A brief biographical sketch followed ending, "Hemingway is considered by American critics one of the best writers of his generation." The next year "Cinquante mille dollars" appeared in the August *NRF*. And early in 1928 Faÿ reviewed the American edition of *Men without Women*, calling Hemingway the "king of dialogue writers, most gifted, most original." When his characters speak they are alive—irrefutable and invincible, the critic continued. Anyone who wants a just and profound perception of American life must read this writer.

In 1928 *Cinquante mille dollars*, a collection of six short stories, was published by Gallimard. In the course of the following months the book received at least nine reviews, all of them full of praise for the new writer. " 'Wring the neck of rhetoric,' Verlaine said. With the strong hands of a young lad from the Middle West Hemingway has obeyed. Neglecting vain compromises he goes right to the goal as a sprinter who dashes, his elbows close to his body." "The bright eye, the clear brain, the play of muscles like the rolling of billiard balls—why cannot this vigor and this health be got down on paper? It has been, now. *Cinquante mille dollars* will not be forgotten by the most absent-minded reader. In its entirety it is a chef-d'oeuvre." "The dialogue of Hemingway is one of the most amusing and dramatic things in

the world." Each reviewer picked out his favorite story. Henri de Régnier preferred "L'Invincible" and wrote of it: "Théophile Gautier and Merimée would have loved this 'planche' à la Goya, which seems to me to represent bullfighting perfectly." Buenzod chose "Le Champion," saying, "It has unbelievable perfection and intensity." Celly wrote of "Le village indien," "The vigor, the rapidity, the poetic expression make of this story a perfect thing." Llona called "Les tueurs" the model of the genre. "It seems impossible that so much emotion can be packed in so few words. My life will not be long enough to explore in my imagination the story which the author here leaves in suspense." A full-page advertisement for the book ran in *NRF* from January to June, 1929, quoting enthusiastic reviews from *L'Intransigeant, L'Avenir, Gazette de Lausanne,* and *Figaro.*

Hemingway was seemingly off to a good start in France. But no other translation appeared until 1931, when Victor Llona edited *Les Romanciers américains.* He chose Hemingway's "Je vous salue Marie" and asked André Maurois to write an article to preface the story. The critic said that he had been introduced to Hemingway's books when he was teaching at Princeton in 1929. He liked especially *The Sun Also Rises.* "Even though the author never intrudes, never comments, his characters are as real as those of Proust." Hemingway writes only what he knows from experience. The final impression is of vigor and courage in a form valuable for its simplicity.

A review by Buenzod of the American edition of *A Farewell to Arms* emphasized Hemingway's Americanism. Hemingway says only what is, what he sees, feels, can prove. He is ingenuous, anti-intellectual, amoral.

Like his immediate predecessors Sherwood Anderson, Waldo Frank, Dos Passos, he is very close to nature, submits to her rhythms, agrees with her laws. He is no *littérateur*. And we cannot judge him by the usual methods. But the book is a success—a work which matters.

In August, 1932, Coindreau's translation of *A Farewell to Arms* was ready for the public. When Hemingway learned this translation was to be made, he asked for Coindreau's copy of the novel. Then in pencil the novelist filled in (with his left hand, since a few weeks earlier he had broken his right arm in an automobile accident) for the translator's use the words which American custom (in 1929) had deleted. For this French edition the well known Drieu la Rochèlle wrote the preface. (Understandably, when Gallimard reprinted *L'Adieu aux Armes* after the war, this preface was omitted. Rochèlle had collaborated with the Germans, and when they lost the war he committed suicide.) The preface compared Hemingway with Maupassant. He has the same gifts—the gifts of the senses. An inexhaustible ability to receive, to register. A man who is at the same time a camera and a photograph but who is nonetheless a man. And Rochèlle, as did almost every other critic, admired Hemingway's dialogue and the use he put it to.

Reviews for this book appeared slowly. The *Revue Anglo-Américaine* commented on the Tauchnitz edition in February, 1933, calling the novel "brilliant, dry, incisive, often cynical, often brutal. It fulfills the promise of his short stories. There are unforgettable pages." In October *NRF* reviewed the French edition. Defeat is rarely a subject to interest writers, but Hemingway blends the retreat of the Italians with the love story and treats his two themes with a sharpness and a visible ease which is his usual manner. As always his dialogue is extraordinary. It would be easy to believe it strictly phonographic. In *Europe* a brief review concluded with the words, "an admirable book."

Jean Prévost was chosen to write the preface to *The Sun Also Rises,* which came out in April, 1933. Prévost bluntly asserted: "Here is a writer famous in his own country but not yet given his rightful place in ours. It is not difficult to discover the reasons." And the first reason listed was that a woman reader would find the six short stories collected under the title *Cinquante mille dollars* too strong, too powerful. She would find no feminine sensibility, no homage to woman. And so Hemingway, though admired, is not pushed by that force the most powerful of all—the conversations around the tea table. Prévost then movingly described the theme of *The Sun Also Rises* and suggested that it will touch more women than did the earlier volume. It is the story of love seen across the strongest prison bars that a man has ever known. Hemingway is here painting hell.

Several months after publication of the novel Philippe Soupault wrote a discussion of the three Hemingway volumes which were now in print in France. He too complained that these books had not received the interest which they merited. "Again in this domain as in many others we find this apathy, this impossibility to interest which seems to be characteristic of the years from 1930 to 1933. It is incontestable however that both in form and content Hemingway brings something very new. Is this the reason that we are suspicious of this writer who refuses to bow to what is fashionable?" Soupault felt sure, however, that Hemingway had qualities which should win over the French reader. He is above all a storyteller. His characters are human beings, not types. They remain the same men in spite of their contradictions—cowardly and brave at the same time, for example. This simplicity and truth gives to the novels of Hemingway their force and should be an aid in getting rid of the paralysis which has stopped the evolution of the modern French novel. Soupault made one adverse comment. There is a danger which lies in wait for Hemingway—one which he has not completely evaded in *The Sun Also Rises—c'est l'automatisme*. It might be possible for him to become too automatically spontaneous.

Two rather brief reviews appeared in the *Revue Anglo-Américaine* in 1933. Professor Charles Cestre wrote of *In Our Time* (American edition) that the psychology there expressed is original and enjoyable, the realism frank without being cynical, the country and the life picturesque. We breathe an atmosphere of action, of adventure, of the senses. The stripped style acquires its firmness by the propriety and *bouquet* of its vocabulary. Some of these short pieces are small marvels of ingenious art, seemingly unpremeditated. The talent of the author here is more even, rich, and pungent than in his novels. M. Cestre did not like, however, *The Torrents of Spring* (Crosby Continental Editions). Of this book he wrote:

Under the influence of Joyce, Hemingway mixes realism and symbol, the conscious and the unconscious. He accentuates the confusion of the reader by throwing in his confessions (or his hoaxes) on the method of composition and his memories (strongly spiced) of Paris after the war. Sentences generally consist of groups of words without verbs. His remarks and his devices are equally bewildering and the author laughs up his sleeve.

Little interest seemed to be shown in Hemingway for the next four years. But in April, 1937, Jeanine Delpech wrote a highly enthusiastic article for *Nouvelles Littéraires*, "Hemingway, romancier de la vie dangereuse," and this literary weekly published during the next few months three excerpts from the forthcoming *Green Hills of Africa*. Mlle Delpech called him the key figure of the young school of writers in America. He shows to his American readers the war and the European scene. He is the first to trace a clear portrait of this confused generation. He creates a new style of writing taken over enthusiastically by a nation too intense, too energetic to put its thoughts into the old moulds of English literature. He speaks neither the language of the Americans cramped by the puritan who makes of pleasure and of death subjects to be spoken of only in religious terms, nor the language of certain intelligentsia who believe they can supply a lack in their culture by cynical sophistication. He is wholly original.

Mlle Delpech's translation of *Green Hills of Africa* appeared in June of this same year, but created little stir. A favorable review in *Europe* treated it as a nature book. In *Etudes Anglaises* the critic admitted that the book was pleasant reading but felt it would hardly add to Hemingway's reputation. He devoted considerable space to complaining about the translation itself. He found too many "anglicisms," asked, "Qu'est-ce qu'une 'expression vacante,' un 'salaud romantique'?" and was generally displeased. The American edition had been discussed in *Le Mois* the preceding year in much more favorable terms. This anonymous critic preferred *Green Hills of Africa* to *Death in the Afternoon*. He felt the atmosphere of Africa was shown "with a consummate art. Hemingway excels in painting both human beings and animals. We feel his love for this immense country."

Notwithstanding the seeming lack of excitement over *Green Hills of Africa,* Gallimard published *Death in the Afternoon,* May, 1938. This gave rise to an article in *Nouvelles Littéraires:* "Un musicien, un comédien, un écrivain, et un peintre nous parlent des livres de Hemingway et de Peyré sur la 'fiesta brava.' " Louis Beyats, Alerme, Marcelle Auclair, and Roger Wild discussed the accuracy of the accounts of bull-fighting in *The Sun Also Rises, Death in the Afternoon,* and *Sang et Lumière.* There was some division of opinion but Peyré won out.

Leiris writing for *NRF* considered the chief quality of *Death in the Afternoon* its being *humaine,* "the quality which gives particular value to so many works coming from American authors and especially from most of the stories and novels of Hemingway."

Two almost diametrically opposed reviews of *To Have and Have Not* (American edition) appeared in 1938—Coindreau in *NRF,* Mayoux in *Etudes Anglaises.* Coindreau, translator of *The Sun Also Rises* and *A Farewell to Arms,* made it perfectly clear that he was greatly disappointed in Hemingway.

Again Hemingway shows us that his conception of society and of man the individual is that of a schoolboy of twelve whose heroes are d'Artagnan, Buffalo Bill, or Jack Dempsey. He gives us as protagonist a man who would have been perfect in the Stone Age but who for our present-day needs is, to say the least, insufficient. And Hemingway admires this man because he drinks whiskey neat, he fights with or kills off his neighbors on the least pretext, or without any pretext at all, and because his wife feels seminal desire stirring within her each time she looks at him. Why isn't Hemingway content to be himself? He is neither a thinker nor a psychologist. He is a painter who feels nature and describes it better than any other of his colleagues. Should he be ashamed of this gift?

Mayoux on the contrary wrote that

each book of Hemingway renews in me the same admiration. Wyndham Lewis has compared Hemingway to Merimée, but it is to Stendhal and his *style Code Civil,* excelled, purified but maintained in the same tradition of absolute limpidity and objectivity that I would compare him. Hemingway has made of pure action a complete experience. Never until this book has the type—man of adventures—been given such human significance. Harry Morgan is a noble individual, the Veterans are a debased and frightening mob. . . . The drinking scene is worthy of Flaubert. Morgan strangles the Chinese as one would kill a fly—and it is affection-tenderness. There is a true beauty in his relationships with his wife. . . . The irony flows; the satire sails along.

With the drawing to an end of the war the Hemingway story accelerates. Before, there had been spurts of violent enthusiasm followed by periods of silence. Partly, of course, that can be explained by Hemingway's own rather slender output.

The French writers themselves had for some time valued his work. But the general reading public really took Hemingway up with *Pour qui sonne le glas.* The fantastic sales story of this novel has been told in Chapter III. The equally amazing critical reception compared Hemingway's book to Stendhal's *Charterhouse of Parma* and *The Red and the Black,* to Tolstoi's *War and Peace,* and compared his characterizations and philosophy to those of Cervantes, Balzac, Joyce, Shakespeare. The book was called "a magnificent work," "a captivating, well told story," "a universal human experience," "a marvelously perfect success," "one of the *oeuvres-clefs* of our time," "an authentic achievement in contemporary literature." It was discussed, dissected, explicated, and praised universally. The obvious comparison to Malraux's *L'Espoir* was made over and over again—with the critics in general preferring the Hemingway volume.

(Sales comparison is interesting also: Gallimard reports 130,000 copies of *L'Espoir* have been sold since its publication in 1937. The Heinemann and Zsolnay figures show that nearly 200,000 copies of *Pour qui sonne le glas* have been sold.) The critics recognized the book as the summit of Hemingway's achievement produced in the full maturity of his powers. Molitor: "By its composition, its use of language, its depth of profound thought and human quality this book takes its place on the highest level." Anglès:

With *For Whom the Bell Tolls* it is no longer a question of an *originale* or *curieuse* or even *bouleversante* work. Nor is it a question of a book which furnishes a typical illustration of such and such a conception of the world. Rather here we find this silence, this harmony, and this calm ease of the truly great work of art, born it would seem of itself, sufficient unto itself, living, but living an ordered and powerful life and unifying in itself all the American vitality with the dignity, the balance, and the rich humanity of the great nineteenth-century European novels.

Certain critics found this book very different from what they were accustomed to consider the American novel. Apropos of this, Molitor wrote: "In Hemingway there is no trace of morbidity, nothing of the pathological mouldiness which disgusts us in some of the others. His vigor and even his brutality remain within healthy limits. Having lived much in Europe, Hemingway thinks in universal terms." Jarlot felt that before this novel "American literature, from Poe to the present, has lacked *conscience*." And, writing with a similar point of view, Lartigue suggested that the book "rehabilitates man. It is optimistic and we need optimistic books." Grenaud said: "Nothing here of mysticism, but the faith of a man put down in the midst of world struggle and judging the value of each human being. Here is an act which carries forward the spiritual possibilities of man."

Other reviewers commented on Hemingway's use of the classical unities or his use of new techniques which the French novelist could well profit by. In some detail they pointed out (as had been done before) the skilful use of the interior monologue and of direct presentation of character. They praised the lyric qualities of Hemingway's work. Typical of many was Las Vergnas's statement:

I consider that the melody of this prose, its plasticity, its clear rhythm (what boldness!), clear yet so charged with far-echoing resonances, make this book a total success. Commentary, discussion are needless. Is there anything more moving in all of Shakespeare than the last passage of this book?

The average French reader had dozens of opportunities to become familiar with the name of Hemingway in these immediate postwar years. In the Algiers special number of *Fontaine* (1943) the second chapter of *For Whom the Bell Tolls* was printed, and the reissue of this anthology in 1945 in Paris got the attention of a good many people. *A Farewell to Arms* was reprinted October 15, 1944. And in the same autumn three stories of Hemingway appeared in publications as diverse as the highbrow *L'Arbalète* and *Cahiers de la Table Ronde* or the popular weekly *Les Lettres Françaises*. In 1945 *L'Arbalète* printed a translation of the entire play, *The Fifth Column*. During the late summer of this year advertisements appeared in various Paris papers announcing a new daily, *Paris-Matin*, which would shortly be on the stands. Hemingway's *To Have and Have Not* under the title *L'Homme qui croyait à la chance* would run serially beginning with the first issue, the advertisements continued. And Duhamel's translation did run each day from October 2 to November 11-12. The book, entitled *En avoir ou pas*, came out also late in 1945 published by Gallimard. *Labyrinthe, Nouvelles Littéraires*, and *Solstice* each printed a Hemingway item during 1946. And Gallimard put out *Dix Indiens*, a collection of twelve short stories. Besides these publications in 1945 and 1946 there were at least thirteen reviews of *For Whom the Bell Tolls*, eleven reviews of *To Have and Have Not*, nine reviews of *Dix Indiens* and ten good-length, general articles on Hemingway and his work.

More than one writer commented that Hemingway had conquered an enormous French reading public. In many ways both critical and popular enthusiasm were made evident. For example, reviews of Coindreau's *Aperçus de Littérature américaine* (1946) angrily asked why was Hemingway not given his rightful place in this work on the American novel. The numerous articles on Hemingway were full of praise. They found him completely representative of America. Tavernier phrased it, "Hemingway well represents the American people with their mixture of realism and idealism, of cynicism and austere Puritanism, of puerility and grandeur . . . a people moody, passionate, tender, ferocious. A young people."

The critics wrote what they could discover about the man Hemingway—his life. Las Vergnas made a point of Hemingway's lack of formal education, his working at many jobs. "When we look at the bulk of his work, we notice the importance of the autobiographical element, utilized directly or indirectly, always empiric and concrete. I wonder if that is not a result of Hemingway's lack of enthusiasm, in his youth, for the rigors of synthesis and abstract formulation." Sans reported that Hemingway does not like Poe or Longfellow but does like Mark Twain. Sans was surprised that the novelist did not express an interest in Jack London, for "they are much alike."

Much ink was spilled on Hemingway's themes— death, sports, men without women, men with women, the active life, the role of the artist. Again and again the critics returned to Hemingway's sense of humanity. Schneider wrote, "Man isolated is always a target for Hemingway. Solitude is the unpardonable sin." Guérard asked, "Has any writer ever described solitude in as poignant and delicate a fashion as Hemingway? But solitude can build a wall, this artist knows, between man and the external world, a wall which must be destroyed at any cost." Lévy wrote, "Hemingway is a moralist. We in France recognize this easily since all writers here are moralists. Hemingway paints man in a modern society in which the social framework has given way. Man wants to find again a stable relationship between himself and other men; he hunts for a place in society, for a society in which there will be a place for him. Hemingway's heroes are adventurers in spite of themselves. Each one is profoundly moral even when outside the law." Maurois raised the question of the conflicts between man's instincts and his reason—or his faith:

The solution of a *post-chrétien* novelist [Hemingway]: all is moral or ethical which brings man a moment's happiness—to eat, to drink, to make love. This ethics takes away sexual taboos. But there remains a conflict between what makes man happy for a moment and what gives him lasting happiness. Sensuality can give quick pleasure, whiskey some moments of agreeable forgetting, but the morning-afters are unpleasant for both mind and body. The life of the heroes of Hemingway could not satisfy a Russian, or a Frenchman.

Long pages were written on Hemingway's techniques, his *style*, his art. Las Vergnas: "He writes a prose more difficult than poetry, a prose of four or five dimensions." Guérard agreed:

Hemingway is above all the *artiste*—a conscious artist and, I believe, the most perfect artist in modern American literature. He speaks of his work as a poet would. He works to control and master emotion. As vehicle he uses prose but I know little poetry more disciplined, more exact, more complex than the prose of Hemingway. This quality is naturally lost in translation. Translated the banality of Poe's style disappears—as does the grandeur of Hemingway's.

A good many explanations were offered for Hemingway's popularity—now full-blown—in France. Perhaps one important explanation is that he is, we have been told by many Frenchmen, easy to read in English. And others find him "simple" in French. But as Guérard and others have suggested, he loses a great deal in translation. There have been more criticisms of the actual translations of Hemingway than we have found for any of the other four novelists. It is understandable that the wartime version of *For Whom the Bell Tolls* was poor (Heinemann and Zsolnay revised it completely in 1948) but critics wrote harsh words also of the translations of *Green Hills of Africa* and of *To Have and Have Not.*

Most critics agreed on a second explanation of Hemingway's popularity. The general reader welcomed his work because it fitted into his ideas of America and Americans. The newspapers had given much publicity to Hemingway's service in World War II. The French knew that he had entered Paris with the first tanks at the time of the liberation. And also his descriptions of the wars and those who fought them—the ordinary soldiers, the peasants in the surrounding countryside— in *Farewell to Arms* and *For Whom the Bell Tolls* were not only all too familiar to the French but were presented in terms the average man responded to. A good many French in World War I and again in World War II knew the Yanks, had fought beside them, chewed their chewing gum, shared their whiskey—knew them as Hemingway described them. Blanzat summed this all up, "If we speak of the American novel, it is Hemingway we are thinking of."

However, certain Frenchmen were not too happy over Hemingway's popularity. Las Vergnas wrote in *Nouvelles Littéraires*, September 4, 1947:

For me, Hemingway is Clark Gable. The people of Hemingway, like the prototype made fashionable by Clark Gable, run after women and race into action. As I understand it, there have been among the feminine readers of Hemingway some millions of Claudette Colberts who have fallen in love with his brutality, spirit, and his handsome mustache. I believe it is under this guise, the Clark Gable of American literature, that Hemingway has seduced the French public.

The actual critical reception of *To Have and Have Not* was in the main unfavorable. The book appeared late in 1945, more than a year after *For Whom the Bell Tolls*. Reviewers made comparisons and to a man preferred *Pour qui sonne le glas*. Varying comments on *En avoir ou pas* were: "As Malraux said of *Sanctuary*, *To Have and Have Not* is the modern equivalent of ancient tragedy." "Rarely has the novelist told a story with such intensity, such sureness of effect, such vivid colors. It is as interesting as a detective story. But the satire is too expected, too systematic, too banal. The last pages recall Lawrence and the naïveté of his psychology." "Hemingway's horizon is limited." "One should not confuse violence with force. Perhaps that is what is wrong with this book. As simple adventure it is good.

But when it makes a pretense of social criticism it is weak."

Hoog wrote a sweeping indictment for *Arts:*

The sound of the machine gun dominates the American novel. *To Have and Have Not* is an example. The Hemingways, Caldwells, Faulkners, Dashiell Hammetts choose to show not the truth but hell. It seems to me impossible to understand the heroes of these machine-gun novels if we forget that young America has given her faith for nearly a century to the heroes of Fenimore Cooper, Emerson, or Rockefeller. This type of superman was very special. The young white god who pursued the bad Indians, or the "representative man" dear to Emerson, or the "self-made man" who began with fifty cents and ended with fifty million—all this expressed the same happy, optimistic point of view. And human destiny reduced itself in the last analysis to *une bonne hygiène interieure et exterieure.* The world was a good place and open to all the benefits of material progress. But neither the world nor the spirit is as simple as this boy-scout philosophy would like to make out.

The reviewers of *Dix Indiens* were much happier. They praised the variety of subjects in this collection of short stories. They emphasized Hemingway's art as a storyteller. They spoke of his essential themes, all illustrated in this volume which "shows very clearly the apparent diversity but the profound unity of Hemingway's art." A few recognized humor. One criticized his basic "nihilism." Another labeled him a "journalist of genius who offers us astonishing flashes but never takes his distance in time or space—which is a necessity for the creation of great works of art."

Finally the seemingly endless flow of commentary died down. But the books continued to sell. Gallimard had reissued the before-the-war volumes and except for fugitive writings and certain short stories which would appear under the title *Paradis perdu* in 1949, all of Hemingway was available in France. Scattered articles about him continued to appear, of course. And in 1948 Guyot's small book devoted fifteen pages to a very favorable presentation of Hemingway's work. Magny's volume contains some twenty pages of serious discussion and praise under the title, "Hemingway ou l'exaltation de l'instant." The critic characterized *A Farewell to Arms* as the only American *roman de guerre* which is truly successful. *The Sun Also Rises* exemplifies individualism leading to a *nihilisme quasi byronien*. *To Have and Have Not* was given a somewhat existentialist interpretation. In *For Whom the Bell Tolls* the critic found Hemingway truly adult. She devoted several pages to the ideas and the techniques of this novel. Simon's book (1950) suggested that in America there had been a reaction against Hemingway beginning about 1935. "Today one must hunt in a conservative periodical like the *Saturday Review of Literature* to see priority still given to Hemingway." Simon himself considered the writer, however, not only as a representative man of first importance but as a "magnificent writer who deserves to endure."

One important article appeared in the *Revue Nouvelle* (1949), "Un grand romantique: Ernest Hemingway." Marie Forestier emphasized the (to French eyes) so different background of American novelists. "Hemingway is typical in going from high school, to war, to journalism, to writing—not to a university. That so many American writers have been reporters helps explain the documentary tendency in their books." She pointed out that

one hears much of American optimism but the great American writers—Melville, Poe, James, and today Faulkner, Caldwell, Hemingway—all have a tragic sense of man and society. Every American who thinks and feels for himself carries within him a

Puritan (the single exception is perhaps Steinbeck, thanks to the influence of the Californians). . . . The genius of Hemingway is fragmentary. He excels in creating silhouettes, scenes, situations. He does not create the single all-important character of the traditional French novel.

The critic spoke of Hemingway's symbols (which she admitted Americans find more easily in Hemingway's work than do the French), of his language sense, of his poor characterization of females, and of the importance of his work as a documentation on the spiritual history of our times. She ended by saying that with certain restrictions one can class Hemingway among *les coeurs purs*. "There are not many artists ancient or modern who merit such praise."

At the end of 1949, as has been said, *Paradis perdu* was published. This included the stories which had not yet been printed in France from *The First 49 Stories* and reprinted *The Fifth Column,* which had appeared in *L'Arbalète* in 1945. Again there was considerable praise, though the reviews added little new to the picture of Hemingway.

Conjecture, criticism, and comment on *Across the River and Through the Trees* have been appearing in France ever since the American publication. The book has not yet been translated into either French or Italian. Gallimard when asked why replies that Hemingway has requested publication be delayed. The early reviewers of the American edition were enthusiastic. Vivet remarked, "This book may well appear to future generations of readers as the most moving witness of one of the last writers who has the sense of man." Muller called Hemingway

certainly the most celebrated American novelist and without doubt one of the greatest living writers. This book opposes the world of brutality to a world of sweetness where art is the essential aim. Beauty against brutality, desire for perfection against desire for power. Hemingway here abandons his stripped style and is limpid, almost *classique*. Perhaps it is this change in style and manner which has deceived certain American critics and made them judge the book a poor one. Hemingway has announced that this is his last novel—henceforward only poetry.

Others were dismayed by the book. Danchin wrote:

This last-born of the American novelist has nothing of the vigorous health of its predecessors. These jerky conversations and disconnected reflections, sprinkled occasionally with coarse slang and profanity, with obscure allusions which tomorrow no one will understand, seem to me to add nothing to the glory of the author. A biographer will perhaps find something here to glean.

Duesburg objected to the book's "senile, stammering love-making" but praised highly the scene of the duck hunt. "For these pages much can be forgiven." Mohrt agreed that *Across the River* was without doubt one of the feeblest works of Hemingway but suggested that it should be read as an epilogue to *A Farewell to Arms*.

One commentator said that Hemingway's criticisms of Montgomery, Leclerc, and Eisenhower were so harsh that they well-nigh led to the banning of the book in the United States. And R. H. de Montalet in the April, 1951, *Critique* attacked the American reviews of *Across the River*. Hemingway, he said, was criticized for the "superficiality of the plot, the banality of the situation, the vulgarity of the dialogue, the constant repetitions of certain trite formulas, and so on." For de Montalet the book is the best Hemingway has written; he does not understand the reason for these attacks. The American critics said they liked Hemingway's other books but not this one. Actually, the French writer continued, these critics never have liked Hemingway or else they have liked him for the wrong reasons. American reviewers compared the book with *A Farewell to Arms;* it should be compared with *The Sun Also Rises.* In one the hero seeks love but is impotent; in the other he seeks love but is dying. Certain themes are common to all of Hemingway's novels. Man is closed within himself, walled in his solitude like a prison. He tries to escape from this solitude by three means: alcohol, dangerous living, and love. Reduced to their simplest terms all three escapes are present in this book and that is the value of the novel. *"Across the River* shows an incontestable progress in the artistry of its author. Our brief analysis tries to illuminate the qualities of *dépouillement* and economy, which . . . are here found raised to an extraordinary degree of perfection."

And a footnote to the commentary on *Across the River* in France can be found in two articles published in *Samedi-Soir,* January, 1951. The newspaper writer reported that many people in Venice think the original for Renata, heroine of the novel, is Adriana Ivanchitch, a member of Venetian aristocracy. The story was, according to *Samedi-Soir,* that Hemingway's wife had broken her ankle skiing in the Dolomites. During her convalescence Hemingway met Adriana, then nineteen. She introduced him to Venetian society and he promised to put her in a book with himself as hero. So went the rumors and conjectures as reported in one Paris paper.

Hemingway's continued popularity was evinced in 1950 when the French Book Club printed a 5,000-copy edition of *Pour qui sonne le glas* for its readers. The entire edition was sold out within three days. And a second printing of 5,000 (Heinemann and Zsolnay had permitted only a total of 10,000) was run off in 1952 and sold with almost equal dispatch. Another indication of the selling power of Hemingway's name could be seen in the ads for

Summer's *Pourquoi ces bêtes sont-elles sauvage?* a book on African big-game hunting for which Hemingway wrote the preface. Even a writer on economics borrowed from Hemingway and entitled his article "Pour qui sonne le glas?" and used the Donne quotation, no doubt thinking to attract attention by the familiarity of Hemingway's title.

In France as in America *The Old Man and the Sea* was, and is, a stunning success. The continental edition of *Life* did not carry the novel, but shortly after American publication a rash of articles and lengthy reviews appeared voicing enthusiastic approval. Hemingway's picture beamed cheerfully from the daily and weekly newspapers. His name got the honor of the largest print on the covers of magazines.

Gallimard had made arrangements to bring out a French translation as soon as possible and had set Jean Dutourd (who just as he saw *Le Vieil Homme et la Mer* appear on the bookstands received the Prix Interallié for his own novel *Au bon Beurre*) to working on the book. They expected to publish in January, probably feeling it just as well to let the November-December furor over the various French *Prix* die down a bit and make room in the papers and magazines for the voluminous comment which they knew a new Hemingway would bring forth. However, Gallimard had sold serial rights on *The Old Man and the Sea* to *Paris-Presse-L'Intransigeant* with the understanding that this daily newspaper would wait until the book hit the bookstores before beginning the serialization. Late Friday afternoon, November 28, Gallimard learned that *Paris-Presse* would print the first installment in Monday's paper. A prompt conference held in the huge *hôtel* on rue Sebastien-Bottin decided to get the book out immediately. And at the end of the second working day—Tuesday—thousands of copies were ready for distribution. *Paris-Presse* ran the novel from December 2 through the issue of the 14-15.

In all the thousands of words written by reviewers of both the American edition in September and the French translation three months later we found only one adverse comment—and that was embedded in an otherwise favorable review: "The book is perhaps just a little too *bien fait.*" As for the praise—"I would put this book on the same level as *Leaves of Grass* by Whitman, *Un Coeur simple* by Flaubert, *Of Mice and Men* by Steinbeck, *La Mort d'Ivan Ilitch* by Tolstoi." "This book reminds us of *Sinbad, Moby Dick,* and Conrad." "Hemingway's impersonality, his description without adjectives, the actions, gestures, simple and vital thoughts of the Old Man are those of Homer and the Bible. . . . Ulysses, Beowulf, Roland are the Old Man's brothers." "In reading this novel we think at times of *Moby Dick,* of the convict in Faulkner's *Old Man,* of the pantheistic lyricism of Steinbeck."

Mohrt in a long and suggestive article for *La Table Ronde* compared the book to the great myths—Hercules, Siegfried, Robinson Crusoe—calling it *un mythe apollinien* where man triumphs over nature or *un mythe dyonisiasque* where nature triumphs over man. The critic suggested we should see it as a mixture, an alternation between the two paganisms. "All victory carries within itself the germ of defeat and all death foretells a resurrection." Muller found Christian symbols in the story. The wounded hands of Santiago, the way he places the mat on his shoulder, the hill leading to his cabin, the manner in which he lies extended, "crucified" in the boat. Nadeau discovered sin, art, and Hemingway's bitter critics [those who found *Across the River and*

Through the Trees a poor book] symbolized in this new book. Lalou also agreed that Hemingway probably thought of his own struggles with the literary critics when he told the story of the struggle with the great fish.

In *Nouvelles Littéraires* an article written on the American edition by Gary, a French novelist, pointed out that young French writers should spend a long time on *The Old Man and the Sea.* "The artist can learn everything about his trade from this book. I myself have already reread the book ten times. Its truth is not new but everlasting—the story of Sisyphus."

A good many of the reviewers were particularly pleased to see that Hemingway had made a striking critical comeback. Erval in *Gazette des Lettres* wrote:

There exists a curious misunderstanding between Hemingway and the American critic who was fond of Hemingway as long as he was relatively unknown or at least unrecognized in his own country and renowned solely in Europe. But then came the war and *For Whom the Bell Tolls* was welcomed with a unanimous enthusiasm by both critics and the general public. It was then that the American critic felt a qualm of conscience. Hemingway a best-seller? Would not his prolonged stay on the best-seller lists along with all the *Gone with the Winds* contaminate this author who had won now not only all the working girls but also Hollywood? Ingrid Bergman and Ava Gardner ended up rendering Hemingway suspect in the eyes of certain people to whom success and quality represent two irreconcilable concepts. After ten years Hemingway published *Across the River and Through the Trees.* American critics did not like this book at all. No one wanted to admit that Hemingway had here written his most beautiful love story, rejoinder of a mature man to *Farewell to Arms,* meditation of a writer who for the first time doubts violence—the supreme value in works of his youth. Now we have *The Old Man and the Sea*—a book universally praised.

Succinctly Mohrt stated: "The former champion has

refound his form and is ready to defend his title. *Le glas ou le gong avait été sonné trop tôt.*"

In the words of the very able translator: "Here is the book. It is finished. It is perfect. It is one of those works of art which live through the centuries like a quietly shining diamond. *The Old Man and the Sea* is a kind of poem, but an epic poem told in the simplest fashion."

9. FAULKNER

THE STORY OF William Faulkner in France is one of a favorable early reception and an increasing critical acclaim going from an "important young American novelist" to the "best of the Americans" to the high pinnacle of being almost universally considered the "greatest living novelist in the world." Faulkner's books never have had the popular sales of Hemingway's *Pour qui sonne le glas* or Steinbeck's *Les Raisins de la Colère*, but they have sold steadily. Though we have been unable to obtain exact sales figures, it seems probable that until *Sanctuary* appeared in America as a twenty-five-cent edition in 1947, sales of Faulkner's books in France surpassed those in America. Many French believe that they taught the United States the importance of Faulkner.

Faulkner's reception in France started in June, 1931, when Maurice E. Coindreau published an article in *NRF*, one of the first extended treatments of the young novelist to appear anywhere. In the article, written shortly after the American publication of *Sanctuary*, Coindreau developed several themes that French criticism of Faulkner has continued to emphasize. First and foremost, Coindreau found the novelist to be a moralist. Like most Americans Faulkner has a bad strain of idealism and cultivates his *fleur bleue*. Already he is the master of a new technique based on the power of the inexpressed. *Sanctuary* demonstrates that the author is one of the most interesting of the young American writers. The subject matter of *Sanctuary*, as is true in all his books, is only a pretext for the displaying of a technique, which here touches on perfection. The reader should forget the subject and occupy himself with the manner in which the book is written.

In November of the same year another article on Faulkner appeared anonymously in *Le Mois* entitled "Les romans horribles de M. William Faulkner." As the title indicates, the author was not as favorably impressed as Coindreau. Based primarily on the English reception of Faulkner, the article commenced by quoting the eulogistic remark by Arnold Bennett, "He writes like an angel." Plots of different novels were summarized, and the homogeneity of Faulkner's books was found to be: "All his subjects are equally horrible. . . . The basis even of existence is a suffering without reason and without expiation." *Sanctuary* was presented as an example of gratuitous horror. Apparently the anonymous author confused Ruby and Temple because he called Ruby "this woman of excellent and formerly rich family who becomes the mistress of a gangster though we know not how or why."

In 1932 Gorham Munson in the August *Europe* continued the attack on Faulkner's subject matter, though admitting the power of his style. In the same year two short stories were published in *Commerce* and *NRF*, both translated by Coindreau. These were the familiar "A Rose for Emily" and "Dry September." Also in 1932 *Nouvelles Littéraires* had a review of the English edition of *Sanctuary*, which spoke of the "cruel lyricism" of the poet-author. Though the reviewer, Levinson, wondered if the book should be relegated to the *Enfer* of public libraries, he thought it better than Lawrence's *Lady Chatterley's Lover*.

In August, 1933, *NRF* published a second short story, "Il était une reine." Three months later *Sanctuaire* was released. The reviews fall into a certain chronological pattern, as is true with many of the books by our five men. Before the French translation appears, reviews are published, particularly in the academic *Revue Anglo-Américaine* or *Etudes Anglaises*, on the American or English editions and sometimes on the Tauchnitz or Crosby. For example, the Crosby publication of *Sanctuary* was reviewed by Charles Cestre in the April, 1933, *Revue Anglo-Américaine*. Professor Cestre spoke of the book's violence, its infernal lyricism, its images employed like those on the screen, and its sinister splendor. Malraux's preface, next step in the pattern, was published as an article in the November, 1933, *NRF*. Its much quoted last sentence has already been given. Elsewhere in the preface Malraux talked about the "irremediable" element in the book and discussed its fascination in terms of tragic art. Reviews after the publication of *Sanctuaire* referred to the somber poetry, the tragic sense of tone, the successful character delineation of Temple Drake, the magnificent drama, the sense of fatality. One dissenting reviewer called the book a nightmare which would give the reader a headache.

Coindreau's translation of *As I Lay Dying* came out in April, 1934, with the preface by Valery Larbaud, who traced parallels between Faulkner and Homeric legends. Addie is the queen, Anse the king Ulysses, and the children the princes. He listed many epic qualities found in the novel and suggested the subject was worthy of a Boccaccio or a La Fontaine. Writing in 1946, Raimbault, one of the translators of *Sanctuary* and some seven other Faulkner volumes, reminisced about the situation in 1933 and 1934, commenting that after the appearance of *Tandis que j'agonise* Faulkner's name was known throughout all of France.

Reviews of the novel were favorable, approving the parallels made by Larbaud. The "great lyric fresco" of the book evoked admiration. Reviewing the book in *Europe*, Eugène Dabit talked about his own experiences a year before in writing a novel, *Un Mort tout neuf*, in which the basic situation was similar to that of *As I Lay Dying*. Dabit's book was the story of a group of petty bourgeois in a small, stuffy French town gathered around the dead body of a member of the family. The reviewer spoke of his envy of Dos Passos, Hemingway, and Faulkner, "who seem to have at their disposition a brute, new, admirable material, and whose works are somewhat on the scale of their country." These new elements cannot help but influence the style and the art of the novel and make of the American novel a thing much different from the French. Faulkner's realism is "pitiless, violent, without smallness, sometimes burlesque with its profound blacks, sulfurous yellows, harsh reds."

The French have continued to regard *As I Lay Dying* as one of the best of Faulkner's novels. It has not sold as widely as *Sanctuary* but its influence on younger French writers has been much greater. In 1935 Jean Louis Barrault, then at the beginning of his career, presented at the Théâtre Atelier a pantomimic adaptation of the novel. He called his production *Autour d'une mère*. And in 1946 a magnificent de luxe edition of *Tandis que j'agonise* appeared, handsomely illustrated by Burins de Courtin. Two hundred copies were printed; each sold for 15,000 francs—$125 at the then going rate for the dollar. One reviewer of this edition called it the "best novel by Faulkner that we know in France. Its realism and form have profoundly impressed our young literature." It is a key book, as essential to one's library as *The Princess of Cleves* or *The Sorrows of Young Werther*. It is a "modern classic."

In January, 1935, *Europe* published the short story, "Soleil couchant." And before Coindreau's translation of *Light in August* was released later the same year, the February *Cahiers du Sud* had given Chapter VII of the book to the public and in April the preface under the revealing title, "Le puritanisme de William Faulkner." In addition to puritanism, so significant in French criticism of American novels, this preface also stressed the subjective quality of Faulkner's realism, a theme developed and emphasized by others.

The American edition of *Light in August* had, in 1933, been reviewed in *Revue Anglo-Américaine* by Cestre and in *NRF* by Coindreau. Cestre spoke of the "overwhelming force" of the book but qualified his admiration by wishing that the author had had both more maturity and more art. Coindreau had no such qualifications for his enthusiasm. The book was evidence of Faulkner's "profound genius." The reviews after the French translation in 1935 were almost universally enthusiastic. The book was called "original from every point of view: subject, atmosphere, composition." One reviewer, in *Cahiers du Sud*, emphasized his preference for *Light in August* over the traditional French novel of psychological analysis. He doubted whether the French form could survive unless it "renews itself by contact with works such as this. Faulkner's novel goes beyond the traditional form and reveals it to be fortuitous, facile, deprived of blood, flesh, and life."

The next year, 1936, saw only a short story by Faulkner published, "Feuilles rouges," in *Europe*; however, 1937 was much busier. Bernard Faÿ in the course of a lengthy article on the new American literature discussed Faulkner in some detail. Faulkner's life and the plots of *Sanctuary* and *Absalom* were summarized. His particular gift is the "faculty of describing a heavily charged emptiness." Faÿ was also impressed by Faulkner's irony and by his "bizarre elegance" like that of a primitive African idol. This same year Coindreau reviewed the American edition of *Absalom*, comparing the house of Sutpen to the Greek house of Atreus. The book was more than a novel, it was a "great barbaric poem." In *Etudes Anglaises* Maurice Le Breton published a full-length scholarly study of Faulkner. His article, "Technique et psychologie chez William Faulkner," placed Faulkner in the novelistic tradition of Joyce and Woolf. The American forces the reader to reconstruct the incidents in the novel so that he may more profoundly experience the individual psychology of the characters. This is the blending of technique and psychology. The critic made a detailed study of three novels: *Soldiers' Pay, As I Lay Dying,* and *The Sound and the Fury;* and he found Faulkner's artistic growth culminating in *Absalom.* He discussed the affinities between Faulkner and Sherwood Anderson and Faulkner and Robinson Jeffers. The concluding note of the article expressed Le Breton's feeling that Faulkner's difficult techniques are justified by the psychological results that he obtains.

In October, 1937, Raimbault and Delgove's translation of *Sartoris* was published by Gallimard. The book was greeted enthusiastically and many reviewers used its appearance as an excuse to discuss Faulkner in general terms now that four of his books had been translated. Thousands of words of praise appeared, and the critics stressed Faulkner's originality. "He is the most original of all the American novelists." "The only European influence on him is perhaps that of Dostoevski." "He has a marvelous poetic magic." Of considerable importance was the six-page article by Jean Paul Sartre in *NRF*. Sartre stressed the admirable silences in *Sartoris* whose meaning is made clear only by indirect suggestions. Even the characters, like young Bayard, act and do not think or talk. This silence is the "impossible dream of a puritan ultrastoicism."

The Sound and the Fury in Coindreau's translation and with his preface appeared in August, 1938. He called the order of the book essentially musical. The four parts are like the four movements of a symphony: first, *moderato*; second, *adagio douloureux*; third, *allegro*; and fourth, a sequence of *allegro furioso, andante religioso, allegro barbaro,* and *lento.* Commenting on the characters, Coindreau found Dilsey the black sister of Flaubert's Felicité.

The critical reception of the book was extremely favorable. Jacques Duesberg, for example, wrote an almost rhapsodic article in *Revue Générale.* The reader of Benjy's soliloquy "identifies himself with Benjy and abandons himself to the lyricism of the poem as to the savor of a great wine, until then unknown." Each rereading, the critic concluded, brings us new beauties. Generally speaking, the first part of the book, Benjy's soliloquy, attracted most attention among the critics. So much discussed was this section, then and later, that Henri Peyre, writing in the Summer, 1947, issue of the *Virginia Quarterly Review,* could call it a *locus classicus* of French criticism.

The publication of *Le Bruit et la Fureur* occasioned another important article by Sartre which was printed in the June and July *NRF.* The recent collection of Faulknerian criticism edited by Hoffmann and Vickery makes this article now available in an English translation, but it might be helpful to point out the ideas in this essay which are picked up by other French critics. Sartre considers the theme of the novel to be time. Time has a value dependent on character and has no absolute existence. No future exists for Faulkner's people, only a present derived from the past, and Quentin's breaking of his watch symbolizes this. Sartre evaluates this treatment of time in metaphysical terms. He finds the lack of future in Faulkner's world to be an untrue description of reality. "Not that life is not absurd, but that it has an absurdity different from what Faulkner ascribes to it." The future may hold only violent change, but that is still a future. Sartre admires Faulkner's art, but "I don't believe in his metaphysic." The existentialist philosopher can be clearly seen in these comments.

The three books the average Frenchmen will name if you speak of Faulkner to him are *Sanctuary, Light in August,* and *The Sound and the Fury.* All three were published before the war and each brought forth great enthusiasm. So Faulkner is by no means a postwar phenomenon in France. Though his books did not, and still do not, have "popular" sale to the masses, nevertheless his name would have been known before the war to even the casual reader of the literary weeklies and monthlies.

The publication of *Treize Histoires* in March, 1939, however, aroused little response. As French publishers have emphasized to us, the French have never accepted the short story form as Americans have; sales for such volumes are low. The few reviews of the book were favorable, but that is about all that can be said. In *Cahiers du Sud* the reviewer, really talking about the whole of Faulkner, said, "He attains a strange music, an unforgettable rhythm of incantation." His universe is by turns "magical, fantastic, and tragic" by means of the newest, most tender, and most piercing poetry.

One other evaluation should be summarized here. René Liebowitz in the November, 1940, *Cahiers du Sud* published an article, "L'Art tragique de William Faulkner." He spoke of two kinds of novelists—one like Balzac stressing objective reality, the other like Faulkner (stemming perhaps from Flaubert) stressing the interior world and requiring the reader to reconstruct the exterior events. This second attitude predisposes the artist to the spiritual atmosphere of tragedy. Early novels in France and England, primarily picaresque, are not tragic. It is Faulkner's achievement to bring back into the novel the sense of tragedy the Greeks had. Time in Faulkner plays the role of a kind of fourth dimension, a spatial quality. Each event in his novels is the synthesis of many anterior events. And each character is the result of many predecessors. This synthesizing gives the epic quality to Faulkner's works. Thus is explained the kind of books Faulkner writes and the difficulty that the reader has with them.

The story of Faulkner is now broken by the war. Between 1939 and 1946 no new translations appeared in France. Nor could the French critics in the occupied zone publish articles on him. So the discussion of Faulkner moves to Algiers or wherever resistance magazines were possible. Because of physical circumstances these magazines were in the hands of young writers. And so there recommences a steady stream of articles on Faulkner or stories by him that has continued to the present day. *Poèsie 43* published "L'Après-midi d'une vache," and this same story, made available by Coindreau before it was published in English, reappeared in the *Fontaine* special issue. In 1944 "Elly" was in *Fontaine,* and the special number of *L'Arbalète* in the fall of the year published "Wash." *Confluences's* "Problèmes du Roman" contained many references to Faulkner throughout its more than five hundred pages. The critics found in him new possibilities for the future postwar French novel. One, harking back to Coindreau, pointed up the techniques Faulkner had borrowed from musical composition. Others talked about his breaking up of the narrative, a movie technique. Some again dealt with the role of fate in Faulkner and made comparisons with Kafka. One critic emphasized the instantaneous feeling, the immediacy, in Faulkner's novels. Whenever his name was mentioned, he was treated as the most important of the American novelists, either implicitly or explicitly.

The postwar years continued the steady flow of stories by Faulkner published in various magazines and anthologies. In 1945 there were 2; 1946, 2; 1947, 4; 1948, 4; 1951, 4; 1952, 3. Each year there were more articles on Faulkner—too many even to list here. It is also true that Faulkner's name appears more and more often as a standard of comparison for other American and French novelists. That his works should be referred to apropos of so many Europeans, both living and dead, indicates something of the universal stature conferred on the writer William Faulkner by the French.

The publication of *Pylon* in a translation by Raimbault and Mme Rousselet in 1946 attracted a great deal of attention. Shortly after its publication a selection from it was printed in the popular weekly, *Samedi-Soir.* As early as 1935 Le Breton had favorably reviewed the American edition of this novel; and in 1945, a year before the French translation, Mme Magny in *Esprit* had spoken of the perfection of the ending of *Pylon* and Pierre Fauchery in the June *Espace* had discussed "La mythologie faulknérienne dans *Pylon*." This critic described the typical Faulkner novel as the "development of an obsession—almost always of sexual character—up to its resolution" either in crime, or suicide, or simply death. In *Pylon* the obsession of the reporter is the principal subject. Fauchery felt that like all mythologies the Faulknerian world is filled with fatality. The puritanism of the writer comes out in his contemptuous treatment of Laverne, the wife of the pilot, and in the writer's repetition of the act of vomiting. His insistence bears all the earmarks of puritan cruelty, concluded the critic.

Samedi-Soir struck a keynote for the reception of the French translation of *Pylon* when its anonymous reviewer said, "It is an extraordinary book—but that is not at all surprising, given the name of the author." Another commentator called the book a "novel-poem"— a new reason for our admiration and gratitude to the "greatest contemporary novelist." Several admitted that *Pylon* was not the best of Faulkner's books, but still found it to be perfect. One reviewer after talking about the black pessimism in the novel and its implied attack on the capitalistic system went on to ask, "Is it true, as we have been told, that Faulkner has sought refuge in an insane asylum? And will madness be for him the ultimate means of escaping from his monsters?" Like the comments on *Light in August* the reviews of *Pylône* emphasized Faulkner's puritanism—"the puritan conviction that sin is never forgiven, a conviction which, from Hawthorne to Faulkner, goes through all American literature."

This same year Coindreau's *Aperçus de Littérature américaine* was published by Gallimard. Though most of the material had appeared before in various prefaces and articles, Coindreau gathered together a thirty-five page chapter on Faulkner, whom he regarded as the culmination of the literary movement starting with Dreiser. One of the principal virtues of the chapter was that Coindreau presented Faulkner's works in the order in which they were written and discussed the books (up to *The Hamlet*) which had not yet been translated into French. As an analysis of Faulkner's artistic development, however, the chapter is incomplete since it dismisses everything Faulkner wrote before *The Sound and the Fury* in one sentence. Several reviews used Coindreau's book as a springboard for considerations of the American novel in general and, because of Coindreau's emphasis, of Faulkner in particular. Julien Sans's review in *Climats,* for example, referred to "William Faulkner or: the artist; William Faulkner or: the genius." This man's books are "the greatest contemporary literature" and Faulkner himself is "the greatest of all." Sans went on, "Not to admire the work of Faulkner is to turn one's back on the Aeschylan art of these American tragedies. . . . Sooner or later, men will feel the grandeur and the importance of his message. We possess no novelist, alas! who is comparable to him." Max Pol Fouchet in *Carrefour,* going again from Coindreau to Faulkner, said, "The United States possesses in Faulkner a very powerful mind, the most powerful mind it has had, beyond a doubt, since Melville. But the capital importance of Faulkner is perhaps explained by the fact that he has gone farther than the others into the soul of his people." André Rousseaux in *Le Littéraire* complained, "It seems to me that the esteem for the work of William Faulkner in France does not follow the ascending curve that his value merits. After having had a great vogue in the years before the war, Faulkner is no more the star for us. The changing mode is infatuated with a Steinbeck." Then the critic continued by pointing out the permanent value in Faulkner's novels.

Monsieur Rousseaux's complaints would seem unwarranted. In 1946 in addition to what has already been mentioned, Brodin's book, *Les Ecrivains américains de l'entre-deux-guerres,* came out with a chapter on Faulkner and Jean Pouillon's *Temps et Roman* contained a lengthy discussion of Faulkner and time. The de luxe folio edition of *Tandis que j'agonise,* noted earlier, appeared also in 1946. Raimbault translated two short stories: "Au-delà" for *Fontaine* and "Chacun son tour" for *Samedi-Soir.* In this same year critical articles on Faulkner were published in *Revue Internationale, Les Temps Modernes, Cahiers des Langues Modernes, Les Nouvelles Littéraires,* and *Gazette des Lettres.* In some ways the most important of these was the one in *Revue Internationale,* March issue. For it was the translation of Malcolm Cowley's introduction to the Viking *Portable Faulkner.* No particular comments accompanied the introduction, but after its publication certain remarks made by French critics seem explainable only granting the critic had read Cowley's discussion. The following February this same magazine printed a translation of Robert Penn Warren's article on the *Portable Faulkner* (the article was originally in the *New Republic*). But judging from later criticism, we can only conclude that few critics read Warren's essay since there are almost no references to it or to the ideas found in it.

During 1947 short stories by Faulkner were published in *Les Lettres Françaises, Les Oeuvres Libres, Samedi-Soir,* and the anthology edited by Albert J. Guérard, *Ecrit aux U. S. A.* In his preface to Faulkner's story

Guérard, now a professor at Harvard, compared the French and American reception of Faulkner:

William Faulkner is generally regarded in France as the most important American writer of our time, though the Americans give this place to Hemingway. The French critique of Faulkner has been more penetrating than the American. . . . The actual interest in existentialism has certainly contributed to prolong in France the debates [on Faulkner]; more than any other modern novelist, more than Joyce, Faulkner seems to put in his works the "philosophy of the absurd." The ever-present macabre humor and horror, the exoticism of places and strangeness of style, the revelation of a *conscience* foreign and profoundly "puritan"—all this gives to the work of Faulkner an originality and a complexity much more striking for the French than for the Americans.

The next year, 1948, found short stories in the *Revue de Paris* and in the anthology *Courtes Histoires américaines*. The pamphlet *Littérature prolétarienne aux Etats-Unis* printed an excerpt from *Tandis que j'agonise* entitled "Dewey Dell." Excerpts from the forthcoming translation of *Soldiers' Pay* appeared in the *Gazette des Lettres*. Publishers this year went back to Faulkner's early works, and translations of *Soldiers' Pay, Mosquitoes,* and *Doctor Martino and Other Stories* were issued. The first two were not published by Gallimard, the only Faulkner volumes of which this has been true.

Soldiers' Pay was translated under the title *Monnaie de Singe*. The expression *monnaie de singe* has its origins in the sixteenth and seventeenth centuries, when many Parisians kept monkeys as household pets. The question arose whether or not the monkeys needed to pay when crossing the toll bridges over the Seine. Many people solved the problem by having their monkeys perform various tricks for the tollkeepers, who would then let the monkeys, and presumably the masters, across free.

In time *monnaie de singe* came to mean these tricks done in lieu of actual payment. A natural extension of meaning made the expression apply to human activities similar to the monkey's. Needless to say, the connotations of the phrase are derogatory.

The French critics realized that the book was Faulkner's first novel and discussed it as such. They spent little time on the merits of the book itself, admitting it not to have too much value, but studied the novel to find traits of the Faulkner they knew so well. Their conclusions were that the novelist had not by then worked out any of the techniques which were later to preoccupy him, but the disillusioned bitterness was already present. The combination of picturesque cruelty and a kind of pity for the characters was commented on. But the pen of Faulkner was still an inexpert one.

Mosquitoes came out with an amusing preface by Raymond Queneau, whose election this same year to the Académie Goncourt probably did not hurt sales. According to the publishers, Editions de Minuit, *Moustiques* has sold only some five or six thousand copies, though there is a steady sale on it even now and it is kept in stock. After Faulkner won the Nobel Prize, a new dust jacket with a picture of a yacht was put on the book, and it was sold as "un roman de vacances." The reviewers were rather favorable, though treating the work as a minor Faulkner. The novel showed the writer's versatility rather than his greatness. Most critics found the work amusing, but the humor had a quality much different from Faulkner's usual *noire* comedy. The reviewer in *Nouvelles Littéraires* said how glad he was to find publishers avoiding the "corned-beef littéraire américain" and printing the best authors like Faulkner, "the most powerful and the most original of his country, one of those rare writers who will mark their epoch."

The volume of short stories attracted little attention, perhaps because the critics had said their say about the other two books and had little else to add. The usual device was to pick one or two stories and comment on them to the exclusion of the rest of the book. The few reviews there were, and there were very few, were favorable enough, but the book added little to Faulkner's French reputation. One critic even complained that, in contrast to Caldwell, Hemingway, or Steinbeck, Faulkner could not be judged on the basis of his short stories. His characteristic qualities do not come out in such short narratives.

Articles appraising the whole of Faulkner's works appeared at different times in 1948. Raymond Las Vergnas found the principal source of Faulkner's prestige in France coming from his Hermetism. The other sources are obscenity and violence. He admitted that Faulkner is uncontestably an artist—very high literary praise from a French critic. Jacques Duesberg said that Faulkner's three best novels are *The Sound and the Fury, Absalom,* and *The Unvanquished.* Faulkner is not a realist but is close to Hawthorne in mood, especially in his love of isolation. Jean Jacques Mayoux wrote a long article in the academic series, *Cahiers du Collège Philosophique,* entitled "Le temps et la destinée chez William Faulkner." As the title indicates, the article continued the discussion of time and fate started by Sartre in 1939. The role of free will in relation to the subjectivity of time and the inevitability of fate was analyzed. The ultimate free will for Faulkner's characters is the suppression of existence through suicide, either literally or figuratively. Castration and incest are, in these terms, partial self-destructions. Characters are the most Faulknerian when they recognize the inevitableness of defeat and yet refuse to accept it. Thus the title *Unvanquished* can be applied to all his books.

Mme Claude Edmonde Magny's book, *L'Age du Roman américain,* gave the place of honor to Faulkner by means of an almost fifty-page chapter on him just before her summing-up remarks. This chapter, "Faulkner: ou l'inversion théologique," contains a good comparison between the *Human Comedy* of Balzac and the Yoknapatawpha Saga of Faulkner; in fact, Mme Magny has been one of the few French critics to recognize the implications of the saga. She admits her indebtedness to Cowley's introduction to and editing of the *Portable Faulkner.* Her primary approach to Faulkner is in moral and even religious terms. And it is this quality—the "remaking of a church"—that makes Faulkner better than his contemporaries. His sense of sin and suffering in an absurd world is the qualitative distinction making him great.

Also in 1948, though attracting less attention than *L'Age du Roman américain,* was the book by Charly Guyot, *Les Romanciers américains d'aujourd'hui.* Guyot's chapter on Faulkner in this slender 125-page volume is not long, but he does present the writer's development in chronological perspective. Guyot's favorites among Faulkner's novels are *Sanctuary* and *Light in August.* The chapter ends: ". . . there is in Faulkner something which reveals the truly original writer: an accent, a tonality, a nonanalyzable *je ne sais quoi* which is the major gift of an authentic poet."

In 1949 *The Unvanquished* was published in a translation by Raimbault and Vorce. The book evoked a considerable discussion of the role of the Civil War in

Faulkner's writings. One critic called Poe and Faulkner greater gifts from America than anything the Marshall Plan would give. Another discussed the "inexhaustible imagination of Faulkner." "Never a novelist, not even Balzac, not even Proust, has received from nature gifts so striking." Probably the most frequent thing said about the novel was its ease of reading in contrast to the usual Faulkner book. Many critics then went on to talk about the "pure classicism" and how the success of Faulkner in writing a book so different from his usual showed his tremendous artistic versatility. One reviewer, apparently disliking this "classical" Faulkner, compared the book with *Gone with the Wind* and complained that the merit of the novel was far from that of Faulkner's greats, such as *The Sound and the Fury*.

Several brief articles were written on Faulkner during 1949. Perhaps the most important one was by Ilya Ehrenburg entitled "Les mains sales. Faulkner et Sartre vus par un écrivain sovietique." Another article, in *Carrefour,* shows how much Faulkner's activities have acquired a news value for the French. This widely read weekly printed a discussion of the American publication of *Intruder in the Dust.* An article in *Les Temps Modernes* appropriately discussed the aesthetics of Faulkner, pointing out that his superiority over all other American writers lies in his forcing the reader to act as creator of art just as the artist does. One critic described Faulkner as the "greatest living novelist" and used his tremendous superiority over all other Americans as proof that there was no *école américaine.* Another writer added the following comment: "Like Edgar Poe, Faulkner has, alas! submitted to the terrible god of Alcohol. The last year he almost died."

Jean Simon published in 1950 his brief critical history, *Le Roman américain au XXᵉ siècle*. Writing as a scholar familiar with French criticism of American authors, Simon spoke of Faulkner as having in France the greatest favor of any American novelist. He discussed Faulkner's works in chronological order from *Soldiers' Pay* to *The Hamlet*. The important critical Faulknerian problems are puritanism, symbolism, pessimism, use of the subconscious, and disarrangement of conventional narrative order.

An important event of the literary scene of 1950 was the awarding of the Nobel Prize to Faulkner. Though Bertrand Russell received the literary prize at the same time, he was almost ignored in France in the well-nigh universal acclaim that Faulkner received. Faulkner passed through Paris on his way from Stockholm, and the literary weeklies were able to get interviews with the rather unco-operative author. Typical was the quoted reply to the question which of his books best expressed his thoughts, "None." Also, in December, 1950, the film version of *Intruder in the Dust* was shown at the Biarritz film festival and attracted several favorable comments, though the movie was not shown commercially in France.

The French busied themselves like bees, and almost everybody had his say in an article on Faulkner. Ignoring daily newspapers, between November, 1950, and April, 1951, there was a total of seventeen different articles in various weekly and monthly magazines. Several of these were fairly long, running from ten to twenty pages. Added to the accumulating material was Faulkner's acceptance speech, printed several times in early 1951. As late as October, 1952, the American editors of *Profils* in their first issue rather redundantly printed this same speech all over again. In the January *La Table Ronde* two of Faulkner's poems from *The Green Bough* were given in a translation by Raimbault. And *Les Temps Modernes* serialized the title story of *The Wild Palms* in its January to May, 1951, issues. The name of Faulkner was really important in France.

One of the common statements made in this deluge of articles was that France had recognized Faulkner as an artist and America was only now learning from France and the Swedish academy what a great artist it had in its midst. American critics were taken over the coals for treating Faulkner as a regionalist, whereas he is, said the French critics, a universal writer in the complete sense of the word. The Americans were also accused of equating the merits of Hemingway and Faulkner and even Wolfe and Faulkner.

Looking over this mass of criticism as a whole, we find little said that has not been said before. The same themes of Faulkner's puritanism, pessimism, and poetry were stressed in these articles. Most noticeable was the unqualified enthusiasm for Faulkner. He is "the greatest living novelist"; his talent "finds no one to confront except the dead: Dostoevski, Tolstoi, and Proust." "Faulkner is a literary miracle, a success of nature; rarely can the word 'genius' be so honestly applied to a writer." He is "one of the rare artists of this century who gives us the savor of immortality." His originality and humanity place Faulkner in the "first rank of the novelists of the world." And there were almost innumerable remarks like these. Though we will not go into detail about them, valuable critical studies of Faulkner were made by Marcel Brion, Albert Guérard, Marius Guyard, and Rabi. This last article, the most metaphysical of the group, has been translated into English in the Hoffmann and Vickery collection of Faulkner criticism. Later in 1951 Maurice Le Breton wrote an article for a special number of the *Journal de Psychologie* entitled "Temps et personne chez William Faulkner," but this article adds little to the one Le Breton wrote in 1937 on the same subject.

That American publication of Faulkner was being closely followed is shown by two reviews of *Requiem for a Nun* (as yet untranslated into French) in *Samedi-Soir* and *Le Figaro Littéraire*. The *Figaro* review spoke of the enthusiasm with which the book had been received in America. In *Samedi-Soir* the relationship of *Requiem for a Nun* to *Sanctuary* was stressed, as the title of the article indicates, "Le nouveau Faulkner est une suite de 'Sanctuaire.'"

Towards the end of 1951 *Knight's Gambit* appeared in the translation by André du Bouchet. The reviews of this in late 1951 and early 1952 were only mildly favorable, but the reviewers did not seem to hold the book against Faulkner. His position was established, and if he so desired there was no reason why he could not relax in writing a volume which, though made up of detective stories, is far above the level of the usual *roman policier*. Morvan Lebesque, who refuses to yield to anyone in his admiration for Faulkner, called the character Gavin Stevens the reincarnation of Descartes. Also, "Faulkner is a poet: when he speaks of men and horses, the tone becomes epic, the story is raised to the dimensions of an *Iliad*, of a *Jerusalem Delivered*." Jean Pouillon wrote an article, beside which almost any Faulkner novel is easy reading, in *Les Temps Modernes* on *Le Gambit du Cavalier*. Appropriately enough Pouillon was defending Faulkner's obscurity though one wonders why he picked this particular book to illustrate the problem.

In February, 1952, appeared *The Wild Palms*, translated by Coindreau, who also wrote the preface, sepa-

rately published in the January *Les Temps Modernes.*
Here Coindreau tackled the difficult critical question—
What is the unity between the two parts of the book?
His answer was in terms of Freudian symbolism, and
he did succeed in finding several symbols specifically con-
trasted—air, wind, and water.

Reviewers called the novel a chef-d'oeuvre "surpassed
only by *Sartoris.*" In fact the usual tendency was to regard *Les Palmiers sauvages* as one of the most important
novels by Faulkner. Much was made of its beauty and
lyricism. In contrast to the American critical attitude
which considers the "Old Man" the better of the two
sections, French critics seemed to prefer the title story,
some almost ignoring the tale of the Mississippi flood.
Michel Mohrt, in *La Table Ronde,* illustrates this difference and his remarks suggest why.

One should not ask too much *vraisemblance* from this fantastic
story of the *Old Man,* in which the leading character fights
strange animals and, in his struggle against the river, accom-
plishes fabulous exploits. Certain points in the story are badly
explained, but that is not important because they are resolved
into a great lyric movement appropriate to the cosmic scale of
the catastrophe. By contrast, *The Wild Palms,* story of a *couple
irrégulier,* is a realistic and even naturalistic novel. There is
then an evident contrast between the two works—realistic novel
and mythical tale.

Again an example of the bewilderment of the French
before the sprawling facts of American life. To no victim of the 1927 Mississippi flood would the "Old Man"
seem a "fantastic" or "mythical" tale. A number of the
reviewers considered this novel as further evidence of
Faulkner's puritanism. That physical love should de-
stroy Wilbourne and that the convict should flee the
woman he saved from the flood were proofs of the puritan's hatred of women.

More articles on Faulkner appeared. In February, 1952, the weekly magazine *Réforme* carried on one page three separate articles on the American novelist. One was biographical, one appreciative, and the third discussed Faulkner and the *roman noir*. *Sanctuaire* was labeled the true father of the genre though the critic added that it is much greater than any of the imitations. The same month, in *Etudes Anglaises,* Jean Jacques Mayoux discussed "La création du réel chez William Faulkner," analyzing in the French tradition of exegesis. Mayoux called Faulkner a philosophical idealist in the Platonic tradition. The novelist is as American, he felt, as Kafka is Judeo-Germanic. And he contrasted the two novelists vividly: Faulkner—"dream of reality"; Kafka—"reality of dream."

Gallimard released Raimbault's translation of *Intruder in the Dust* in April, 1952. As might be expected, the reviews harked back to Malraux's preface to *Sanctuary*—the intrusion of Greek tragedy into the detective story. Several remarked that *L'Intrus* is more detective story than Greek tragedy though the lyric hand of the writer Faulkner is present throughout the whole book. That Faulkner should here let justice triumph aroused some comment. The "unexpected freshness" of the book surprised one critic. René Lalou complained that the speeches of Gavin Stevens were much too long and ended by boring the reader—a comment also made by many American reviewers.

The May, 1952, festival, *Oeuvres du XXe Siècle,* featured in addition to the Boston Symphony Orchestra and the New York City Ballet and renowned groups from European countries a series of talks by writers from Europe, Asia, and America. The final session was in the Salle Gaveau on the afternoon of May 30. Denis de

Rougemont presided; W. H. Auden, André Malraux, Salvador da Madariaga, and William Faulkner spoke. The auditorium was completely filled and many people were standing by the time de Rougemont opened the program. Though there were present several visiting Americans like us, the audience of perhaps fifteen hundred to two thousand people was mostly French and included a good many students. The program went along about as one would expect with sometimes perfunctory or sometimes hearty applause. The one variation from this pattern occurred when Faulkner was introduced by de Rougemont. Faulkner stood up; and he had to stand there for several minutes while the audience bravoed, cheered, and gave vent to their enthusiasm in true French fashion. As one French paper described the scene, "The ovation enveloped Faulkner like a tornado —the applause of the single-minded crowd offered him a memorable greeting." And it was this single-mindedness that attracted our attention. That audience had come there to see and hear William Faulkner. They had come to the Salle Gaveau that afternoon as an expression of their adulation and almost worship of the writer William Faulkner.

10. CALDWELL

CALDWELL'S RECEPTION in France really begins with the publication of *God's Little Acre* by Gallimard in May, 1936. The translator was Coindreau, by then a familiar name to those who read American translations, and André Maurois's prestige made him an appropriate person to write the preface. Caldwell was, at first, clearly an exotic and did not reach the popular level until after the war, but the book sold and favorable criticism appeared. In June, 1937, Gallimard published *Tobacco Road* and in May, 1938, *We Are the Living*.

Before 1936 there had been scattered mention of the American editions of Caldwell's books—the most important was a review of *Tobacco Road* in *NRF* July, 1934, in which the germs of future Caldwell criticism appeared. Coindreau pointed out here that the writers of the twenties had been fundamentally romantic in their reaction against the war and their world, but that the younger writers are resigned to an evil world. Caldwell laughs at human stupidities. He is both an observer and a satirist. His book is really farce in spite of the constant atmosphere of tragedy—it reminds us of the Guignol. His farmers hold immovably to a faith in the ferocious god of the Puritans. Later in the same year Philippe Soupault wrote an article on "La nouvelle littérature américaine" for *Europe*. He felt that writers like Faulkner in *Sanctuary* and *As I Lay Dying* and Caldwell in *Tobacco Road* and *American Earth* are particularly symptomatic of the new state of mind which attaches itself to essential problems. It seeks to find the true American and not a phantom or a superficial caricature pushing his glasses up on his forehead or chewing a cigar like Babbitt, who seems, when one knows the citizens of the United States, a pseudo-American pictured by a badly informed European. Faulkner and Caldwell, the critic continued, seek to portray the American soul considered not as a literary motif or a picturesque subject but as a living and intense reality.

Maurois, in the preface to *God's Little Acre,* began by pointing out that "this strange book, cynical and remarkable, needs no commentary." He briefly described Caldwell's early life and then explained that when the book appeared in the United States it was loudly condemned in some quarters for its obscenity. Forty-five prominent American writers protested and the attorney for the state of New York dropped the case. "Wise decision. The book is certainly brutal and harsh as were in a totally different sense Rabelais and Lawrence, but it is impossible to deny that it is a work of art."

Six months after *God's Little Acre* appeared Coindreau wrote an article of some consequence for *NRF.* In it he defended Caldwell's "indecency" as having in it something of the innocence of the profoundly instinctive. This writer, Coindreau said, glorifies man's instincts, especially his animal instincts. In the same month, November, a review of the book came out in *Europe.* The critic believed that *God's Little Acre* is an admirable tonic which should embolden the reader to accept his own vagrant outbursts of passion. And M. Hertz agreed that Maurois was right in protesting the charge of obscenity. "We learn from this book something of childlike folly, of innocent sensuality, of tragedy tempered with humor in a primitive and jovial society which has all the beauties and cynicisms of youth." A review in *Esprit* suggested that the descendants of the Puritans are in the process of taking a revenge against their heritage which puts to shame the French *petites pornographies romancées.* Lawrence, Faulkner, and now Caldwell. "We used to speak of *gauloiserie;* now we must say *américainisme.*"

Pierre Brodin in his book *Roman régionaliste américain* (1937) also took up the cudgels for Caldwell. He recalled that in America not only was the novelist accused of pornography but of downright lies; however, *God's Little Acre* and *Tobacco Road* actually show accurately enough the conditions which existed among many poor whites during the depression. Brodin called *Tobacco Road* a work having two great qualities—an undeniable picturesqueness and a profound accent of truth. And *God's Little Acre* seemed to Brodin, from a literary point of view, even better. Thiébaut in the *Revue de Paris* ("Trois romanciers étrangers: Huxley, Morgan, Caldwell") discussed both books. He emphasized Caldwell's poetic sense, which gives to his burlesque an incontestable grandeur. Lelis reviewing *Tobacco Road* in *Europe* wrote first of *God's Little Acre,* the book which a year before had revealed to the French the name of Caldwell. Echoes of the power of this book still resound, he felt, of its force, originality, and sexual exacerbation. The second novel is just as good as the first. In both, Lelis continued, we find bitterness, humor, despair. We are astonished to discover hungry people in the United States, but Caldwell has depicted men and women as he has seen them. So much the worse for us if it seems too much *nature.*

Jeanine Delpech wrote an article for *Nouvelles Littéraires* in January, 1938, entitled "Visite à Erskine Caldwell, le Céline américain." She put Caldwell outside the pattern of the American regional novelists. His characters, she said, are unforgettable for their wild passions and the force of their *idée fixe*. Their illogical acts seem a reflection of the illogicality of nature; if they are cruel, they are no less cruel than the elements. The scene of Caldwell's novels is a nightmare universe where time no longer exists, where instincts express themselves with such brutality that they come close to perversions. These are not thesis novels, though they arouse in the reader either impotent anger or a desire for immediate action. He is never left indifferent. These novels force us, in spite of our embarrassment, in spite of the laughter Caldwell uses to lighten our agony, to be aware of a suffering humanity whose existence is a shame to the America so proud of her youth, of her civilization. This is Caldwell's aim, which he attains without descending to propaganda but by means of a Rabelaisian vigor and purity of style.

For *We Are the Living,* translated by Ed. Michel-Tyl, Coindreau wrote a six-page preface. In it he emphasized the importance of Caldwell's "The Sacrilege of Alan Kent," which for him contains the germ of all Caldwell's work. In the last sentence of the story Alan Kent says, "And I knew now that I would always be alone in the world." To Coindreau that confession is Caldwell allying himself to the *grands anxieux* of present day Anglo-American literature—to Lawrence, Sherwood Anderson, Faulkner. Coindreau went on to speak of Caldwell's lyricism, to compare it with Faulkner's, and then to emphasize Caldwell's comic sense based on unconscious burlesque and incongruities. It is a humor *pince-sans-rire* whose American forebear is Mark Twain. The French reader will think rather of Maupassant—the same stripped story, dry irony, latent pessimism. But in Caldwell this pessimism turns toward sadism and atrocity. In depicting horror and cruelty, the American triumphs easily over the Frenchman. Finally Coindreau said the short stories in this volume, taken from *We Are the Living* and *Kneel to the Rising Sun,* illustrate all the aspects of Caldwell: social satire, humor and lewdness, atrocities now and then unbearable, pantheistic feeling for nature translated by symbols as old as the world but eternally beautiful, and the final unifying trait—a profound originality rising out of an intense savor of terror.

One critic alone in this first burst of enthusiasm strikes a somewhat sour note. Wessberge, reviewing *Tobacco Road* in *Etudes Anglaises* January, 1938, wrote that though these primitive characters are amusingly superstitious, that is not enough to give them an interest truly human. Caldwell's realism, brutal and cynic, is here as arid as *la Route maudite.* It does not have the comic nor the dramatic power which made *God's Little Acre* a bitter epic. If *Tobacco Road* does not disgust the French reader, it will be only because of Coindreau's remarkable translation.

Even during the war years Caldwell received some attention. *Fontaine* printed his "Fin d'été" and *L'Arbalète* "L'homme de dieu"—a chapter from *Journeyman.* In 1943, Marc Barbezat, in "Caldwell et le mythe," wrote: The society of Caldwell is a jungle, and the writer takes no pains to hide the claws and the fangs of his characters. If Ty Ty were a Negro, how picturesque he would be, the critic continued, but Ty Ty Walden is you—he is me. We cannot escape from him any more than he can escape from his misery, a cosmic misery—as of shipwrecked beings thrown upon a desert isle or of fallen angels on a continent hostile and sterile. Barbezat put Caldwell above Dostoevski, saying that in *Crime and Punishment* Rechetnikov by his monotony loses the attention of the reader but Caldwell in his books holds it by his humor. This humor is the magnificent proof of the health and youth of America. The reader's laughter never mocks but pays homage to the vitality of the characters, to their ruggedness, to their rage to live. They resemble the people of the first books of the Old Testament. Ty Ty, Noah—Lester, Adam. That a twentieth-century novelist has refound the power of the myths of Exodus and Genesis interests us, the critic continued. We ask ourselves if the method of Caldwell is perhaps not indispensable to the modern writer, if it will not give us back force in our novels, help us grow out of our sterile psychological analyses. Caldwell's characters pertain to eternity; however young, they carry within themselves all the experience of humanity; they invite us to live in a mythic universe.

Not too different from Wessberge's adverse criticism written six years before was Charles Lucet's comment in "Les Français et l'Amérique" published in *La Nef* (Algiers) August, 1944. First the critic quoted William Byrd on the life which the early Americans lived on the *frontière géorgienne*—where the utterly lazy men left all the work to their wives and at the end of the year found themselves with nothing to eat. Monsieur Lucet added:

Such was certainly the life of the first pioneers—a life which today, describing the same regions, the great novelist Erskine Caldwell offers us again in his *Tobacco Road* and *God's Little Acre*. His characters are lewd villagers, dirty and sly, ignorant of the civilization which has detoured around their mountains, examples little to be recommended to touch the heart of a civilized man.

In 1945 appeared Maurois's *Etudes américaines.* One

chapter discussed the American edition of *Tragic Ground*, pointing out that Caldwell's characters might better be described as beasts in their tranquil shamelessness rather than as savages, for savages at least have their code and taboos. The family in *Tragic Ground* respects no longer the taboos of Christian civilization. Maurois suggested that when Mavis describes her new job to her family the situation recalls certain scenes by Zola, though the tone is different. Zola gives his characters a sense of sin and the feeling that they are violating the moral law. Caldwell's people walk about nude and candid; they have shame neither for their bodies nor for their habits. And then the critic, as others had, placed Caldwell in the tradition of the revolt against puritanism in Anglo-Saxon literature.

The postwar burst of enthusiasm for the American novel carried Caldwell to popular success though critical reception of *Poor Fool,* which Gallimard got out early in 1945, was mixed. Coindreau had translated the book before the war. In his preface, dated 1940, he again presented to the French the historical background of the modern American novel—the breaking away from the traditional after 1914 by Sherwood Anderson, Dreiser, Sinclair Lewis. He said that *Poor Fool,* published in America in 1930, is the birth of the true Caldwell. We see already his taste for the horrible and cruel, his approach to sex, his tragic-comic puppets. *Poor Fool* illustrates both the Oedipus and castration complexes.

The reviewers were numerous. Vagne wrote:

We have delighted in the American novel as the source of new adventures for the mind. How impatient we have been to break the silence of the war years. Now Caldwell returns! Horrors! Is this what we have loved so dearly? This tissue of gratuitous violence, of sordidness? This nightmare which is closer to psychoanalysis than to literature?

Astruc concluded that no other writer could get away with offering to the French public right after the war a work so full of horror. He dismissed the book as awkward but agreed with Coindreau that it shows the themes and tendencies later developed by Caldwell. De Laprade decided the novel left him rather indifferent. Others were favorably impressed and went into long discussions of Caldwell's techniques and ideas. "This novel is man crushed by his world, dominated by what is stronger than he, the incarnation of the ancient Greek and the modern American conception of the wretched, the unlucky being vomited out by his world, the victim of obscure gods."

Blanzat took this occasion to consider the vogue of the American novel. He felt there were many reasons for it, but most important was the ability of Faulkner, Steinbeck, and Caldwell to express clearly the brutality of the age. That gives them their universal audience. Although each differs from the other, they have the same philosophy. Man as they see him lives in a kind of middle age without the faith of the Middle Ages. Modern civilization, far from helping him, enriching him, actually enfeebles him. He is alone and more than ever powerless before his destiny. This image of man is not new. We find it from Greek tragedy to the naturalistic novel. American novelists have much of both in them, but they deviate from naturalism because they are not realists though they begin from the real. They seem to copy reality—to give detail after detail, effacing themselves. All this is why their literature is filled with idiots, drunks, perverts—each with a symbolic value. So builds up a literature of myths and allegories which turns into a neoromanticism. But this new romanticism is not talkative, not sentimental, and its lyricism is always masked under a precise, dispassionate tone. If such are the traits of the American novel, then we can say that no one is more American than Erskine Caldwell. The desolate world of Steinbeck and Faulkner appears civilized and flourishing compared with Caldwell's.

Poor Fool sold. By June, 1946, one critic at least, Sans, was suggesting that certain American novelists were better known in France than in their own country. As a proof he said, "Several thousand copies of Caldwell's story *Poor Fool* have been run off in Paris although in New York the printing, solely for devotees, was limited to 300 copies!"

Over the months from May, 1945, to September, 1946, a group of artists in Paris were working to produce a magnificent de luxe edition of *Tobacco Road* "to honor the great American writer Erskine Caldwell." Nine hundred copies were printed. There were eleven copperplate illustrations by Denyse de Bravura. Marcel Chapuis directed the work. The printing was done at the press of Ernest Puyfourcat fils, the copper plates in the workshop of Paul Haasen. The folio pages were folded chez Jossé, the box cover chez Adine, and the paper chez Mertens. All was under the imprint of Editions du Pré aux Clercs. A review of this handsome book said, "This novel appears to us one of the most remarkable of the young American literature. It has a force at the same time realistic and lyric—the power of the great literary fables where the characters were called Misery, Hunger, Pride, Love, Desire."

In 1946 also, *Action,* a leftist weekly, published three short stories: "Beechum le Beau," "Abe Latham, homme de couleur," and "Le Nègre dans le puits." In August Jacques Vallette wrote "Erskine Caldwell: plan de son oeuvre" for *La Nef* summarizing and praising the American novelist's work. And two books appeared: Brodin's had a seventeen-page chapter on Caldwell, straight biography and criticism, and Coindreau's a twenty-eight-page section which gathered together the opinions on Caldwell he had expressed in his articles and prefaces.

When Caldwell paid a visit to Paris in the summer of 1947, half a dozen papers carried articles or interviews. One of the most entertaining was in *Figaro Littéraire*. The interviewer, Arban, asked:

"Why did you choose such people to write about, such horror?"

"Because I knew them as a boy. All the people of *Tobacco Road* exist. It is 100 per cent reality. But *Poor Fool* is 100 per cent imagination."

"Tell me—have you read especially carefully Edgar Poe?"

"What?"

"Edgar Poe. There are in your *Poor Fool* passages which evoke him particularly. This tendency to necrophilia. *L'histoire de cette robe de morte.*"

"Poe. No." Caldwell smiled gently in excuse. "I never read. In any case, not Poe!"

Also in 1947 Guérard in his preface to the short story "Dorothy" by Caldwell in *Ecrit aux U.S.A.* attempted to give the French a picture of American criticism of Caldwell. Guérard asserted that Caldwell is much more admired in France than in the United States, where more and more his last books are unanimously judged not to be fulfilling the promises of his youth. He seems to have lost the indignation he once had. In *Tragic Ground* the condition of children uprooted seems humorous rather than terrible. This kind of thing is hard to see in translation. But certain American critics find in Caldwell as in James Cain or Henry Miller a sort of sadistic compliance in the tortures of their victims and a desire to titillate or scandalize the bourgeois reader. In Caldwell this tendency seems more pronounced in his novels than in his short stories where his greatest qualities—mastery of dialogue and choice of detail—appear to best advantage. But it is in his novels that French readers find this *absurde,* this vision of a world in disorder which interests them so much today.

The same year, 1947, brought Caldwell success on the Paris stage. *La Route au Tabac* opened March 15 at the Renaissance Théâtre. Simon recalls that the play was a striking success though only mediocrely produced. There were favorable reviews which emphasized the play's "fantastic lyricism" and its "deep tenderness hidden under surface ferocity." One in *Europe* admitted:

Unquestionably *Tobacco Road* dominates this theatrical season as did *Of Mice and Men* the year 1946. But the road of tobacco never attains the emotion produced by the mice. We speak of its naturalism—that it is a slice of life, that it allies the grotesque and the sublime. But the play does not reach its goal. The ideas are too denuded and at the same time too violent to allow the onlooker time for breath. We lose the social significance of suffering humanity.

Another critic, in *Paru,* complained, "It is difficult to be moved by such sordid beings who have no vitality except in their sexual debaucheries (rather disagreeable on the stage)."

Seven thousand five hundred copies of the play version were printed in the winter of 1947 by Editions Laffont, we were informed, and all but a few copies sold. This, according to one French literary agent, was a good sale; the French do not ordinarily buy plays. A well-known play by a French writer might sell as few as five hundred copies.

Finally, near the end of this year which had seen Caldwell's name achieve prominence again and again, Gallimard published the French translation of *Trouble in July*. The book got a mixed critical reception, though the weight was on the favorable side. Again the emphasis on "humor held in check by profound human sympathy." "The writer is not a simple painter of certain customs. Here is the eternal struggle between man and society." "This tragedy classic in its unities," "this whirlwind of astonishing poetry." One critic, agreeing with others bored with lynching, called *Trouble in July* the hundredth version of a hackneyed theme and asked, "Is Caldwell commercializing his subject matter?" Several pointed out that Richard Wright had a more profound approach to the Negro problem.

During these early years after the war Gallimard and other presses also, as quickly as they could get paper, put out new impressions of the prewar publications by all five of our novelists. Discussing the reissues in December, 1947, Blanzat wrote in *Figaro Littéraire* that Caldwell's two first novels done in French, *La Route au Tabac* and *Le petit Arpent du Bon Dieu*, "gave the impression of a novelist particularly American: brutal, cruel, obscene, painter without nuances of people simplified to the point of caricature." *Nous les Vivants* shows an inspiration "more flexible, more varied, closer to reality." This book, the best of his eight, "forces us to reconsider the somewhat premature evaluation we have made of Caldwell." And thus we see that "in the detail as in the whole, each creation of Caldwell has a double dimension. Only by an unjustifiable simplification do we speak of Caldwell's 'caricatures and puppets.' "

Two Caldwell translations appeared in 1948—*Tragic Ground* early in the year, translated by Coindreau, and *A House in the Uplands* just at the end of the year, translated by Robert Vidal. Neither received as many reviews as had *Poor Fool*. So much had been written on Caldwell since the war that perhaps the critics found little new to add. Also it is a familiar pattern to see a novelist somewhat ignored by the intellectuals as he becomes more popular. Third, of course, the question arises whether these books actually have the power of Caldwell's earlier writings. And it is clear enough that by the publication of the seventh volume in French the original shock value of Caldwell had lessened. One critic said of *A House in the Uplands,* "A bad, a very bad Caldwell. Written to measure with all the tricks showing." But Gérard d'Houville, although suggesting that the influence of American novelists on French writers was probably not good, continued, "But let us speak of one of the novels that does please us and does transport us to another world—*A House in the Uplands.* Here the heady atmosphere, the feverish climate of the South, the odor of the marshes, the chants of the Negroes on the plantations, the melancholy of ruined fortunes, the old hopes now become shameful—it is all this that gives value and interest to Caldwell's brief and somber story."

The critical scales swung back and forth. Guyot's slender volume gave Caldwell three pages of extremely favorable comment. Magny refers to him, however, only in passing. The anthology *Courtes Histoires américaines* omitted him, as had the one published at the end of 1946 by *Cahiers des Langues Modernes.* Reviewing this in 1948, Duvignaud wrote, "It is indeed strange that Caldwell, without doubt one of the most original American writers, does not figure in this collection."

In 1949 *Georgia Boy* appeared but made little critical stir. Two short stories were printed during this year, "Dans la prairie" in *Arts-Lettres* and "Fichue journée" in *Lettres Françaises,* and there were several interviews when Caldwell visited Paris. *Journeyman* came out in

January, 1950, and the French recognized this as one of Caldwell's best novels—classed it with *Tobacco Road* and *God's Little Acre*. Robert Merle, whose prestige was enormous—he had won the Prix Goncourt two months before for his novel *Week-End à Zuydcoote*—wrote the preface for *Journeyman*. He considered it technically the most successful of Caldwell's novels because it has more unity. Humor, he said, dominates it from beginning to end. But Caldwell is a critic of capitalistic society as well as a novelist. He "has eaten with the people he describes, he has gathered cotton with them, he has thrown dice with them, and at night behind the barn he has slept with their daughters." As economist he deplores their kind of life; as a man he delights in it. The reviewers agreed with Merle's vigorous praise of the novel—"a master work," "of high quality," "perhaps his chef-d'oeuvre," "one of the summits."

Simon's book, *Le Roman américain au XXe Siècle,* published in 1950, devotes a dozen enthusiastic pages to Caldwell. He wrote: "American puritans detest him, the intellectuals pretend disdain. But each has read him. Popular editions have made him known everywhere and it is only just." His work, so simple in appearance, hides a wealth of richness which too many hurried readers fail to see. He is one of the absolute masters and he characterizes his period; heir of the realists, he has considerably enlarged their domain. The time for perfect but impersonal photography is past. Caldwell is an artist and an artist *qui prend parti*.

Later in the same year *The Sure Hand of God* translated by J. L. Bost and Marcel Duhamel under the title *Le Doigt de Dieu* appeared. *This Very Earth* was published in 1951 and occasioned a serious discussion by Raymond Las Vergnas in *Hommes et Mondes*. *Episode à Palmetto* came out in the summer of 1952 and in November appeared *Soleil du Sud,* which contains twelve of the fourteen stories printed in *Southways.* There is no question but that Caldwell continues to be read in France—four translations in two years. Yet the reviews of these books, and there were not many, showed Caldwell's critical decline.

But the critics' lack of enthusiasm does not worry the general public. And Monsieur Queneau at Gallimard told us that *Place Called Estherville* will be published soon and also *Call It Experience.* M. Hoffman, Caldwell's literary agent in Paris, reported that he is looking for a translator for *A Lamp at Nightfall,* which he feels will greatly interest the French although they may have difficulty understanding the pictured degeneracy of Maine whites and their hatred of new, foreign blood coming in. And so the story of Caldwell in France continues.

11. STEINBECK

JOHN STEINBECK was the last of our five novelists to appear on the French literary scene. Even though two of his books were translated before the war, in 1939 and 1940, world circumstances did not make for thorough discussion of works by a new American author whether the critics were interested in him or not.

The first critical notice of Steinbeck was by Jean Catel in the November, 1937, *Mercure de France*. The article reviewed the American edition of *Of Mice and Men* devoting much space to a plot summary which ended, "George killed his friend Lennie in a fit of jealousy." Catel spoke of the influence of psychoanalysis, which "has always had a particular attraction for the Anglo-Saxon. Emerson in 1840 studied the turbid agitation of this interior force to which he gave a happy name, the over-soul, and which was nothing more than the unconscious of the moderns."

Of Mice and Men was the first Steinbeck to be issued in French. Coindreau's translation came out in June, 1939, a few months before war broke out. Coindreau wrote an introduction and Joseph Kessel did the preface, which began with this paragraph: "This book is short. But its power is long." He emphasized the absence of any analysis by the author of the characters and his dependence on dialogue and action but said that these characteristics do not prevent the book's being bathed in poetry. The reader ends with a profound admiration for the author, "who in so few pages, with words so simple, and without any explanations has written a book so lasting, so profound, and so strong." The introduction, though primarily biographical, compared Steinbeck as a mystic with D. H. Lawrence and Jean Giono, names recurring often in French criticism of Steinbeck, and stressed the American's vigorous idealism and the good Samaritan tenderness towards his characters. Coindreau announced: "The work of this man is above all the work of a romantic and of a poet with keen sensibility." Steinbeck is definitely "in the first rank of the writers of his generation."

The few reviews of the book were favorable. Although Arland in *NRF* complained of the book's rudimentary psychology, he praised the novel as "remarkable, well conceived and realized, with simple lines and a striking tone." The *Nouvelles Littéraires* review reemphasized that the minds of the characters are revealed only through their actions and words. The novel was the "best that Steinbeck has written." His power as a writer lay in his giving to a simple fact of daily life a tragic amplitude.

The same month *Des Souris et des Hommes* was published, the weekly *Gringoire* printed a Steinbeck short story, "Le Meurtre." In a brief introduction the editor said that Steinbeck "is considered incontestably the greatest American writer of the moment."

In April, 1940, Gallimard released *In Dubious Battle*, only a few weeks before the German invasion of France and occupation of Paris. In the melee the book was practically ignored by the press. Shortly after the Germans moved in and with their approval Drieu la Rochèlle took over the editorship of *NRF*. It is interesting to find *En un Combat douteux* reviewed in the January,

1941, issue by Henri Thomas. The review, appropriately enough for a collaborationist journal, disapproved. Thomas called the book unconvincing, "a composition of the mind, rather cold and definitely incomplete."

Much different are the remarks made by André Gide in his journal under the date of September 27, 1940. His notes were published in the April-May (1944) *L'Arche,* one of the literary magazines that sprang up in Algiers during the war, this particular one sponsored by Gide himself. He wrote:

> *En un Combat douteux* of Steinbeck. Impeccable translation of a very remarkable book. . . . It is the best painting (psychological) that I know of communism and has a perfect clarity. . . . The crowd is the protagonist, but from this unformed and irresolute mass are detached diverse figures who expose the chameleon aspects of the problem without ever encumbering or holding up the action. . . . But what Steinbeck *montre* admirably (without however *démontrer* anything) is how those to whom all other means of struggle are denied are led, and even forced into, perfidy, injustice, resolute cruelty; and how the most noble and generous characters find themselves corrupted. From this comes the great anguish which, from one part to the next, breathes through this beautiful and cruel book.

The wartime story of Steinbeck's books has already been told in Chapter II, but a listing of the titles published during the war may not be amiss. *The Grapes of Wrath* under the title *Grappes d'Amertume* had been printed in Brussels. *The Moon Is Down* was published in Lausanne under one title and in Paris by the Underground under another. And in 1944, before Parisian publishers were in full operation again, Jean Marguerat in Lausanne put out *Tortilla Flat* and the Overseas Editions did a translation of *Bombs Away* entitled *Lâchez les Bombes!* The last book, written as avowed propaganda at the request of the armed forces, is of no importance to us beyond its being another indication of what the name of Steinbeck meant to wartime France. In 1940 only the literati had known Steinbeck. In 1944 his name was a symbol of resistance and known by the average man on the street. And Gide's praise of *In Dubious Battle* and comparison of Steinbeck's stories to Chekhov's had not hurt his critical reputation.

As soon as it was possible to get them out, translations of various Steinbeck stories appeared. *Confluences* published "Fuite" in the February-March issue and the whole of "The Red Pony" in two installments, August and November, 1944. In three November issues *Les Lettres Françaises* (just out of the clandestine) also published the entire "Red Pony" sequence. In 1945 six short stories appeared in six different newspapers or magazines.

During the later part of 1944 and early 1945 the critics began to write about the Steinbeck books that had by then been published. The critical reception to *The Moon Is Down* was mixed. The "accent of truth" was remarked upon, but other critics noted the difference in their feelings for the book during the war and now after liberation. As one put it:

When during the oppression, the Editions de Minuit revealed to us *Nuits noires,* I suppose that many readers like me experienced a sense of gratitude. From before the war we had held Steinbeck as one of the best and noblest writers of his generation. How could we not be touched to learn that from 1942 the great California novelist had given to the victims of Nazism this evidence of fraternal sympathy?

The postwar feeling was expressed by another: "However, on rereading *Nuits noires* today, I find a real disappointment, for these happy formulas are a little too glossy, this measured tone is not always the right tone, and this sober grandeur seems too well-made." "A brilliant exercise, the book of an intellectual who defends a just cause and tries to understand: all is *vraisemblable,* but all is artificial." Yet not all critics dismissed the work so easily. One referred to the sobriety and dignity "which make of this work of circumstance a moving and durable book." And another talked about the role of an all-powerful fate, "so dear to most of the American novelists of today who are the heirs of Greek tragedy."

A long article by Blanzat in *Poésie 44* discussed all three volumes: *Of Mice and Men, In Dubious Battle,* and *The Moon Is Down.* He began by suggesting that as the French were about to renew their acquaintance with the Anglo-Saxon novel, it would be well for them to realize the enormous differences between the two branches of it: (1) the English, which has behind it a long literary tradition expressing most often the customs of an evolved society and of complex human relationships; and (2) the American, which is new—its principal initiators are alive or like Joyce dead but a brief time. The American novel describes generally man alone or man in obscure but elementary human relationships: erotic love, nearly animal friendship, fury, hate. It simplifies and magnifies and takes place at the lowest level of a civilization brutal and in certain respects terrifying. By all this it recalls at times, strangely, the literature of the great Greek myths. The gods are never absent, particularly Fate. Neither Hemingway—more cosmopolitan and diverse, nor Faulkner—more complex and singular, nor Caldwell—more *rapide,* is as significant in these terms as Steinbeck. With him for the first time perhaps the contemporary novel goes back not to the themes but to the spirit of Greek tragedy. Nor is Steinbeck an imitator. His heroes are not Orestes or Oedipus changed into unemployed or vagabond Americans. But as in

Sophocles, there is at the end the abyss and the destruction of man. And in man's spilled blood the gods see their eternal victory.

Early in 1946 Gallimard published *The Long Valley* and reissued *Of Mice and Men*. The short stories were widely acclaimed, reviewed, and bought. The critics took the occasion to consider the short-story form—one remarking it had been an American monopoly since O. Henry. They overwhelmingly agreed that Steinbeck was a master of the art, and each quoted Gide's famous remark (p. 21). Steinbeck's stories have "a simplicity, an ease, a tenderness." He conceives the art of the short story "not as a pretext for sharp surprise but as the poetic revelation of the most intimate secrets of the soul." "He is the poet of the unutterable." Steinbeck "shows more diversity in this collection than Faulkner does in *These 13* or Caldwell in *We Are the Living*." Steinbeck "penetrates to the most intimate heart of his characters. He seeks to present, to suggest obscure sentiments, incoherent thoughts—the purity of personality." His "short stories have an admirable precision. Their formula is classic." " 'The Red Pony' is a masterpiece." It is "a true work of art which expresses the childhood of all the children of the earth." The reviewers preferred "The Red Pony" without fail, but certain of them added "The White Quail" and "The Chrysanthemums" as perfect examples of the storyteller's art. There was no doubt this volume enjoyed a great welcome.

On April 28, 1946, the play *Of Mice and Men* opened at the Hébertot Théâtre. It was an immense success and in the fall, November 14, was moved to Théâtre Edouard VII to continue its run. (The play was revived at Hébertot September 16, 1948.) Most critics agreed it was one of the best plays of the season. René Laporte, reviewing the past year in the theater for the *Almanach des Lettres,* 1947, placed Camus's *Caligula,* Obey's *Maria,* and Giraudoux's *La Folle de Chaillot* at the head of his list of plays by Frenchmen. Then he continued, "But the real strength? Let us frankly admit it is in the plays from abroad." And first among them Laporte indicated was *Of Mice and Men* (*Our Town* and *Winterset* were two other American imports that season). Two long articles appeared in *Carrefour,* one on *l'interprétation,* the other on *la pièce.* Both were extremely laudatory. *Of Mice and Men* is "more original and its interpretation is newer than *Cocu magnifique* or *Caligula.*" Long reviews of the play considered the themes—the loneliness of man, the friendship between these two waifs, and the "nomadism"—a subject which fascinates the French in American literature. "No family, no land, no resting place. These nomads reflect certain aspects of *la condition humaine* in the modern world." But on an even deeper level, one reviewer stated, appears a theme in this play which touches our most secret inquietudes. George and Lennie are two clowns who ordinarily provoke our laughter—here transposed to a tragic plane. They are *L'Enfariné,* industrious, eloquent; and dull, doltish *L'Auguste.* When we accept this concept we begin to get at the profound meaning of the play. These two men represent two human types, two tendencies frequently at battle within the same individual. We recognize the echo of our own secret debates. Each tends to show us one of the two sides of a single temperament— our own. *Beau sujet tragique, en vérité.*

There were some adverse criticisms, of course. Lalou, though agreeing that the play was one of the best of the season, felt it lacked the highest values found in the novel. Several praised the play itself but said it was neither too well acted nor too well put into play form. Bernard criticized it severely as being a Freudian case history.

When Gide wrote *Le Dixième Arbre* twenty years ago, it was to satirize the infatuation of French writers and public alike for the work of the Viennese doctor. Now today this infatuation is evident in American literature. It is in the corncob of *Sanctuary*, the bag of turnips in *Tobacco Road*, the unnecessary horrors in *Poor Fool*. No American novels translated in the last ten years except those of Hemingway have escaped the demonology of Freud.

To take advantage of the success of the play, Robert Laffont published *Des Souris et des Hommes* (the play version). It sold 14,000 copies according to the figures given us—an astonishing sale for a play. And this same version had run in the *Magasin du Spectacle* for June and July. A half dozen or more general articles on Steinbeck also appeared during the course of the year. This last to be known on the French scene of the *cinq grands* was equaling the critical enthusiasm engendered by the other four and in certain respects surpassing it. Beigbeder believed him to be "one of the greatest and certainly the most open-hearted. The simplicity, the primitivism flows easily from this writer—in Faulkner it has to be striven for." Another critic expressed his opinion that "the conception in *Big Money* is less supple, less diverse, less warm, the lyricism more suppressed than in Steinbeck's two novels, *In Dubious Battle* and *Of Mice and Men*." Lalou had an important article, "Le Réalisme lyrique de John Steinbeck," in "Romanciers américains contemporains," the special 325-page issue of *Cahiers des Langues Modernes*. He called Steinbeck a *conteur-poète*, emphasized the "Our-Father-who-art-in-nature," reminded the reader that the novelist had dedicated one of his novels to an unknown god, and stated his belief that Steinbeck should be considered a pantheist uniting mysticism and sensuality.

We are still in the year 1946, and next we must pick up the story of *The Grapes of Wrath*. Evidently the Brussels translation, *Grappes d'Amertume*, had some wartime circulation, for Marie Forestier told of seeing it in the windows of the book stores. She explained:

> The name of the author (Steinbeck is of German origin) seemed at first to class the book among those coming from the educators of New Europe. The reader could persist in this mistaken notion because *Grapes of Wrath* is clearly a powerful instrument of propaganda against the social setup in America and certain California canners could with difficulty pose as champions of democracy.

At the end of the war Gallimard was anxious to get out the Coindreau-Duhamel translation as soon as possible. And it appeared, first serialized in *Les Lettres Françaises* from May to December, 1946. (Book publication is dated 1947. Considering that the entire book had come out in one of the most popular literary weeklies, Gallimard's sales figures for the book—120,000—are interesting.)

Les Lettres Françaises, in advertising their coming serialization, had firmly stated: *C'est le chef-d'oeuvre du roman américain.* Some reviewers agreed. "Steinbeck has a rare gift of blending the drama of society with the drama of the individual without one eclipsing the other. This book is one of the most beautiful American novels." Lalou, repeating his earlier judgments, praised the book highly for the "lyric realism by which the odyssey acquires a general value and an epic allure." Kanters in the *Gazette des Lettres* spoke of the prestige of American literature in France. He asked what this particular novel could bring to French literature.

There are no technical eccentricities; the construction is solid and in the main classical. Steinbeck gives us amazingly beautiful passages on nature, minute realistic description in action and dialogue, and passionate lyricism. These are familiar elements. But what we can relearn from this book is a sort of honesty in the evocation of a man stripped of his intellectual tinsel, reimmersed in his vital current, in his profound interior climate. And we can relearn the necessity not to separate this man from his historic context, from the precise economic and social contexts which determine his drama and his destiny.

Fauchery in *Action* thoroughly approved and pointed out that in Steinbeck the reader is not annoyed by verbal labyrinths or metaphysics as sometimes happens in Faulkner or Dos Passos. Steinbeck does not plunge us into the fatality of solitude as in diverse ways do Dos Passos, Faulkner, Hemingway, Caldwell. His last word is always fraternity.

On the other hand Jouve in *Etudes*, though praising *The Grapes of Wrath* for its social and economic criticism and its descriptive passages, wrote that the French reader would prefer *The Long Valley* or *The Moon Is Down*. Others too agreed that the book was excellent social documentary but did not find it a complete literary success. Roux believed the characters were too excessively schematic, that the book lacked dramatic interest. Guilleminault was bothered by a certain puerility of thought. Minet felt that this writer had a very great ability but mostly a utilitarian talent which aimed constantly and legitimately at the effect desired. Sans in an article entitled "D'un nouveau poncif" lashed out bitterly against all American novelists (except Faulkner) and called *The Grapes of Wrath* a tour de force in reverse. "The author piles horror upon horror without being able to make the reader the least sympathetic—or without even being able to interest him."

In spite of the minority adverse criticism, enthusiasm for Steinbeck continued through 1947. Not only did the book publication of the long-awaited *The Grapes of Wrath* fall in this year, but Gallimard brought out *Cannery Row* and Marguerat reissued *Tortilla Flat*. There were a dozen interviews with or articles about Steinbeck in the magazines and newspapers. For part of the year at least *Of Mice and Men* was still on the stage and the dramatic version of *Nuits noires* was presented at the Théâtre Saint Georges, starting April 20. The French adaptation was by Mme M. R. Belin. The play had a fair success and elicited several favorable comments. The one in the June, 1947, *Europe* complained of the mediocrity of the Paris theater for the previous two months. Five different French plays were listed as being downright bad. "Only the three American works deserve attention: *Tobacco Road, The Moon Is Down,* and *The Glass Menagerie.*"

The wartime edition of *Tortilla Flat* by the Swiss publisher sold poorly in France even after the liberation. Swiss book prices were too high, for one thing. The book's reissue in 1947 got little critical attention, though we have been told that sales were good. Delfosse wrote that this book was not a major Steinbeck but was nevertheless pleasant to read. The nonconformist philosophy of the paisanos of California, he said, is most congenial in spite of its encouraging an immoderate love of wine. The adventures of Danny and his friends make us smile and move us. A French radio adaptation of *Tortilla Flat* made by Mlle Bataille was well received. John Villars played Danny.

In general the articles written on Steinbeck in 1947 were complimentary, but one critic, de Laprade, writing a review of the two plays, *Des Souris et des Hommes* and *Nuits noires*, was bitterly condemnatory. "Quelle platitude, quelle vulgarité, quelle épaisse sottise!" *The Moon Is Down* was the "exercise of a schoolboy. Oh, that we would not continue to confuse Steinbeck with Caldwell, Hemingway, or Dos Passos!" Forestier discussed the whole of Steinbeck's output and labeled *Tortilla Flat* an original story but awkwardly put together, a sort of rough draft of the extraordinary *Cannery Row*. She classified *The Grapes of Wrath* as belonging to an American literary genre—the glorification of the pioneer. The satiric story "Saint Katy the Virgin" is puerile and coarse anticlericalism, which recalls Anatole France in his worst moments. "I do not believe Steinbeck is actually the best American writer. Faulkner or even Hemingway has attained summits which he is incapable of climbing. But he is without doubt the most *complet* and the most human. He redeems his faults by qualities of the heart. It is the heart, it is the sympathy which stimulates in him the creative imagination." Vallette had no such misgivings. "Two things make Steinbeck's work good: his ability to catch the feeling of a group, and his warm human sympathy." Bailly summarized: "Steinbeck is a writer of the highest quality, feeble in his understanding of the psychology of the individual but nearly always right in his interpretation of the group. He has also a sense of humor, a taste for the mysterious, and a profound feeling for poetic values." Duché in an interview with the American novelist called him a man of strong emotion, humor, simplicity. There is something of the romantic, of the epic in Steinbeck. "Do you know, I said to him, that here in France we consider

Of Mice and Men a work of pure classicism in the line which goes from *La Princesse de Clèves* to *Diable du Corps?*" Steinbeck replied, "Yes? I have never read those books." And Duché noted, "I did not doubt it. Happily he had not read them."

The numerous reviewers of *Cannery Row* pointed out much the same virtues in this book that they had found in others by this novelist—realism, lyricism, love for mankind. Certain critics objected in one way or another. Roy accused Steinbeck here of not equaling *Tortilla Flat* or *In Dubious Battle* and said Steinbeck had found no substitute for the Catholic faith of Danny. Minet found that in *The Grapes of Wrath* Steinbeck had offered his readers a point of view singularly revealing of American life. "This is true again in *Cannery Row*. Banal this time, monotonous, painted in pale colors and insignificant details. But certainly not less exact. Here we have photography rather than painting. And we recognize as authentically given certain people characteristic enough of Americans." Kanters expressed his feeling: "In a sense the people we find in *Cannery Row* are 'primitive Americans,' human beings who beyond puritanism and conformism have found again innocence, as people beyond crimes and laws find again the sense of honor."

By 1948 the critical furor had somewhat died down. Early in the year the movie version of *The Grapes of Wrath* was showing and occasioned this amusing comment by Claude Mauriac: "In Russia this picture was hastily withdrawn from the screens, M. Denis Marion says, because the misery of the Okies seemed Edenlike to the Russian spectators." Gallimard published *The Pastures of Heaven*, and a de luxe edition of *Des Souris et des Hommes* was published by Arts et Métiers Graphiques, 390 copies being printed. The book was illustrated with 37 lithographs in color by Reynold Arnould. Reviewers of *The Pastures of Heaven* found little new to say but they approved the book. Blanzat wrote for *Figaro Littéraire,* February 14, an article comparing and contrasting *Cannery Row* and *Tortilla Flat.* He preferred the later book and said, "Since *Ulysses* we have read nothing more ample, more true, more sensual than certain evocations of the sea which illuminate here and there the humor of *Cannery Row.*"

In January, 1949, the play version of *Of Mice and Men* was published again—this time in *Paris Théâtre.* The play had been revived in the fall at the Théâtre Hébertot (September 16). Also in 1949 Le Club Français du Livre published the play version of *Of Mice and Men* and the novel *Tortilla Flat.* For this edition of the play Madeleine Paz wrote a preface. She spoke glowingly of Steinbeck and of the values of American literature and its techniques. She concluded: "Alone—we are always alone is the cry of mankind. This human torment has re-echoed from one end of the earth to the other and has given a masterpiece to men; he who has created it is John Steinbeck."

In this same year Gallimard published both *A Russian Journal* (10,000 copies), which had few reviews, and *The Wayward Bus* (20,000 copies), which was rather generally unfavorably reviewed. Weidlé in commenting on the American edition had said that "if we judge a work on the intention of the author and according to the laws which he recognized, we would approve and praise *The Wayward Bus* without reserve. But the American novelists in their attempt to simplify and improve on the realists and naturalists of the last century have attained their hoped-for perfection at the expense of grandeur, at the expense of man, at the expense of all we used to call ideas or signification. We have a better right to refuse to read than to criticize their works." Jouve asked why after *The Long Valley* and *Cannery Row* Steinbeck had bothered to take up his pen, and then answered his question by supposing that Steinbeck had in mind a little psychoanalyzing since in the bus there is no man who does not want a woman, nor any woman, save one, who does not want a man. "One alone attains her goal but the thoughts of those frustrated—we know all that the American attaches to this word 'frustration' —are not any nobler or better for all of that." Roy objected that Steinbeck was, in *The Wayward Bus,* not writing about his usual characters. "Apparently Steinbeck wrote this book for an American audience only, for we can hardly comprehend the so-called lack of comfort faced by the passengers. The bathroom of the garage man is hardly less luxurious than the millionaire's." There were critics, however, less harsh. The anonymous writer for *Bulletin Critique* felt that though *The Wayward Bus* is not up to *The Grapes of Wrath* or *Of Mice and Men* it still shows proof of Steinbeck's great talent as a novelist. Fouchet wrote that Steinbeck "possesses an extraordinary gift of bestowing artistic significance upon the most common of people." Blanc-Dufour said, "I love Steinbeck and recommend reading him." He disparaged another critic who had said this book has no "message." Blanc-Dufour asked, "Why under heaven's name should Steinbeck have to give us his 'annual message'? Steinbeck is a novelist, not a prophet, not a preacher, not a licensed reformer."

In 1950 Gallimard published both *The Pearl* (15,-000 copies) and *To a God Unknown.* The reviewers gathered up again their most favorable adjectives for

The Pearl. "This book is in the tradition of the exotic story and the philosophic tale—short, packed, artistic, beautifully conceived. The art of the storyteller is here at its height, precise and subtle." Marchal wrote:

The Pearl is the definitive proof of Steinbeck's mastery. The literary quality and the human value of this tale make it an authentic chef-d'oeuvre of American literature worthy of a very large audience. So perfect is this story that we know not what to admire most: the magical precision of detail, the blending of epic and poetic themes, the constant lyricism, the tragic sense, the logical rigor of the story, or the poignant force of the great scenes.

When the critics considered *To a God Unknown*, they placed it properly as an early work, compared it to Lawrence, suggested that it held within it the germs of Steinbeck's genius, decided that with it the writer had freed himself from a certain poetic excess. Bosc said, "This somber novel is magnificently poetic, morbid, but fascinating." Several analyzed at some length Steinbeck's paganism. Blanc-Dufour:

One of the brothers, bored with the placid life of the farm, opens a store in the village. It is necessary to underline here Steinbeck's intention. He shows this man to be the only one in the family who believes in one god, personal and all-powerful—that is to say the Jewish God, the God of the Bible of whom Christ is only the human projection. Monotheism equals trade. Paganism equals breeding of cattle and cultivation of the soil.

The unknown god, to Blanzat, is a mixture of Pan and Jehovah.

This passionate paganism curiously impregnated with Biblical ferocity seems a bit disconcerting to us. But without "believing it" we are aware of the strange romanticism of the setting. And beyond the fable there remains enough of the real—of men and women, of the countryside, of beasts, of sky, of forest—for us to abandon ourselves to Steinbeck the storyteller here at the dawn of his gifts.

Lalou was enthusiastic. In his review he took Coindreau to task for saying in *Aperçus* that the importance of *To a God Unknown* was to free Steinbeck from a kind of druidic romanticism. Instead, said Lalou, the book is beautiful, moving, as tragic as poetic.

Simon's literary history published this year, 1950, gave Steinbeck high honors. The French critic objected to the American critical attitude which saw little value in Steinbeck's production during the forties. And he pointed out, "It would be foolhardy to affirm that a writer forty-seven years old, in full physical and mental vigor, might not, at any time, produce a new masterpiece, completely different from his early work." Simon divided Steinbeck's writings into (1) picaresque novels: *Tortilla Flat, Cannery Row*; (2) social novels: *In Dubious Battle, The Grapes of Wrath, The Moon Is Down;* and (3) poetic novels: the early ones—*Cup of Gold, The Pastures of Heaven, To a God Unknown*—the mature and completely successful short stories in *The Long Valley* and the masterpiece, *Of Mice and Men.* Simon did not hestitate to point out Steinbeck's weaknesses: something of the too systematic, even oversimplification, occasional sentimentality, and a too primitive psychology. But he felt that the sum of Steinbeck's values is so high that it is foolish to quibble over his defects. "Certainly Steinbeck remains in some respects indebted to Dreiser. But more than his predecessors or his contemporaries, he has shown that the conquest of the real does not imply the renouncement of the beautiful."

The year 1951 saw the French edition of *Burning Bright* on the bookstands. The reviews were few and divided. Rousselot, for example, felt that Steinbeck had solved his technical problems but that the psychological solution was unconvincing. In August of this year Las

Vergnas, prompted by the recent appearance of *To a God Unknown* and *Burning Bright,* wrote a general evaluation of Steinbeck for *Hommes et Mondes*. He saw *Burning Bright* in the tradition of *Of Mice and Men* and *The Moon Is Down*. He called Steinbeck

a man of action and adventures . . . laborer, salesman, or reporter. But under this apparent ruggedness, he has a taste for the natural, the simple, a sort of astonishing and considerate candor. I believe this combination of vitality and sensibility explains the success as well as the weaknesses of John Steinbeck. Pure intellect has no place in his work. Extraordinarily receptive and curious concerning the world about him, he need not fall back upon himself; introspection does not seem to him either necessary or sufficient for the exploration of reality. Reality for him takes the multiple forms, changing yet immutable, of nature—vegetable, animal, human. His metaphysics, his ideas spring forth of their own accord. All the prose of Steinbeck seems to obey a sort of lyric necessity. Far from being the impassive witness in the naturalistic tradition he is the much moved spectator.

In 1952 Gallimard brought out *Cup of Gold,* which the critics found interesting as an early work but nothing more. But the interest of the general reading public in Steinbeck does not seem to flag. We have been told that plans are on foot to stage *Burning Bright* both in Paris and in Belgium. And M. Hoffman, Steinbeck's Paris agent, has contracted with Editions Mondiales to bring out *East of Eden,* and the French critics as well as the reading public are eagerly awaiting this book.

12. FRANCE—AMERICA

THROUGHOUT the preceding pages of this book we have been seeing what happened to the contemporary American novel in the hands of the French. They seem to have ignored certain of our novelists, called others *les cinq grands*, and deified Faulkner. What is the situation today? What of the future?

How much the American novel has become a part of the Frenchman's literary vocabulary is shown in an article by Michel Roux in *Réforme*, October 4, 1952, "En 7 années (de la sixième au baccalaurèat) tout lycéen devrait avoir lu ces 100 livres qui ne font pas parti des programmes scolaires." This list reveals not only how high is the prestige of the American novel but also how inaccurate still is French knowledge of it. The titles are arranged according to the age of the student; these are the American books included:

11 Alcott, *Little Women*
12 Stowe, *Uncle Tom's Cabin*
     London, *White Fang and Other Stories*
13 Twain, *Tom Sawyer*
14 Poe, *Short Stories*
15 Melville, *Moby-Dick*
     Mitchell, *Gone with the Wind*
17 Faulkner, *God's Little Acre* [sic]
     Hemingway, *For Whom the Bell Tolls*
           (*A Farewell to Arms* was also rec-
           ommended though not one of the
           one hundred books)

Steinbeck, *The Grapes of Wrath*
        (*The Moon Is Down* was also recom-
        mended though not one of the one
        hundred books)
Cain, *Double Indemnity and Other Stories*

And of interest in indicating the present-day attitudes of the French is an *enquête* published in the January, 1953, *France-U. S. A.* Five well-known French critics were asked, "What were the best books from America in 1952?" All agreed on two—Hemingway's *Le vieil Homme et la Mer* and Faulkner's *Les Palmiers sauvages*. And scheduled for publication in the coming months are books by all five of our men. A volume of Caldwell short stories is on the list and *A Lamp at Nightfall* has been contracted for. Gallimard expects to bring out *A Place Called Estherville* and *Call It Experience*. The only Hemingway not translated, *Across the River and Into the Trees*, is being held up at the request of the author against the wish of the publisher. Steinbeck's *East of Eden* is appearing from the press of Edition Mondiales in 1954. Gallimard is publishing a translation by Jean Collignon of *Number One* by Dos Passos. Raimbault's translation of *Absalom, Absalom!* appeared in July, 1953. As time permits, Raimbault works on Faulkner's volume of poetry, *The Green Bough,* and *The Collected Stories of William Faulkner* is going through the mill of various negotiations before the French translation of the stories not yet available can be given to the reading public.

In addition to translations of our five men we find scheduled for publication, according to the 1953 *Almanach des Lettres*: William Styron, Orson Welles, Irving Stone, Henry James, Ernestine Gilbreth, J. D. Salinger, and W. Van Tilburg Clark. The popular novel will be represented by Ben Ames Williams, Taylor Caldwell, Frances Parkinson Keyes, Vicki Baum, and Pearl Buck. And the publications of the *Sèrie Noire* and similar series continue to flood the bookshops of Paris and the provinces. Young American authors whose books have attracted attention during the past year or so include: Frederick Buechner, John Hersey, James Jones, Chester Himes, Tom Lea, James Michener, Truman Capote, Gore Vidal, and Calder Willingham. Occasionally treated as heir to Faulkner is Robert Penn Warren.

Early in 1953 the publisher Hachette (France's most important book distributor) began a series in imitation of the American pocket-books, called *livre du poche.* The present plans call for a printing of 50,000 copies of each title chosen; each volume sells for 150 francs. Among the titles either announced or, according to the agents, contracted for are: Hemingway's *A Farewell to Arms* and *For Whom the Bell Tolls,* Steinbeck's *Of Mice and Men,* and Caldwell's *Tobacco Road* and *God's Little Acre.* One of the first titles was a two-volume edition of *Forever Amber.* The publishers of the series have approached Faulkner's French agent to obtain rights to *Sanctuary.*

Another indication of the sales value of the American novel in France is the activities of the Club Français du Livre, founded in 1946. Except for a club specializing in de luxe and semi de luxe editions, this is France's only book club. There are approximately 160,000 members and the club operates on a plan similar to its American counterparts. The chief difference between the Book-of-the-Month Club and the Club Français du Livre is that the French club does its own publishing. The regular French book trade has not as yet taken to the idea of a book club wholeheartedly and severely limits the number of copies that the Club Français du Livre can print of each title. The usual practice is to print an edition of 5,000 copies; occasionally, as with Hemingway's *Pour qui sonne le glas*, a second 5,000 will be printed. All five of our men have been represented on this book club's list. Each month the club prints five different titles ranging, as an advertisement has it, "from Homer to Jacques Prévert and from Cervantes to Steinbeck." Almost always one of these five titles is American. Recent selections include books by Kay Boyle, William Gardner Smith, Merle Miller, Robert Penn Warren, Willliam Saroyan, and Paul Bowles.

From the French readers to the writers—are the French novelists still writing books in imitation of Faulkner or Dos Passos? French critics say no, but the typical French novel of 1953 is obviously far from that of 1933, and the most important influence on the French novel during these past twenty years has been the *style américain*. A simple tangible difference is that present French novels tend to stress readability much more than did those of twenty years ago. Many novelists are consciously striving to combine the virtues of the novel of psychological analysis with the immediacy and the interest in the external world of the American novel.

Au bon Beurre by Jean Dutourd, all of whose books have been written since the war, well illustrates this present trend among the French writers. This novel, one of the best sellers on the French market of latter 1952 and early 1953, is a gently satiric story of the rise to riches of a b-o-f dealer during the occupation. The book is not influenced by any particular American, nor even the *style américain*, but it is much different from the usual French novel of 1919 to 1939. In the preface

Dutourd says, "I love the exterior world. I find that this world, even when it is the most conventional, the most commonplace, is more interesting than my reveries." It is perhaps too early to speak of a "trend," but there is striking evidence that one of the principal aesthetic results of the American influence is the return of the present-day French novel to Lesage, Voltaire, Stendhal, and Balzac. The American novel has contributed to the intellectual influences which made possible the shift in aesthetic emphasis from the interior world of Proust and Gide to the exterior world of Zola and Balzac.

Undoubtedly one of the most important of the influences in France maintaining the interest of the French in American books is the privately endowed American Library in Paris. This was started for the American colony in Paris shortly after World War I from a book collection gathered together for American soldiers on leave. If this library were used only by Americans living in France, there would be no need to mention it here. But the fact is that 60 per cent of its subscribers are French, not American. Even during World War II this library remained open in Nazi-occupied Paris, thanks to the efforts of Comtesse de Chambrun (née Clara Longworth). Today the main library at 9, rue de Teheran has a collection of 80,000 books and a membership of 2,000. In 1948 a left-bank branch was opened on boulevard Saint-Germain, which now has some 3,000 books and a membership of almost 600. In these two libraries about 99 per cent of the books are in English. During 1951 and early 1952 five branch libraries were established in the French provinces at Roubaix, Toulouse, Rennes, Montpellier, and Grenoble. In these branches 70 per cent of the books are in French, though mostly translations from American. The circulation figures for 1952 give an idea of the importance of the library's activities. In the two Paris libraries 138,236 books circulated; in the provincial branches 126,602. The story of the Roubaix branch tells something of the service this institution gives. Roubaix is an industrial town of 98,000 in northern France. There was no circulating library at all in the town when the branch was opened in March, 1951. The townspeople, including many workmen, became so much interested in having books available for all to read that they are opening their own municipal library in 1953. The American library has been offered two rooms in this building. Because the Bibliothèque américaine is dependent upon private funds, its activities are limited and the future of these branch libraries is in doubt as these lines are being written.

American literature has played a role in French higher education. Even the French lycées have included in their curriculum work in American civilization, but it is the universities which we would like to speak of here. In many ways the story of American literature in the French universities dates from 1918, when Charles Cestre came to the Sorbonne from the University of Bordeaux as a professor in the department d'Anglais, specializing in American literature. Later, in 1926, an endowed chair in American literature and civilization was set up with Professor Cestre as the first holder. Students in America as well as in France are familiar with the name of Professor Cestre through his works on American literature. He retired some years ago and Professor Maurice Le Breton now occupies this chair. A certificate in American literature is part of the student program for the licence in English. Throughout France more than a thousand students prepare for this certificate each year. For the agrégation in English, the competitive examination students take to obtain appointments in lycées and universities, each year approximately three hundred and fifty prepare themselves. One of the examinations required for the *agrégation* is on a list of ten texts, given out a year in advance. Each year two or three are American. The list in the spring of 1952 included Frost's poetry and Faulkner's *Absalom, Absalom!* The question on Faulkner was, *"Qu'est-ce que la condition humaine chez Faulkner?"* On the list for the May, 1953, examination were Melville's *Moby-Dick,* Crane's *Red Badge of Courage,* and Eliot's *Waste Land.* (Needless to say, these students are expected to be able to read and write English.) To facilitate these studies in American literature, the National Ministry of Education has, since the war, encouraged many French universities to set up courses in American literature and civilization. Before the war only the Sorbonne, Lille with Professor Jean Simon, and Lyon with Professor Lèonie Villard had such programs. Now, at the Sorbonne for example, Professors Le Breton, Las Vergnas, Mayoux, and Landré devote all or part of their time to work in American literature. Courses in American literature and civilization are also given now at Aix-Marseille, Alger, Bordeaux, Caen, Clermont, Dijon, Rennes, Strasbourg.

French scholarship in American literature had its outlet before the war in the *Revue Anglo-Américaine* and its successor, *Etudes Anglaises.* In the spring of 1952 *Etudes Anglaises* appeared for the first time since 1940. Many doctoral dissertations on subjects pertaining to American literature are defended each year at the Sorbonne and other French universities. Recent subjects have included work on Thomas Wolfe, Mark Twain, James Fenimore Cooper, Gertrude Stein, Eugene

O'Neill, Henry James, Walt Whitman, and William Faulkner.

Of some importance in French university life are the exchanges of teaching personnel under the Fulbright program. This has provided means for Americans to teach in French universities and vice versa. The Fulbright funds for France still have fifteen years to run, and each year's selection of eight American professors to teach in French universities includes three for American literature. These three professors usually lecture in at least two different universities, and a conscious attempt is being made to scatter their services around. Besides these Fulbright teaching awards there are also research awards for both pre- and postdoctoral study.

A question that has no doubt occurred to readers of these pages is this: How has reading the novels of the five men discussed here affected the French concept of America? These novels are not exactly noteworthy for their optimistic picture of American life. Does this mean that the French readers picture America as a land filled with Benjies, Lennies, Popeyes, and assorted Okies? To say that these novels have no social influence would be absurd, since we know the average Frenchman still has some weird notions about America based on his reading of James Fenimore Cooper and James Oliver Curwood. Thorough knowledge of America is hardly revealed in such a remark as this by a critic in the January, 1946, *Esprit*: "Indeed we are accustomed to the brutalities of the American novel, but we are not astonished at them from a literature which expresses a society in which the atavisms of redskins and the manners of cowboys still weigh heavily."

The French critics have frequently asked themselves

what is the relationship between American life and its literature. Usually the question took the form of a paradox—Why is American life so optimistic and American novels so pessimistic? In 1939 André Maurois raised this question apropos of *The Grapes of Wrath*. His answer was: (1) America is going through a literary crisis of romanticism. (2) The average American seeks thrills in his reading. From this comes the taste for brutality, the sensual violence of Caldwell, and the cruelty of Steinbeck. (3) The easy means that were at one time available to all Americans to go from poverty to wealth are no longer available. This loss results in a literature more nearly revolutionary. (4) The intellectuals in the United States are antisocial because their own social position is not secure. No established American institution gives to the savant, the artist his proper place in the social hierarchy. "That is imprudent. A well-made society must assimilate its elite."

But André Maurois was writing in 1939, when the effects of the depression were still evident. A more common answer to this same question is the one given in 1947 by George Adam in his book, *L'Amérique en Liberté*: "We [the French] appreciate Faulkner and Caldwell, not for their documentary value, but for the novelistic world that they give us. We do not expect that in America young girls are raped with corncobs every day or that your countrymen resemble, without exception, Ty Ty Walden of *God's Little Acre*." In other words, the French readers have read the novels of our five men as fiction, not as mirrors of American life. Critics frequently discuss the distorting role of art in its relation to life, and this distortion is particularly stressed apropos of the American novels.

The resolution of the seeming paradox between

American optimism and its pessimistic literature goes frequently something like this. A country that is prosperous and overly optimistic has need of a literature of criticism. A country that is down on its back in the dirt demands a literature of optimism so that it can be encouraged to get back on its feet. The only literature in the world today that is uniformly optimistic is that of Soviet Russia. Should American literature become uniformly optimistic, the European reader would feel that America had adopted, whether by laws or by force of social conformity, an intellectual atmosphere inhibiting the human mind as in Russia.

What then are the sources for the picture of America the French hold? One source is certainly the scene presented in books by our five men and other serious American novelists. But influencing more strongly the man on the street are the hard-boiled detective stories published in such collections as the *Sèrie Noire*. Though probably most readers treat the style and language of these books as conventions, no doubt there is a cumulative effect from reading so many novels all alike in their presentation of America. Other influences, even stronger, are American movies, still so popular throughout France; various American manufactured products, such as refrigerators and cars; and the personal contacts with American tourists. It is a combination of all these influences that made a European hotelkeeper say to us, "But I thought all Americans slept in twin beds!" Hollywood delineates America for more Europeans than does Yoknapatawpha.

Political events in America are, of course, influential in determining how favorable or unfavorable the French picture of America is. One of the reasons for the welcome to the American novel immediately after the liberation was the tremendous reservoir of good will built up during the war. Even the Communists joined in the acclaim for *les choses américaines*. But the era of good feeling did not last long. The Communists soon started their hate-America campaign, and various right-wing nationalistic groups also began to attack American influence. Jean Simon in an article in *Etudes Anglaises* in 1937 traced the pattern of the reactions to America of French novelists between 1917 and 1937. His conclusions were that from 1917 to 1920 the reactions to Wilsonian democracy were favorable. From 1920 to 1932 French novelists stressed the unfavorable aspects of American life. From 1933 to 1937 Roosevelt's New Deal caused the pendulum to swing back again. It would be foolish to think that political factors are not still important in determining the French attitude towards America.

In spite of these fluctuations in attitude certain characteristics seem to remain constant in the French idea of the average American and his country. American materialism is one of these. This idea goes back at least as far as the 1850's and turns up in remarks by Baudelaire on Poe. American materialism had rejected Poe; it was up to the more aesthetically aware Frenchmen to rescue him and his writings. This same attitude can be recognized in the frequently heard remarks which parallel the money materialism of the United States and the power materialism of Soviet Russia. The speakers feel that it is the duty of France in the present world situation to remain aloof from the deteriorating influences of both the United States and Russia. To do otherwise would, for them, mean the end in our present civilization of respect for aesthetic beauty and the arts of living. Many who think in these terms find in our culture one antimaterialistic force—the novels of *les cinq grands*. America's ability to produce works of aesthetic greatness indicates to these French intellectuals that, though our society may be dominated by materialism, there is hope for us.

What is known as the "American man" comes in for almost as much discussion in France as the "average Frenchman" in America. Most often the American man is found to be immature and totally dependent upon his psychoanalyst for guidance in the world about him. Several erudite articles argue the question—Is the American man infantile or adolescent? His lack of maturity is assumed. This inability to grow up into the post-Hiroshima world leads to the ironic picture of the most powerful nation on earth obsessed with the most fears. Thus for the French, Americans are a mixture of puritan-inspired neuroses and essential loneliness. Internal values are not developed because ersatz external standards are all the American man can either comprehend or utilize in his own life. And, it must be admitted, one of the evidences introduced to demonstrate the diseased, warped mind of the American man is what our five men have written. As artists, these five authors have been sensitive to the currents of life about them, and therefore the pessimism, cruelty, and violence in their books.

Little is known about what happens when one culture impinges on another. Within the limits of the material presented here, what hypothetical conclusions concerning intercultural relationships can we make? Because the material utilized is literary, our terminology and hypotheses must be literary. Let us look at the French scene in the 1930's when the American novel first made its critical inroads. The traditional French novel of psychological analysis was in a state of decline, of decadence. As many then young French writers put it, "What is there to say in this form after Proust and Gide?" So two elements of a pattern are present: (1) a decline of a literary mode and (2) a desire for renovation. These are the two important factors within the culture being impinged upon. Now let us turn to what the American novel was offering. It represented a different approach to the problems of the world. As part of this different approach were new techniques of plot and character presentation. In particular terms, the American novel through its violence, concreteness, and immediacy was a kind of literary opposite to the traditional French form. The American approach was through the external world; the French through the internal world.

Decline and desire are present in one culture. In another culture there is a form which seemingly fulfils the wants of the first country. Also this foreign form seems best to express the current intellectual attitudes towards the world—pessimism and despair. Therefore the first culture borrows the approaches and literary techniques from the second. Because this is not an imposition of one culture on another but rather the active borrowing of one from another, the first culture interests itself only in those aspects of the other which it feels the need of. For our particular intercultural problem this means that the French are interested only in the hard-boiled pessimistic novels of America to the exclusion of the so-called realistic novels of a Willa Cather or an Ellen Glasgow. Because it is an active process of selection, not of imposition, the novels of our five men become *the* American novel. The one culture has emphasized and taken from the other what it lacked, what it wanted.

It is easy for an American reader to say that the French have distorted the picture of the American novel in their process of selection. Yet the very process of selection, added to the traditional French logicality and the perspective of three thousand miles of ocean, makes for certain insights. We as Americans must not ignore what the French have said and thought of us. What can we learn from the French criticism of the American novel?

Have we underestimated Faulkner, at least until he won the Nobel Prize? Is Faulkner a puritan? Is Caldwell another writer whom we undervalue, particularly in his short stories, *Tobacco Road, God's Little Acre,* and *Journeyman?* Is the Steinbeck of *Of Mice and Men* and *Tortilla Flat* a classicist in his formal unities?

In general terms, we can ask ourselves the questions the French have asked about us. Does our alleged immaturity result in an epic period of American literature? Is the dominant problem of American writing one of intellectualizing itself, as Malraux has said? Is the determinism of American novels similar to that of Greek tragedies? Whether we agree or not with the French answers to these questions is not important, but we have much to learn by asking them of ourselves.

CHECK LIST

TO MAKE THE MATERIAL written in France on the contemporary American novel available to the American scholar, we have compiled this check list of books, articles, and reviews. As in the text, five authors are used as a focus: Dos Passos, Hemingway, Faulkner, Caldwell, Steinbeck. So that they may be seen in context, a list of articles on the contemporary American novel in general terms is included first. Most of the material has been published in France, obviously, but we have added several Belgian and Swiss publications widely read by the French and a few pertinent articles from recent American magazines. Because French practice in numbering issues and volumes of magazines is inconsistent, it has seemed practicable to give date of issue and page only. Consistency here, however, has been sacrificed to clarity when necessary.

Magazine and newspaper titles are abbreviated according to the following table. Those marked with an asterisk have been completely searched in the files of the Bibliothèque nationale (Paris) from 1940 through December, 1952. For the twenties and thirties we have used the bibliography of Félix Ansermoz-Dubois (see 4), making additions and corrections. However, those magazines marked with two asterisks were completely searched through their runs (though in the twenties and/or thirties) because of their importance. We have added the Bibliothèque nationale call number to this table, should the reader want to write to that library for a microfilm of any article. Finally, the symbol (#) has been used to indicate which of these titles are weekly or daily newspapers rather than magazines.

	*#	*Action* (Fol. Z. 1391)
AC	*	*Annales (Les) Conferencia* (8° Z. 17347)
AF	*	*Aspects de la France* (Fol. Lc². 6761)
AL	*	*Arts Lettres* (8° Z. 29750)
AN	*	*Age (L') Nouveau* (8° Z. 27831)
Arb	*	*Arbalète (L')* (4° Z. 3698)

	* *Arche* (*L'*) (8° Z. 29621)
	*# *Arts* (Gr. fol. V1185)
Bat	*# *Bataille* (*La*) (Gr. fol. Z. 195)
BCLF	* *Bulletin Critique du Livre Français* (8° Q. 6937)
BFLS	* *Bulletin de la Faculté des Lettres de Strasbourg*
BURG	*Bibliothèque Universelle et Revue de Genève* (Z. 22543)
Car	*# *Carrefour* (Gr. fol. Z. 190)
Cli	*# *Climats* (Gr. fol. Z. 212)
CLM	*Cahiers des Langues Modernes* (4° Z. 3996 [1])
CMN	*Cahiers du Monde Nouveau* (8° G. 15204) [Merged with *Paru* under title of *Monde Nouveau-Paru* in 1951.]
	# *Combat* (Gr. fol. Lc². 6705)
Com	*Commerce* (Rés. pZ. 1605)
Con	* *Confluences* (8° Z. 8220)
Cor	*Correspondant* (4° Z. 3201)
CP	* *Cahiers de Paris* (4° Z. 3373)
CPl	* *Cahiers* (*Les*) *de la Pléiade* (8° Z. 30542)
CR	* *Cahiers du Rhone* (16° Z. 87)
Crit	* *Critique* (8° Z. 29838)
CS	* *Cahiers du Sud* (8° Z. 24037)
CT	* *Cheval* (*Le*) *de Troie* (8° Z. 30681)
	* *Delta* (8° Z. 29668)
	* *Divan* (*Le*) (8° Z. 18035)
DN	* *Démocratie Nouvelle* (4° R. 6002)
EA	** *Etudes Anglaises* (8° N. 628)
Emp	* *Empédocle* (8° Z. 30669)
ER	** *Echange et Recherches* (4° Z. 3321)
	* *Espace* (8° Z. 29749)
	** *Esprit* (8° Z. 26070)
Eto	*# *Etoiles* (*Les*) (Gr. fol. Z. 198)
EtR	* *Eternelle* (*L'*) *Revue* (8° Z. 29583)
	* *Etudes* (D33939)
	** *Europe* (8° Z. 22011) [searched since 1932]

FicL	*	*Fiches Littéraires* (4° Q. 2994)
FL	*#	*Figaro (Le) Littéraire* (Gr. fol. Lc¹³. 9 [10])
Fon	*	*Fontaine* (8° Z. 28480)
FUSA		*France—U. S. A.*
Gav	*#	*Gavroche* (Gr. fol. Z. 228)
GL	#	*Gazette de Lausanne* (Jo. 9537)
GLet	*#	*Gazette (La) des Lettres* (Fol. Z. 1416) [monthly starting October, 1950 (8° Z. 30983)]
GR		*Grande (La) Revue* (8° Z. 15129)
Grin	**#	*Gringoire* (Gd. fol. Z. 142) [searched since 1933]
HM	*	*Hommes et Mondes* (4° Z. 3889)
Int	#	*Intransigeant (L')* (Quot. Lc². 3980)
Lab	*#	*Labyrinthe* (Gr. fol. 200) [Geneva]
LE	*	*Liberté de l'Esprit* (4° R. 6347)
Let	*	*Lettres (Les)* (8° Z. 29591)
LetF	*	*Lettre de France* (8° Z. 29936)
LF	*#	*Lettres (Les) Françaises* (Gd. fol. Z. 197)
Litt	*#	*Littéraire (Le)* (Gr. fol. Lc¹³. 9 [10]) [Became *Le Figaro Littéraire* in 1947.]
	*	*Livre (Le)* (8° Q. 7317)
LM	*	*Langues (Les) Modernes* (8° X. 13072)
Main	*	*Maintenant* (4° Z. 3830)
Mar	#	*Marianne* (Gr. fol. Z. 143)
Mes		*Mesures* (4° Z. 3138)
MF	*	*Mercure de France* (8° Z. 12830)
MI	#	*Monde (Le) Illustré* (Fol. Lc². 2943)
	*	*Mois (Le)* (8° G. 12424)
	*#	*Mondes* (Gr. fol. Z. 196)
MonF	*	*Monde (Le) Français* (8° G. 14707)
MNP	*	*Monde Nouveau-Paru* (8° G. 15204)
MS		*Magasin (Le) du Spectacle* (8° V. 56277)
NA	**	*Navire (Le) d'Argent* (8° Z. 23525)
NAge		*Nouvel Age* (4° Z. 2922)
NC	*	*Nouvelle (La) Critique* (8° R. 51575)
	*	*Nef (La)* (8° Z. 29601)

NL	**#	*Nouvelles (Les) Littéraires* (Gr. fol. Z. 133)
NR	*	*Nouvelle (La) Revue* (8° Z. 1287)
NRF	**	*Nouvelle Revue Française* (8° Z. 17955)
Ob	*#	*Observateur (L')* (4° Z. 4405)
	*	*Paru* (8° Q. 6861) [Merged with *Cahiers du Monde Nouveau* under title of *Monde Nouveau-Paru* in 1951.]
	*	*Pensée (La)* (4° R. 5108)
	*	*Poésie* (8° Ye. 15260)
Pre	*	*Preuves* (4° R. 6820)
Quad	*	*Quadrige* (Fol. Z. 1395)
QV	*	*Quatre (Les) Vents* (16° Z. 610)
RA	*	*Revue d'Algiers* (4° Z. 3785) [Became *Revue de la Mediterranée* in 1945.]
RAA	**	*Revue Anglo-Américaine* (8° Z. 24096)
RDM	*	*Revue (La) des Deux Mondes* (8° Z. 30370)
RE		*Revue (La) Européenne* (8° Z. 22987)
Ref	*#	*Réforme* (Gr. fol. Z. 227)
Ren	*	*Renaissances* (8° Z. 29582)
RF	*	*Revue Française* (Fol. Z. 1458)
RG		*Revue Générale* (8° Z. 12106)
RHL	*	*Revue d'Histoire Littéraire de la France* (8° Z. 13998)
RHP	*	*Revue d'Histoire de la Philosophie et d'Histoire Générale de la Civilisation* (8° R. 35149) [Became *Revue des Sciences Humaines* in 1947.]
RI	*	*Revue (La) Internationale* (4° R. 5795)
Riv	*#	*Rivarol* (Gr. fol. Z. 237)
RLC	*	*Revue de Littérature Comparée* (8° Z. 21190)
RM		*Revue (La) Mondiale* (4° Z. 600)
RMed	*	*Revue de la Mediterranée* (4° Z. 3785)
RN	*	*Revue (La) Nouvelle* (8° Z. 29616) [Brussels]
RNou	**	*Revue (La) Nouvelle* (4° Z. 2773)
	*	*Roman* (4° Z. 4558)
RP	*	*Revue de Paris* (8° Z. 13887)
RS	**	*Revue (La) du Siècle* (8° Z. 24110)

RSH	*	*Revue des Sciences Humaines* (8° R. 35149)
Sem	*#	*Semaine (Une) dans le Monde* (Gr. fol. Z. 219)
Sol	*	*Solstice* (8° Z. 29733)
SS	*#	*Samedi-Soir* (Gr. fol. Lc². 6699)
Syn	*	*Synthèses* (8° Z. 30000)
TH	*	*Terre Humaine* (8° Z. 31174)
TM	*	*Temps (Les) Modernes* (8° Z. 29682)
TP	*#	*Temps Présent* (Gr. fol. Z. 159)
TR	*	*Table (La) Ronde* (8° Z. 30371)
		Verve (Rés. grZ. 122)
VI	*	*Vie (La) Intellectuelle* (8° Z. 24765)

GENERAL

BOOKS:

1. Anon. *American Books in French Translation.* Paris: Services Américains d'Information, 1951. American books translated into French and French books on U. S. A. in print as of May 1, 1951. Revised edition 1952 under the title: *Les Etats-Unis à travers les Livres* includes books in print up to May 15, 1952.

2. *Almanach des Lettres françaises.* Paris: Comité National des Ecrivains, 1944. "Cet almanach des lettres françaises a été achevé d'imprimer à Paris sous l'occupation nazie en mars 1944." *Almanach des Lettres.* Paris, yearly beginning in 1947. From 1947 to 1950 the publishers were Editions de Flore and Gazette des Lettres; from 1951, Pierre Horay, Editions de Flore, and Gazette des Lettres.

3. Adam, George. *L'Amérique en Liberté.* Paris: Robert Laffont, 1947. Factual account of trip in U. S. Discussion of American literature, its reception in France, and its value as an indicator of American life, 284-9.

4. Ansermoz-Dubois, Félix. *L'Interprétation française de la Littérature américaine d'entre-deux-guerres (1919-1939).* Lausanne: Imprimerie la Concorde, 1944. Bibliographical essay, 1-150; bibliography, 151-211.
   Review: Delpech, J. *NL,* 18 oct. 1945, 3.

5. Baiwir, Albert. *Abrégé de l'Histoire du Roman américain.* Bruxelles: Editions Lumière, 1946. Brief history. Dos Pas-

sos, 77-9; Faulkner, 81-3; Hemingway, 85-7; Steinbeck, 90-3; Caldwell, 94-6.

6. ————. *Le Déclin de l'Individualisme chez les Romanciers américains contemporains.* Bruxelles: Editions Lumière, s.d. Part I: Individualism in American literature; Part II: Chapters on Upton Sinclair, Theodore Dreiser, Sherwood Anderson, Sinclair Lewis, Waldo Frank, Dos Passos, 266-90; Hemingway, 291-312; Faulkner, 313-32; Caldwell, 333-52; Thomas Wolfe.

7. Brodin, Pierre. *Les Ecrivains américains de l'entre-deux-guerres.* Paris: Horizons de France, 1946. Chapters on Robert Frost, Sinclair Lewis, Eugene O'Neill, Dos Passos, 103-24; Hemingway, 125-43; Faulkner, 145-70; Thomas Wolfe, Caldwell, 193-210; James Farrell, John P. Marquand, Steinbeck, 245-68. Bibliography, 269-84.
   Reviews: Anon. *BCLF,* nov. 1946, 14 (brief); Anon. *TP,* 22 nov. 1946, 5 (brief); Clavel, M. *LM,* nov.-déc. 1947, A70-2; Miauray, J. *NL,* 21 août 1947, 3.

8. ————. *Les Ecrivains américains du vingitième Siècle.* Paris: Horizons de France, 1947. Chapters on Theodore Dreiser, Gertrude Stein, Sherwood Anderson, Upton Sinclair, Ellen Glasgow, Pearl Buck, F. Scott Fitzgerald, Henry Miller, William Saroyan, Richard Wright, Henry James.

9. ————. *Le Roman régionaliste américain, Esquisse d'une Géographie morale et pittoresque des Etats-Unis.* Paris: G. P. Maisonneuve, 1937. Préf. M. E. Coindreau.
   Review: Delpech, J. *NL,* 26 juin 1937, 5.

10. Cahen, Jacques Fernand. *La Littérature américaine.* Paris: Presses Universitaires de France, 1950. (Que sais-je? 407) Brief general history. Chapter VI on writing between the wars, "La littérature noire," 93-118.

11. Carisey, Maurice. *Images des Etats-Unis.* Paris: Editions Défense de la France, 1946. Discussion of American books and publications, 113-23.

12. Cestre, Charles. *La Littérature américaine.* Paris: A. Colin, 1945. General history.
    Reviews: Le Breton, M. *LM,* mars 1946, 117-18; Prévost, R. *RMed.,* sept.-oct. 1947, 635-6; Simon, J. *RHP,* avril-juin, 1946, 198-200.

13. Coindreau, Maurice E. *Aperçus de Littérature américaine.* Paris: Gallimard, 1946. Part I: Discussion of contemporary novel, Hemingway, 76-94; Part II: Faulkner, 111-46; Caldwell, 147-75; Steinbeck, 176-97; Thomas Wolfe.

    Reviews: Anon. BCLF, juillet-août 1946, 16; Bailly, R. *Paru,* fév. 1947, 77-82; de Saint Jean, R. *Fon.,* nov. 1946, 657-60; Fourbeure, M. *Gav.,* 29 août 1946, 5; Lalou, R. *NL,* 17 oct. 1946, 3; Launes, E. *Action,* 1 nov. 1946, 14-5; Le Breton, M. *LM,* sept.-oct. 1947, A55-6; Nadeau, M. *Gav.,* 19 nov. 1947, 5; Peyre, H. *Books Abroad,* Spring 1947, 175 (Comments on vogue of American novel in France); Pons, C. *CS,* 1er semestre 1947, 168-9; Sans, J. *Cli.,* 25 juillet 1946, 8; Simonnet, C. *RI,* nov. 1946, 294-300.

14. ————. *Quadrille américain.* Les Oeuvres nouvelles. Tome I. N. Y.: Editions de la Maison Française, 1942. Part I: *Faulkner,* 139-64; Part II: Steinbeck, 164-81. Tome II, 1945. Part III: Caldwell, 61-102. Essays later expanded in *Aperçus.*

15. de Beauvoir, Simone. *L'Amérique au jour le jour.* Paris: Editions Paul Morihien, 1948. References to American writers *passim.*

16. de Lanux, Pierre. *New-York 1939-1945.* Paris: Hachette, 1947. American books, 170-81.

17. Desternes, Jean. *Littérature prolétarienne aux Etats-Unis.* Paris. Editions Nouvelles, 1948. Pamphlet. Int. 1-12; brief quotes from 19 writers: Dos Passos, 21-2 (from *La grosse Galette*); Faulkner, 22-3 (first "Dewey Dell" from *Tandis que j'agonise*); Caldwell, 27-8 (from *La Route au Tabac*).

18. Guérard, Albert J. (ed.). *Ecrit aux U.S.A. Anthologie des Prosateurs américains du XXe Siècle.* Paris: Robert Laffont, 1947. Int. 7-34. Brief biography of each author prefaces selection. Cather, W. C. Williams, Lardner, E. M. Roberts, Aiken, D. Parker, K. A. Porter, Fitzgerald, Faulkner, S. V. Benet, Hemingway, J. Lewis, Tate, Wolfe, Y. Winters, Caldwell, Steinbeck, O'Hara, D. Baker, Saroyan, M. Schorer, Welty, I. Shaw, McCullers.

    Reviews: Anon. BCLF, avril 1948, 213; Anon. *RDM,* 15 mars 1948, 383 (brief); Delpech, J. *NL,* 1 mars 1948, 3 (brief); Magny, C. *Sem.,* 12 juin 1948, 8; Paz, M. *Paru,* sept.

1948, 43-4; Sigaux, G. *GLet.*, 10 juillet 1948, 6; Sigaux, G. *TR*, avril 1948, 669-71.

19. Guyot, Charly. *Les Romanciers américains d'aujourd'hui.* Paris: Editions Labergerie, 1948. Chapters on Dos Passos, 29-44; Faulkner, 45-60; Hemingway, 61-76; Steinbeck, 77-92; sketches of Wolfe, H. Miller, Caldwell, 100-3; Saroyan, R. Wright.

Reviews: Anon. *BCLF*, avril 1949, 239 (brief); Asselineau, R. *LM*, sept.-oct. 1949, A96 (brief).

20. Kazin, Alfred. *Panorama littéraire des Etats-Unis de 1890 à nos jours.* Paris: Robert Marin, 1952. Tr. Gabrielle Rousseau. Translation of *On Native Grounds.*

Reviews: Anon. *BCLF*, déc. 1952, 729 (brief); Mallet, R. *FL*, 10 mai 1952, 8; Sigaux, G. *GLet.*, juillet 1952, 91-3.

21. Lebettre, Francis. *Mémento d'Histoire des Littératures anglaise et américaine.* Paris: E. Belin, 1950. General history of American literature, 177-231.

22. Llona, Victor (ed.). *Les Romanciers américains.* Paris: Denoël et Steele, 1931. Anthology. Brief introduction to each author prefaces selection. S. Anderson, Bromfield, Cabell, Dos Passos, Dreiser, Hemingway, S. Lewis, Lewisohn, London, U. Sinclair, G. Stein, Westcott.

Reviews: Lalou, R. *NL*, 7 mars 1931, 3; Petit, G. *RNou.*, mars 1931, 100-1.

23. Magny, Claude Edmonde. *L'Age du Roman américain.* Paris: Editions du Seuil, 1948. Part I: Roman américain et cinéma; Part II: Temps et impersonalité dans le roman américain—Dos Passos, 117-58; Hemingway, 159-77; Steinbeck, 178-95; Faulkner, 196-243.

Reviews: Anon. *BCLF*, fév. 1949, 97-8; Aubier, D. *Paru*, juillet 1949, 56-60; Braspart, M. *TR*, avril 1949, 652-5; Delpech, J. *NL*, 17 mars 1949, 3; d'Houville, G. *RDM*, 15 mars 1949, 359; Forestier, M. *RN*, 15 mai 1949, 513-16; Roy, C. *Action*, 5 jan. 1949, 10; Schérer, M. *TM*, mars 1949, 563-6; Sigaux, G. *GLet.*, 24 juin 1950, 1, 9.

24. Mandé, Philippe. *Ecrivain U.S.A., Ecrivain U.R.S.S.* Paris: Editions Téqui, 1952. Comparative sociological study. Bibliography on U.S.A., 83-102; on Russia, 103-26.

25. Maurois, André. *Etudes américaines.* N. Y.: Editions de la

Maison Française, 1945. Collection of book reviews which appeared 1944-5 in *Pour la Victoire,* a French newspaper published in New York. Reviews of Caldwell's *Tragic Ground* and Coindreau's *Quadrille américain,* 190-200; and of Dos Passos's *State of the Nation,* 221-31.

26. Michaud, Régis. *Panorama de la Littérature américaine contemporaine.* Paris: Kra, 1928. General.

27. ————. *Le Roman américain aujourd'hui.* Paris: Boivin, 1926. Begins with Hawthorne. American edition: *The American Novel Today.* Boston: Little, Brown, 1928.

   Review: Lalou, R. *NRF,* août 1927, 270 (brief).

28. [Moore, Nicolas (ed.)]. *Courtes Histoires américaines.* Paris: Editions Corrêa, 1948. Anthology. Int. Henri Delgove. Brief biography of each author prefaces selection. W. van Tilburg Clark, Westcott, K. A. Porter, W. C. Williams, Faulkner, K. Boyle, O'Hara, B. Field, M. Callaghan, Welty, P. Goodman, S. Anderson, Saroyan, H. Miller, Hecht.

   Reviews: Anon. *BCLF,* juillet 1948, 488 (brief); Herr, M. *Pensée,* mai-juin 1949, 157; Magny, C. *Sem.,* 12 juin 1948, 8; Paz, M. *Paru,* sept. 1948, 43-4.

29. Narcejac, Thomas. *La Fin d'un Bluff.* Paris: Le Portulan, 1949. Essay on the "roman policier noir américain."

30. Pouillon, Jean. *Temps et Roman.* Paris: Gallimard, 1946. Dos Passos, 117-37; Faulkner, 238-60.

31. Rousseaux, André. *Littérature du vingtième Siècle.* Paris: Albin Michel, 1949. Faulkner, 238-46; Hemingway, 247-53.

32. Roy, Claude. *Clefs pour l'Amérique.* Genève-Paris: Editions les Trois Collines, 1947. Reprinted Paris: Gallimard, 1950. Chapter XXIII on the new American literature.

33. Sartre, Jean Paul. *Situations I.* Paris: Gallimard, 1947. Two essays on Faulkner: "Sartoris," 7-13, and "A propos de *Le Bruit et la Fureur,*" 70-81; one essay, "A propos de John Dos Passos et de *1919,*" 14-25.

34. Schaeffer, Pierre. *Amérique nous t'ignorons.* Paris: Editions du Seuil, 1946. Brief section on American literature, 130-2.

35. Simon, Jean. *Le Roman américain au XXᵉ Siècle.* Paris: Boivin, 1950. Dos Passos, 100-8; Hemingway, 108-18; Faulkner, 119-31; Caldwell, 146-50; Steinbeck, 159-70 Bibliography, 185-8.

Reviews: Anon. *BCLF,* déc. 1950, 764 (brief); Le Breton, M. *LM,* juillet-août 1951, A70-1; Schmidt, A. *Réf.,* 30 sept. 1950, 7.

36. Simon, Yves (ed. and trans.). *La Civilisation américaine.* Paris: Desclée de Brouwer, 1950. Collection of essays written, with two exceptions, by professors at the University of Notre Dame. "Littérature américaine et littérature mondiale," by Frank J. O'Malley, 239-68.

37. Vaucher-Zananiri, Nelly. *Voix d'Amérique. Etudes sur la Littérature américaine d'aujourd'hui.* Le Caire: R. Schindler, [1945]. Dos Passos, 26-8; Faulkner, 29-31; Hemingway, 32-5; Steinbeck, 61-9.

SPECIAL ISSUES OF MAGAZINES:

38. *L'Arbalète,* n° 9, automne 1944. LE ROMAN AMERICAIN. Anthology: G. Stein, D. Baker, Caldwell, D. H. Clarke, P. Cheyney, Hemingway, MacCoy, W. Edmonds, Faulkner, N. Z. Hurston, H. Miller, Runyon, Saroyan, N. West, Wilder, Wolfe, Wright.

    Review: Picon, G. *Con.,* avril 1945, 314-21.

39. *L'Age Nouveau,* juin-juillet-août 1952. VISAGES DES ETATS-UNIS. Short stories by Faulkner, B. L. Burman, R. Lowry. One-act play by Wilder. Critical articles on American literature by K. Woods, A. Kazin, L. Galantière.

40. *Cahiers de Paris,* mai 1939. LE ROMAN CONTEMPO-RAIN AUX ETATS-UNIS. Critical articles on Dreiser, S. Lewis, S. Anderson, W. Frank, Dos Passos, P. Buck, J. Johnson.

41. *Cahiers des Langues Modernes,* déc. 1946. ROMANCIERS AMERICAINS CONTEMPORAINS. Critical articles on Dreiser, Rölvaag, U. Sinclair, S. Anderson, S. Lewis, Wilder, Hemingway, Steinbeck, S. V. Benet, Bromfield, Faulkner, Saroyan; also general critical articles.

    Review: Duvignaud, J. *Pensée,* jan.-fév. 1948, 154.

42. *Confluences,* n° 21-24, 1943. PROBLEMES DU ROMAN. Discussions by about sixty prominent French writers of the aesthetics, possible crisis, and future of the contemporary novel.

43. *Esprit,* nov. 1946. L'HOMME AMERICAIN. Descriptions

of the American man by regions, the American way, and French reactions.

44. *Etudes et Documents,* 1947. LA PROSPERITE AMER-ICAINE. Economic problems in the U. S.

45. *Fontaine,* n° 27-28, août 1943 (Algiers). Reprinted Paris, 1945. ECRIVAINS ET POETES DES ETATS-UNIS. Several prefatory articles. Anthology: Eliot, Hemingway, Steinbeck, Faulkner, H. Miller, W. C. Williams, Saroyan, G. Stein, Prokosch, Caldwell, Frost, Crapsey, Hagedorn, W. Stevens, Teasdale, Jeffers, Aiken, L. Ridge, MacLeish, H. Gregory, L. Bogan, Sandburg, M. Van Doren, Tate, Hillyer, H. P. Putnam, Ransom, Cummings, H. Crane, L. Hughes, M. Moore, J. Agee, Patchen, J. Laughlin, Lindsay. *Reviews:* Laffay, A. *LM,* juillet 1946, 291; Rode, H. *Con.,* août 1945, 669-75.

46. *La Gazette des Lettres,* 14 sept. 1946. LE ROMAN AMER-ICAIN. Critical articles on the American novel.

47. *L'Illustration,* 10 avril 1937. FRANCE-AMERIQUE. Historical and sociological articles.

48. *Mesures,* 15 juillet 1939. HOMMAGE A LA LITTERA-TURE AMERICAINE. Anthology: R. P. du Poisson, C. Mather, Franklin, John Paul Jones, de Crévecoeur, Irving, Poe, Whitman, W. H. Herndon, Dickinson, Lindsay, J. W. Johnson, H. Crane, J. P. Bishop, L. Hughes, Jeffers, Mac-Leish, H. Miller, M. Moore, Dos Passos, Ransom, W. Stevens, Tate, W. C. Williams.

49. *Le Navire d'Argent,* mars 1926. LA LITTERATURE AMERICAINE. Anthology: Whitman, R. McAlmon, Hemingway, W. C. Williams, E. E. Cummings. Previously this magazine had carried a bibliography of American literature translated into French: Part I: From Franklin to Whitman appeared Dec. 1925, 350-5; Part II: From Whitman to the Contemporary Writers appeared in Jan. 1926, 477-86. The special issue in March printed "Remarques et Addenda" to this bibliography, 221-4.

50. *Renaissances,* n° 18, fév. 1946. DE L'AMERIQUE ET DES AMERICAINS. General and critical articles. Short stories by Saroyan, Fitzgerald.

51. *La Revue Nouvelle,* oct. 1928. NUMERO SPECIAL CON-SACRE A LA LITTERATURE ETRANGERE CONTEM-

PORAINE. Short story by S. Anderson. Article on Waldo Frank and general article on American literature.

52. *Les Temps Modernes,* n° 11-12, août-sept. 1946. U.S.A. General articles on the American scene.

CRITICAL ARTICLES:

53. Anon. "Au pays des dollars et des huit cylindres les écrivains exploitent la poésie du désespoir." *SS,* 5 oct. 1946, 2.

54. Anon. "Le bec de la plume." *GLet.* (see 46), 1. Brief editorial on the importance of the American novel.

55. Anon. "Best-sellers 1951 aux U.S.A." *Car.,* 20 fév. 1952, 7. Brief article based on *Publisher's Weekly* annual listing.

56. Anon. "Cartes d'identité." *GLet.* (see 46), 4-5, 15. Brief biographical sketches and pictures of Faulkner, MacCullers, U. Sinclair, S. Lewis, Betty Smith, Steinbeck, Saroyan, Bromfield.

57. Anon. "En découvrant l'Amérique, les romanciers français n'enrichissent pas notre littérature." *SS,* 3 nov. 1945, 2.

58. Anon. "Les jeunes lettrés américains sont-ils iconoclasts?" *FL,* 18 août 1951, 3.

59. Anon. "Les livres les plus vendus en 1946." *Car.,* 9 jan. 1947, 7.

60. Anon. "Les livres les plus vendus en 1947." *Car.,* 14 jan. 1948, 8.

61. Anon. "Quels sont les meilleurs livres venus d'Amérique en 1952?" *FUSA,* jan. 1953, 3, 2.

62. Anon. "Le roman américain à l'étranger." *Arts,* 20 sept. 1946, 2. Based on an article by Malcolm Cowley in the *New Republic.*

63. Anon. "Traductions récentes, littérature américaine." *RLC,* jan.-mars 1947, 122-3. Brief listing of translations of 17 American writers published in France in 1945-46.

64. Anbert, Camille. "Roman américain et littérature totale." *TP,* 1 fév. 1946, 5. Aesthetic discussion.

65. Ansermoz-Dubois, Félix. "Le merveilleux dans la littérature américaine." *Lab.,* 15 déc. 1944, 13.

66. Antonini, Giacomo. "Le roman anglais depuis la guerre." *TR,* avril 1952, 157-61. Brief comparison of the vogue of the English and American novel in France.

67. Arland, M. "Sur les conditions du roman." *CPL.*, hiver 1948, 31-4.

68. Astre, Georges Albert. "L'apport américain au roman contemporain." *AN*, déc. 1951, 29-34.

69. ————. "Les origines de lettres américaines." *Crit.*, mars 1949, 206-14. Discussion of Van Wyck Brooks, *World of Washington Irving*.

70. ————. "Le roman aux Etats-Unis et la crise de-l'homme américain." *AN*, avril 1951, 25-35.

71. ————. "Sur le roman américain." *Crit.*, avril 1947. 302-15.

72. Astruc, Alexandre. "Lectures américaines." *Con.*, mars 1945, 230-2.

73. ————. "Le roman américain." *Action*, 6 oct. 1944, 8.

74. Baldensperger, Fernand. "La France s'américainise-t-elle?" *MonF*, sept. 1949, 405-17.

75. Bataille, Georges. "La souveraineté de la fête et le roman américain." *Crit.*, août 1949, 675-81.

76. Beigbeder, Marc. "Le théâtre." *Esprit*, juillet 1947, 152-5. Discussion of American realism in *La Ménagerie de Verre, La Route au Tabac, Des Souris et des Hommes*.

77. Beloff, Max. "The Projection of America Abroad." *Am. Quart.*, Spring 1949, 23-9.

78. Bergman, Alix et M. L. Becker. "Les écrivains américains et leurs oeuvres depuis 1939." *Paru*, avril 1945, 7-16. From N. Y. *Her. Trib.*

79. Blanc-Dufour, A. "A propos de romans américains." *CS*, 1re semestre 1949, 291-8. Reasons for success of the American novel in France after the liberation.

80. Blanchot, Maurice. "Chroniques: Traduit de. . . ." *Arche*, juillet 1946, 114-28. Difficulty of translation and influence of American novels in translation.

81. Blanzat, Jean. "Les lettres." *MonF.*, nov.-déc. 1945, 131-6. Brief discussion of influence of American novelists on young French writers.

82. ————. "Les romans." *Poésie 43*, oct.-nov. 1943, 75-82. Influence of American novelists on Simone de Beauvoir, *L'Invitée* and Louis René des Forêts, *Les Mendiants*.

83. —————. "Romans policiers." *FL*, 28 août 1948, 5. Discussion of Série Noire, Cheyney, Chase in relation to Faulkner *et al.*

84. Blondel, Jacques. "Connaître la littérature américaine." *Réf.*, 17 juillet 1948, 7.

85. Bousquet, Joe. "Le cabinet de lecture." *CS*, n° 280, 1946, 494-99. H. Miller and the *roman noir* in America.

86. Brée, Germaine. "The 'Interpenetration' of Literatures." *Mod. Lang. Jour.*, Dec. 1949, 619-23.

87. Brion, Marcel. "L'actualité littéraire à l'étranger." *NL*, 25 fév. 1933, 6. Discussion of Ludwig Lewisohn, *Expression in America*.

88. —————. "Les tendances nouvelles de la littérature américaine." *Arts*, 30 nov. 1945, 6.

89. Brodin, Pierre. "Les écrivains américains de l'entre-deux-guerres." *Ren.*, fév. 1946, 65-8. Summary of ideas in his book.

90. —————. "Panorama du roman américain." *Arts*, 1 mai 1952, 6.

91. Bromfield, Louis. "Les chroniques nationales. Etats-Unis. 'La nouvelle découverte de l'Amérique.'" *BURG*, mars 1927, 333-44.

92. Brown, John. "Les lettres américaines en 1944." *Esprit*, mars 1945, 598-602.

93. —————. "Tendences du roman américain moderne." *CLM* (see 41), 275-85.

94. Buenzod, Emmanuel. "Quelques romans américains." *GL*, 13 nov. 1932, 1. Hergesheimer, Heyward, Leonard Falkner.

95. Cahen, Jacques Fernand. "Du roman américain. I: Conceptions littéraire." *Divan*, juillet-sept. 1948, 393-406; "II: Cause et déchéance de la littérature noire." oct.-déc. 455-69. Survey of American novel between the wars.

96. Camus, Albert. "Art and Revolt." *Partisan Rev.*, May-June, 1952, 268-81. Defines and gives weaknesses of the American novel.

97. C[arré], J. M. "La vogue du roman américain en France." *RLC*, jan.-mars 1947, 95-6.

98. Catel, Jean. "Le roman 'en masse.'" *CP*, mai 1939, 128-32.

99. Chabrier, Agnes. "L'Amérique, elle aussi a sa crise du roman." *Bat.*, 14 jan. 1948, 4. Discusses Book-of-the-Month Club and relation of best sellers to literature.

100. Clouard, Henri. "Littérature." *RF*, avril 1950, 46-8.

101. Coindreau, Maurice E. "L'Amérique et le roman alcoolique." *CS*, avril 1932, 166-72.

102. ————. "Le crime dans le roman américain contemporain." *Les Cahiers des Hommes de Bonne Volonté.* IV. Paris: Flammarion, mars 1950, 54-7.

103. ————. "William Maxwell." *RP*, fév. 1948, 120-6. Includes general commentary; reprinted as preface to *La Feuille repliée.*

104. Cormeau, Nelly. "Ethique de la littérature française d'aujourd'hui." *Syn.*, mai 1946, 63-81; juin 60-73. Questions whether French writers have been contaminated by foreigners such as Faulkner, Caldwell, Cain.

105. ————. "Révolte contre le temps chez les romanciers d'aujourd'hui." *AN*, mai 1951, 37-44.

106. Daix, Pierre. "Servitude et décadence du 'roman américain.'" *LF*, 20 jan. 1949, 8. Communist point of view.

107. d'Astorg, Bertrand. "Les faussaires de' l'obscénité." *Esprit*, fév. 1947, 337-40.

108. d'Aubarède, Gabriel. "Roman français et roman américain." *Arts*, 5 juillet 1946, 2. Attempts to prove that American novelistic technique goes back entirely to individual French writers.

109. de Beauvoir, Simone. "An American Renaissance in France." N. Y. *Times B. R.*, June 22, 1947, 7, 29.

110. de Belleville, Joseph. "Le point de vue du librairie. La librairie amèricaine à Paris." *GLet.* (see 46), 8. Brief account of the Bibliothèque américaine and of Gallignani's.

111. Debu-Bridel, Jacques. "L'avenir du roman." *Con.* (see 42), 388-90.

112. de Fréminville, Claude. "Le vagabond américain." *Ren.*, mai 1946, 146-52. Discussion of Dos Passos, Steinbeck, Miller, Saroyan.

113. de Jouvenel, Renaud. "D'une bibliothèque américaine." *Europe*, mars 1949, 108-15. Communist point of view.

114. de Peyret-Chappuis, Charles. "Comment expliquer l'influence de la littérature anglo-saxonne." *Gav.*, 7 août 1947, 1, 5.

115. de Rougemont, Denis. "Conseils à un français pour écrire à l'américaine." *Litt.*, 13 juillet 1946, 1, 2.

116. ————. "La jeune littérature des Etats-Unis devant le roman américain." *FL*, 7 juin 1947, 1.

117. ————. "Rhétorique américaine." *Fon.* (see 45), 15-7.

118. Desternes, Jean. "Que pensez-vous de la littérature américaine?" *Combat.* Interview with Jean Paul Sartre, 3 jan. 1947, 2; Louis René des Forêts, 4 jan., 2; Georges Charensol, 5-6 jan., 2; Jacques Lemarchand, 7 jan., 2; Alfred Rosmer, 8 jan., 2; Albert Camus, 17 jan., 2; Roger Caillois, 21 jan., 2; André Bay, Mouloudji, 23 jan., 2; François Mauriac, 26-27 jan., 2; Henri Parisot, 28 jan., 2; Emile Henriot, 2-3 fév., 2; Pierre François Caillé, 6 fév., 2; Claude Edmonde Magny, 7 fév., 2; Thierry Maulnier, Henry Poulaille, 13 fév., 2.

119. Doolaard, A. D. "A Study in Misunderstanding." *SRL*, Sept. 24, 1949, 6-7, 39-40. European attitudes towards America derived from contemporary American literature.

120. du Parc, Robert. "Revue des livres." *Etudes*, nov. 1949, 276. Review of Sartre, *Les Chemins de la Liberté* with comment on American influence.

121. Ellmann, Richard. "Lettre de New-York. Mars et les muses américaines." *Con.*, jan.-fév. 1945, 96-9.

122. Elsen, Claude. "Quelques nouveaux venus." *TR*, oct. 1950, 148-51. General influence on the novel.

123. ————. "Le roman est-il un genre périmé?" *TR*, nov. 1950, 141-4.

124. ————. " 'Série Noire,' panorama de la littérature américaine du second rayon." *GLet.*, 2 avril 1949, 11.

125. Emmanuel, Pierre. "Romanciers et poètes américains." *TP*, 20 avril 1945, 5.

126. Erval, François. "Tendances actuelles." *GLet.*, 15 jan. 1951, 20-3. Discussion of the translations which appeared in 1950.

127. Etiemble, [René]. "Petit supplément à des 'Aperçus' de littérature yanquie." *TM*, fév. 1947, 913-27. Merely men-

tions Coindreau's book; denounces American materialism as shown in *Reader's Digest*, best sellers, etc.

128. Farrell, James T. "L'avenir de la littérature américaine." *AN*, jan. 1949, 116-23.

129. ————. "Le héros de roman américain." *RI*, fév. 1947, 117-25; mars, 226-33.

130. ————. "Situation présente de la culture américaine." *TM*, avril 1947, 1327-35.

131. Faÿ, Bernard. "L'école de l'infortune ou la nouvelle génération littéraire aux Etats-Unis." *RP*, 1 août 1937, 644-65. Depression upset American physical and intellectual life; Wolfe, Faulkner, M. Mitchell.

132. Flandrau, Grace. "On What It Is to Be French." *Am. Quart.*, Spring 1949, 9-22.

133. Forestier, Marie. "Lettres anglo-saxonnes." *RN*, 15 avril 1948, 399-403. French rage for American books.

134. Fouchet, Max Pol. "Littérature américaine." *Car.*, 24 oct. 1946, 7.

135. ————. "La littérature américaine se détache du réel." *Car.*, 28 sept. 1949, 8.

136. ————. "Si nous ne devons pas lire les américains. . . ." *Car.*, 29 oct. 1947, 7. Article refuses to accept the party line as expressed in *L'Humanité*, 24 oct. 1947, 4—"L'Amérique dégrade l'esprit."

137. Gadenne, Paul. "Efficacité du roman." *Con.* (see 42), 248-57.

138. ————. "Recherche de l'objectivité dans le roman américain." *Sem.*, 11 mai 1946, 8.

139. Gersennes. "Entrepénétration des littératures: présentation des Etats-Unis." *AN*, jan. 1947, 111-15. What America is like and what her people think.

140. Gide, André. "Interview imaginaire." *Fon.* (see 45), 7-11. Gide's opinions on contemporary American novelists.

141. Green, Julien. "Au seuil des temps nouveaux (en guise de préface)." *Fon.* (see 45), 12-14. Green hopes the war will arouse the French from the lethargy of the nineteenth century.

142. Guérard, Albert. "French and American Pessimism." *Har-*

per's, Sept. 1945, 267-72. American novel in France during World War II.

143. ————. "Puritanisme, solitude et violence." *Con.,* sept. 1945, 736-45.

144. ————. "Les relations culturelles entre la France et les Etats-Unis. Il faut d'abord établir des relations normales entre les écrivains et les éditeurs de nos deux pays." *Eto.,* 25 sept. 1945, 1, 2.

145. ————. "Le roman américain depuis 1939." *LM,* oct. 1945, 111-20.

146. ————. "Les romanciers américains." *TP,* 17 août 1945, 3. Tells French readers of American writers unread by them.

147. ————. "Voici l'état actuel de la littérature américaine." *MI,* 22 sept. 1945, 20.

148. Guth, Paul. "Ce que demande 'le grand public.'" *Car.,* 23 jan. 1947, 7. Discussion of what books have sold most.

149. ————. "Deux heures de meeting littéraire à l'Ecole Normale Supérieure." *Litt.,* 18 mai 1946, 1, 2. Brief evaluation of American literature by students.

150. Hauger, Raymond. "L'évolution de la littérature américaine." *Mondes,* 8 août 1945, 5.

151. Hessel, Vitia. "Romans américains en France." *TM,* jan. 1951, 1293-6.

152. Hoog, Armand. "Tous les écrivains américains sont seuls." *Car.,* 31 mars 1946, 8.

153. Hubaux, Jean. "Le roman anglo-saxon depuis la guerre." *Syn.,* avril 1946, 75-94.

154. Jacquier, Claude. "Cinéma et crise du roman." *Con.* (see 42), 205-7.

155. Jaffe, Adrian. "Franz Kafka et le héros solitaire dans le roman américain contemporain." *Roman,* mars 1951, 142-9.

156. Kanapa, Jean. "Il y a deux littératures américaines." *LF,* 5 fév. 1948, 3. Communist point of view.

157. Kanters, Robert. "Ambassadeurs d'Amérique." *AN,* déc. 1950, 109-11. American novels.

158. ————. "Les livres de la semaine. C'était une histoire

d'amour." *SS*, 24 nov. 1951, 2. Brief comment on the return of French literature in 1951 to the traditional forms.

159. ————. "Nouvel âge du roman américain?" *GLet.*, avril 1951, 97-102. Discussion of changing tastes in the American novel; reviews of books by John Kelly and John Horne Burns.

160. Lafore, Larry, et Eugénie Helisse. "L'Amérique est en guerre jusque dans sa littérature." *Arts*, 30 mars 1945, 3. Books read in the U. S. during the war.

161. Lalou, Etienne. "Vers une 'Culture atlantique'? Défense du roman français." *Gav.*, 3 mai 1945, 4. Discussion of American influence on French novel.

162. Lanoux, Armand. "Emile Zola: pére du roman américain moderne." *Car.*, 1 oct. 1952, 7.

163. Lartigue, Jean. "Notes sur le roman américain." *CS*, n° 271, 1945, 395-6.

164. Las Vergnas, Raymond. "Lettres étrangères." *HM*, juillet 1946, 192-7. Hemingway, H. Miller, K. Winsor, Harry Brown.

165. ————. "La littérature américaine pendant la guerre." *NL*, 13 sept. 1945, 1, 2.

166. ————. "La littérature romanesque en Amérique pendant cette guerre." *Ren.* (see 50), 68-77.

167. ————. "Y a-t-il une crise du roman français?" *NL*. This article precedes a number of interviews conducted by Jeanine Delpech. Replies to the question by David Rousset, Roger Vailland, Celia Bertin, Jean Malaquais, René Barjavel, Morvan Lebesque, 30 oct. 1947, 1, 2; Francis Ambrière, Julien Blanc, Georges Govy, Jean Jacques Gautier, Gilbert Sigaux, 6 nov., 6; Julien Gracq, Henri Calet, Robert Morel, Jacques Lemarchand, 13 nov., 5; Dominique Rollin, Françoise d'Eaubonne, Pierre Molaine, Jean Orieux, Paul Gadenne, 20 nov., 8; (the preceding are all young novelists who have risen since the war; the following are the older generation) Marcelle Auclair, Marcel Aymé, Marc Blanc pain, Joseph Delteil, Yves Gandon, Joseph Peyre, Charles Plisnier, Paul Vialar, 18 déc., 5.

168. Lavergne, Edouard. "Il n'y a pas de roman américain." *GLet.* (see 46), 1, 3.

169. ————. "Le nègre: héros tragique du roman américain." *GLet.*, 24 jan. 1948, 1, 2.

170. Le Breton, Maurice. "L'avenir de la littérature en Amérique." *ER*, 15 mars 1938, 320-2.

171. ————. "Note sur les Etats-Unis." *LM*, juillet 1946, 270-4.

172. ————. "Les tendances du roman américain contemporain." *RHP*, 15 oct. 1933, 241-64.

173. ————. "Tendances du roman américain d'aujourd'hui." *CP* (see 40), 122-7.

174. Lemonnier, Léon. "Le roman contemporain aux Etats-Unis." *CP* (see 40), 120-1.

175. Leroux, A. G. "Propagande et littérature américaine." *LF*, 3 mars 1945, 1, 3. On Lewis Galantière and the opening of the USIS in Paris. Galantière reminisces over the American writers in Paris during the twenties.

176. Levin, Harry. "Some European Views of Contemporary American Literature." *Am. Quart.*, Fall 1949, 264-79.

177. Lévy, Marguerite. "Aperçus sur le tragique américain." *AN*, sept. 1949, 14-17.

178. Llona, Victor. "Américains expatriés." *NL*, 18 avril 1933, 6. Long review and discussion of the anthology, *Americans Abroad*.

179. Lynes, Carlos. "The 'Nouvelle Revue Française' and American Literature, 1909-1940." *French Rev.*, n° 3, 1946, 159-67.

180. Magny, Claude Edmonde. "A bâtons rompus." *Esprit*, mars 1945, 596-8. Critical comments on what is appearing in French magazines.

181. ————. "La critique aux limites de la littérature." *Esprit*, jan. 1945, 161-84. Reprint of preface to *Les Sandales d'Empédocle*; problems of criticism.

182. ————. "Le roman américain depuis la guerre." *Poésie 45*, fév.-mars 1945, 72-8.

183. ————. "Roman américain et cinéma. I. La technique objective dans le roman: Dashiell Hammett." *Poésie 44*, juillet-oct. 1944, 108-16; nov.-déc., 126-31; "II. L'ellipse au cinéma et dans le roman." *Poésie 45*, avril-mai 1945, 59-

72; "III. La succession des plans au cinéma et dans le roman." juin-juillet, 71-9; oct.-nov., 74-84. Reprinted in her book (see 23).

184. ————. "Le temps de la réflexion." *Esprit,* avril 1948, 686-703. Primarily criticism of Sartre.

185. Malherbe, H. "Les français n'achètent plus les romans américains. Réflexions sur le déclin de la littérature commerciale." *LF,* 24 mars 1949, 1, 2. Communist; objects to lengthy, trashy American books but specifically exempts from the accusation Dreiser, Faulkner, Westcott, Steinbeck, Caldwell.

186. Malraux, André. "Après un silence de quatre ans André Malraux expose pour notre journal ses vues et ses idées sur les problèmes du monde actuel." *Lab.,* 15 fév. 1945, 1, 2. On American literature and civilization. Translated and reprinted in *Horizon,* Oct. 1945, 236-42 (under the title "An Interview with Malraux").

187. Marion, Denis. "Roman anglais et roman américain." *LF,* 21 juillet 1945, 3.

188. Maulnier, Thierry. "Feuilleton littéraire. Le sort du roman." *HM,* sept. 1946, 194-202. Influence of American novelists.

189. ————. "Position de la littérature française." *HM,* juillet 1946, 186-91.

190. Maurois, André. "Ce qu'on lit aux Etats-Unis." *NL,* 1 août 1946, 1, 7. Maurois had just returned from the U. S.

191. ————. "Ecrivains américains." *RP,* avril 1947, 9-24. Dorothy Parker, Frank Dobie, James Burnham, Henry James.

192. ————. "Les romanciers américains." *NL,* 25 avril 1931, 1. Lewis, Dreiser, Anderson, etc.

193. Mazars, Pierre. "Les généraux et leurs romanciers." *TR,* déc. 1950, 145-8. Hemingway, Mailer, Fast.

194. Michaud, Regis. "La littérature américaine d'aujourd'hui: de New-York à Montparnasse." *MF,* 15 juillet 1928, 310-23.

195. Miller, Perry. "Europe's Faith in American Fiction." *Atlantic,* Dec. 1951, 53-6.

196. Mithois, Marcel. "Les étrangers vus à leurs microscopes."

GLet., 15 jan. 1951, 24-7. Discussion of the translations which appeared in 1950.

197. Mohrt, Michel. "Une enquête sur les tendances actuelles de la littérature américaine." *TR*, déc. 1948, 2118-27. Summary of opinions of John Berryman, R. P. Blackmur, Robert Davis, Leslie Fiedler, Clement Greenberg, Mencken, Ransom, Wallace Stevens, Lionel Trilling; appeared originally in *Partisan Review*.

198. Mouillaud, Maurice. "Le romancier aux prises avec la facticité." *Con.*, mai 1945, 373-82.

199. Munson, Gorham. "Le roman d'après-guerre aux Etats-Unis." *Europe*, 15 août 1932, 617-23.

200. Muray, Jean. "Regards sur les lettres anglo-américaines." *RF*, mai 1949, 63-4.

201. Nadeau, Maurice. "Une littérature d'urgence." *GLet.*, 15 jan. 1951, 17-20. Discussions of the translations which appeared in 1950.

202. —————. "Que pensez-vous de la littérature américaine?" *RI*, fév. 1947, 113-16.

203. Parrot, Louis. "Les livres et l'homme. Caldwell au Tessin." *LF*, 6 sept. 1946, 5. General discussion of influence of various Swiss and American writers on the French.

204. —————. "Les livres et l'homme. De Faulkner à Henry Miller." *LF*, 9 août 1946, 5.

205. Peyre, Henri. "American Literature through French Eyes." *Va. Quart. Rev.*, Summer 1947, 421-38.

206. —————. "La culture et la littérature aux Etats-Unis." *MonF*, sept. 1948, 485-90. Warns French that Faulkner, Caldwell, Hemingway do not present a complete picture of American life.

207. Pierhal, Armand. "L'âme américaine à travers sa littérature." *GLet.* (see 46), 10.

208. —————. "Défense du roman français." *NL*, 10 avril 1947, 1, 2. Almost entirely a discussion of the American novel.

209. —————. "Une littérature sans espérance." *NL*, 2 oct. 1947, 1, 2. General discussion of need to turn from the *littérature noire*.

210. Pons, Christian. "Position du roman américain." *CS*, n° 274, 1945, 801-6.

211. Renaud, Georges. "Pour connaître la littérature américaine." *GLet.* (see 46), 8.

212. Rice, Howard C. "Seeing Ourselves as the French See Us." *French Rev.*, May 1948, 432-41.

213. ———. "Témoignages américains, livres américains sur la France parus depuis 1940." *Paru*, nov. 1945, 5-12.

214. Roux, Martin. "Pas d'orchidées pour M. Duhamel." *RI*, août 1946, 76-9. Comment on the *Série Noire* edited by Duhamel.

215. Roy, Claude. "Air d'Amérique." *LF*, 17 mars 1945, 3. General article including comment on the special issues of *Fontaine* (see 45) and *L'Arbalète* (see 38).

216. ———. "Clefs pour l'Amérique et sa littérature." *Fon.*, oct. 1947, 655-63.

217. ———. "Panorama des livres." *Europe*, juillet 1946, 114-19. Dos Passos, Saroyan, Steinbeck.

218. Sans, Julien. "D'un nouveau poncif." *Cli.*, 3 déc. 1947, 4. Steinbeck, Caldwell, Taylor Caldwell. Violently opposed to American novelists with the exception of Faulkner.

219. ———. "Romans de France et d'Amérique." *Cli.*, 27 août 1947, 8; 3 sept., 8. Comparison of basic techniques.

220. ———. "*La Lettre écarlate* de Hawthorne." *Cli.*, 6 juin 1946, 7. Remarks on the vogue of American literature in France.

221. Sartre, Jean Paul. "American Novelists in French Eyes." *Atlantic*, Aug. 1946, 114-18.

222. Schakowskoy, Zinaïda. "Les américains." *Lab.*, 15 mai 1945, 10.

223. Sigaux, Gilbert. "Etapes du roman américain." *GLet.* (see 46), 11. Historical perspective.

224. S[igaux], G[ilbert]. "Le point de vue de l'éditeur. L'édition américaine." *GLet.*, 1 fév. 1947, 8. Summary of books which were published in the U. S. in 1946.

225. S[igaux], G[ilbert]. "Le point de vue de l'éditeur. Sur l'édition aux Etats-Unis." *GLet.* (see 46), 8. General comment on publishing on the U. S.; twenty-five-cent books, enormous printings, book clubs, etc.

226. S[igaux], G[ilbert]. "Point de vue du libraire. L'édition américaine en 1947." *GLet.*, 17 avril 1948, 6. Summary of books which were published in the U. S. in 1947.

227. Sillen, Samuel. "Crise du livre aux U.S.A." *DN*, nov. 1952, 629-32. Communist point of view.

228. Simenon, Georges. "L'âge du roman." *Con.* (see 42), 358-61.

229. Simon, Jean. "L'Amérique telle que l'ont vue les romanciers français (1917-1937)." *EA*, nov. 1937, 498-520.

230. —————. "French Studies in American Literature and Civilization." *Am. Lit.*, May 1934, 176-90. Primarily bibliographical. Lists translations, books, articles, reviews.

231. —————. "Romanciers américains et critiques français." *RSH*, jan.-mars 1948, 60-4.

232. Singer, André. "Lectures en 1951 (1)." *FUSA*, jan. 1952, 2, 8. American novels in translation.

233. Soupault, Philippe. "Connaissons-nous la vraie littérature américaine?" *GLet.*, 18 oct. 1947, 1, 7.

234. —————. "La nouvelle littérature américaine." *Europe*, 15 oct. 1934, 272-9.

235. Spears, Monroe K. "Les romanciers américains devant le public et la critique des Etats-Unis." *CLM* (see 41), 287-313.

236. Sutherland, Donald. "Time on Our Hands." *Yale Fr. Stud.*, no. 10 [1953], 5-13. Discussion of time in American and French novels.

237. Tavernier, René. "Les problèmes du roman." *Con.* (see 42), 9-17. "Roman et bonheur." 258-66.

238. Tournier, Jacques. "M. E. Coindreau découvre la littérature américaine." *TR*, sept. 1948, 1547-50.

239. Trédant, Paul. "Ecrivains de Californie." *NL*, 18 déc. 1952, 1, 5.

240. —————. "Eisenhower et Stevenson ouvrent la saison littéraire aux Etats-Unis." *NL*, 30 oct. 1952, 1. Survey of fall literary scene in the U. S.

241. —————. "Lettre de New-York." *NL*, 3 mai 1951, 1. Literary scene in New York City.

242. —————. "Littérature et cinéma." *NL*, 24 avril 1947, 1. Discussion of American novels made into movies.

243. ————. "U. S. A. 1952." *NL,* 10 jan. 1952, 1, 5. Literature, movies, theater at the end of 1951.

244. Ulmann, André. "Sur la littérature américaine." *Eto.,* 15 oct. 1946, 5. General article mentioning Faulkner, Winsor, Dos Passos, Caldwell, Steinbeck, Hemingway, H. Miller.

245. Vagne, Jean. "Note sur le roman américain et le public français." *Ren.,* août-sept. 1945, 145-50.

246. Vallette, Jacques. "Etats-Unis: le phénomène américain." *MF,* fév. 1947, 349-51.

247. ————. "Prosateurs et poètes américains." *MF,* mai 1948, 148-52. Review of books on American literature since the war.

248. Venaissin, Gabriel. "Les livres." *Esprit,* oct. 1951, 581-4. John Kelly, John Horne Burns, Henry Morton Robinson: comparison with older generation.

249. Viel, Marie Jeanne. "Aux Etats-Unis les livres préférés sont actuellement des livres sévères." *Bat.* 7 déc. 1944, 4. Survey of literary scene; mostly nonfiction.

250. Villard, Léonie. "La vie américaine d'après le conte et la nouvelle." *MF,* 1 déc. 1923, 289-331. Short story in America from Irving to S. Anderson.

251. Woods, Katherine. "Remarques sur la littérature américaine." *AN* (see 39), 142-51.

DOS PASSOS

BOOKS TRANSLATED:

252. [*The Big Money*] *La grosse Galette.* Paris: Gallimard, 1946. Tr. Charles de Richter.

253. [*The 42nd Parallel*] *42ᵉ Parallèle.* Paris: Bernard Grasset, 1933. Tr. N. Guterman.

254. ————. Paris: Le Club Français du Livre, 1949. Tr. N. Guterman. Préf. Claude Edmonde Magny.

255. ————. Paris: Gallimard, 1951. Tr. N. Guterman.

256. [*In All Countries*] *Sur toute la Terre.* Paris: Gallimard, 1936. Tr. Albine Loisy et May Windett.

257. [*Manhattan Transfer*] *Manhattan Transfer.* Paris: Gallimard, 1928. Tr. M. E. Coindreau. First printed in two volumes, later in one.

258. [*1919*] *1919*. Paris: Editions Sociales Internationales, 1937. 2 vols. Tr. Maurice Rémon.

259. ————. *L'An premier du Siècle (1919)*. Paris: Gallimard, 1952. Tr. et préf. [biographical] Yves Malartic.

260. [*One Man's Initiation*] *L'Initiation d'un Homme*. Paris: F. Rieder, 1925. Tr. Marc Freeman.

261. [*State of the Nation*] *Bilan d'une Nation*. Paris: Editions du Pavois, 1946. Tr. Jean Castet.

262. [*Three Soldiers*] *Trois Soldats*. Paris: Editions de Flore, 1948. Tr. R. N. Raimbault. Brief preface entitled "Note de l'éditeur."

263. [*Tour of Duty*] *Service commandé*. Paris: La Jeune Parque, 1947. Tr. Yves Malartic.

OTHER TRANSLATIONS:

264. "Avec Roosevelt à la Maison Blanche." Tr. Jean Castet. *Bat.*, 28 août 1946, 1, 5. Excerpt from *Bilan d'une Nation*.

265. "Les deux bouts de Pennsylvania Avenue: le Congress s'ennuie." Tr. Jean Castet. *Bat.*, 14 août 1946, 1, 5. Excerpt from *Bilan d'une Nation*.

266. "Le feu." *Verve*, dèc. 1937, 35. Paragraph on the burning of Madrid.

267. "La grève de Harlan." Tr. Guilloux et Brumm. *Europe*, 15 mars 1932, 328-47.

268. "La grosse galette." Tr. Charles de Richter. (See 17), 21-2.

269. "L'homme qui disait s'appeler Jones." Tr. M. E. Coindreau. (See 22), 113-32.

270. "L'initiation d'un homme." Tr. Marc Freeman. *Europe*, 15 fév. 1924, 153-73. Excerpt. Note on Dos Passos by L. B., 172-3.

271. "Jour d'action de grâces, bleu, blanc, rouge." Tr. F. Auberjonois. *Mes.* (see 48), 311-18.

272. "Manhattan Transfer." Tr. M. E. Coindreau. *RNou.*, 15 mai 1926, 8-14. Excerpts from Am. ed. *Manhattan Transfer*, 20-1; 43-5; 118-21.

273. "Meester Veelson." Tr. M. E. Coindreau. *CS,* avril 1933, 257-65.

274. "1919." Tr. Maurice Rémon. *NL,* 27 nov. 1937, 8. Excerpt.

275. "Orient-Express." Tr. M. E. Coindreau. *RNou.,* nov. 1927, 3-12. Excerpts.

276. "Retour d'Europe." Tr. Yves Malartic. *Fon.,* oct. 1947, 587-601.

277. "Sacco et Vanzetti." Tr. Henry Muller. *NAge,* avril 1931, 303-4. Poem.

278. "Tableaux de l'Amérique en guerre." [Tr. Jean Castet.] *RI,* avril 1946, 380-6. Excerpt from *Bilan d'une Nation*; brief note by Maurice Nadeau, 380.

279. "Trois Soldats." Tr. Victor Llona. *NAge,* nov. 1931, 1029-31. Excerpt.

280. "Trois Soldats." Tr. R. N. Raimbault. *GLet.,* 30 oct. 1948, 11, 12. Excerpts.

281. "Washington, ville solitaire." [Tr. Jean Castet.] *Eto.,* 9 avril 1946, 4; 16 avril, 4; 23 avril, 4; 30 avril, 4. Excerpts from *Bilan d'une Nation.*

CRITICAL ARTICLES:

282. Anon. "Les romans de John Dos Passos, ou une épopée de l'Amérique moderne." *Mois,* juin 1932, 176-83.

283. Acaste. "John Dos Passos." *Mois,* jan. 1938, 190-2.

284. Clouard, Henri. "Faulkner, Dos Passos, Maupassant, Flaubert." *TR,* oct. 1950, 152-6.

285. de Massot, Pierre. "Leviathan 1937." *NL,* 11 déc. 1937, 5. Biographical sketch and picture of Dos Passos; review of *1919.*

286. Duché, Jean. "Déclarations au 'Littéraire' du romancier américain Dos Passos sur Le Miracle qui pourrait sauver quelque chose des ruines de la civilisation occidentale." *Litt.,* 8 fév. 1947, 1, 2. Interview.

287. Guth, Paul. "L'interview de Paul Guth: John Dos Passos." *GLet.,* 15 oct. 1949, 1, 2.

288. Las Vergnas, Raymond. "Dos Passos." *NL,* 25 sept. 1947, 1, 5.

289. ————. "Lettres anglo-américaines." *HM,* mai 1951, 777-80.

290. ———— "Lettres étrangères: Itinéraire de Dos Passos." *HM,* fév. 1949, 334-8.

291. Leuwen, Pierre. "Dos Passos ou le romancier sacrifié." *Action*, 17 nov. 1944, 12.

292. Magny, Claude Edmonde. "Introduction à la lecture de Dos Passos. A propos de *La grosse Galette*. I: Technique et métaphysique chez Dos Passos." *Poésie 46*, avril 1946, 62-78. "II: Le temps chez Dos Passos." *Poésie 46*, mai 1946, 99-114. Reprinted in her book (see 23).

293. ————. "Plaidoyer pour Dos Passos." *Sem.*, 18 mai 1946, 8.

294. Muller, Henry. "Dos Passos confesse trois engouements: Paris, notre cuisine, et 'Les Mariés de la Tour Eiffel' [play by Cocteau]." *Car.*, 12 oct. 1949, 1, 9. Interview.

295. Pazos, José Robles. "John Dos Passos, écrivain américain." *RNou.*, 15 mai 1926, 3-5.

296. Pierhal, Armand. "Le grand romancier Dos Passos est à Paris." *NL*, 5 juin 1937, 9. Interview in which Dos Passos speaks of his techniques.

297. Pozner, Vladimir. "L'écrivain devant l'actualité; John Dos Passos, romancier américain, nous dit." *NL*, 5 sept. 1936, 6. Interview.

298. Sartre, Jean Paul. "A propos de Dos Passos et de '1919.'" *NRF*, août 1938, 292-301. Reprinted in *Situations I* (see 33).

299. Savitzky, Ludmila. "John Dos Passos." (see 22), 109-12.

300. Simon, Jean. "John Dos Passos." *CP* (see 40), 152-6.

301. Sinclair, Upton. "John Dos Passos: écrivain américain." Tr. Henry Muller. *NAge*, jan. 1931, 27-8.

302. Soupault, Philippe. "John Dos Passos." *Europe*, fév. 1934, 282-6.

REVIEWS:

[*The Big Money*] Bay, A. *GLet.*, 13 avril 1946, 11; de Laprade, J. *Arts*, 30 août 1946, 2; Fauchery, P. *Action*, 22 mars 1946, 12-13; Guilleminault, G. *Bat.*, 27 mars 1946, 6; Jouve, R. *Etudes*, juin 1947, 411-14; Pierhal, A. *TP*, 12 avril 1946, 5; Simon, J. *EA*. jan. 1937, 84-5.

[*The 42nd Parallel*] Anon. *BCLF*, juin 1951, 437 (brief); Cestre, C. *RAA*, août 1931, 574 (brief).

[*In All Countries*] Bousquet, J. *CS*, fév. 1937, 150; Catesson, J. *CS*, août-sept. 1936, 690; Dabit, E. *NRF*, sept. 1936, 562.

[*Manhattan Transfer*] Buenzod, E. *GL*, 9 sept. 1928, 1, 2; Celly, R. *RNou.* (see 51), 172-5; Cestre, C. *RAA*, déc. 1933, 175-6 (brief); Coindreau, M. *RNou.*, 15 mai 1926, 6-7; Crémieux, B. *NRF*, déc. 1928, 877-9; Finot, L. *RM*, 1 oct. 1928, 297; Gilson, P. *NL*, 22 sept. 1928, 3 (brief); Poulaille, H. *NAge*, jan. 1931, 79; Rapin, R. *BURG*, juillet 1927, 109-10; Villard, L. *RAA*, juin 1930, 467-8.

[*1919*] Anon. *BCLF*, déc. 1952, 728 (brief); Coindreau, M. *NRF*, août 1932, 313-16; Lalou, R. *NL*, 21 août 1952, 3.

[*One Man's Initiation*] Lalou, R. *RE*, jan. 1926, 67-8 (brief); Petit, G. *RNou.*, 15 déc. 1925, 52-3; Rocher, L. *RAA*, déc. 1926, 183.

[*Orient Express*] Coindreau, M. *RNou.*, août-sept. 1927, 63-6.

[*State of the Nation*] Anon. *BCLF*, fév. 1947, 15-16 (brief); Bay, A. *GLet.*, 15 fév. 1947, 11; Fauchery, P. *Action*, 31 jan. 1947, 11; Jouve, R. *Etudes*, juin 1947, 411-14; Nadeau, M. *Gav.*, 13 fév. 1947, 5; Rabaud, J. et G. *Paru*, août 1947, 79-82; Schmidt, A. *Réf.*, 8 mars 1947, 7; Thiébaut, M. *RP*, oct. 1947, 157-60.

[*Three Soldiers*] Anon. *BCLF*, mars 1949, 172 (brief); Authier, J. *NL*, 6 jan. 1949, 3; B., J. *Etudes*, avril 1949, 140; Cestre, C. *RAA*, juin 1933, 465-6 (brief); Sigaux, G. *Nef*, jan. 1949, 129; Sigaux, G. *Livre*, jan. 1949, 65; Sigaux, G. *TR*, déc. 1948, 2056-9.

[*Tour of Duty*] Gersennes, *AN*, mars 1947, 111-12.

HEMINGWAY

BOOKS TRANSLATED:

303. [*Death in the Afternoon*] *Mort dans l'Après-Midi*. Paris: Gallimard, 1938. Tr. René Daumal.

304. [*Farewell to Arms*] *L'Adieu aux Armes*. Paris: Gallimard, 1932. Tr. M. E. Coindreau. Préf. Drieu la Rochèlle.

305. [*The Fifth Column and the First 49 Stories*] *Cinquante mille dollars*. Paris: Gallimard, 1928. Tr. Ott de Weymer. Contents: Cinquante mille dollars, Mon vieux, L'invincible, Le champion, Le village indien, Les tueurs.

306. *Dix Indiens*. Paris: Gallimard, 1946. Tr. Marcel Duhamel.

Contents: Dix indiens, Les neiges du Kilimandjaro, La capitale du monde, Hommage à la Suisse, L'heure triomphale de Francis Macomber, Le vieil homme près du pont, C'est aujourd'hui vendredi, La lumière du monde, La fin de quelque chose, Une journée d'attente, Là-haut dans le Michigan, Trois jours de tourmente.

307. *Paradis perdu* suivi de *La cinquième Colonne*. Paris: Gallimard, 1949. Tr. Henri Robillot et Marcel Duhamel. Contents: Paradis perdu, Histoire naturelle des morts, Course poursuite, Après la tempête, Un endroit propre et bien éclairé, Sur le quai à Smyrne, Le docteur et la femme du docteur, Une très courte histoire, Un soldat chez lui, Le révolutionnaire, Monsieur et Madame Elliot, Un chat sous la pluie, Hors de saison, La neige sur les champs, La grande rivière au coeur double, Dans un autre pays, Che ti dice la patria? Le vin de Wyoming, Le joueur, la religieuse et la radio, Pères et fils, Simple enquête, Un Canari voyage, Idylle alpestre, Histoire banale, Maintenant je me couche, Il est né le divin enfant, Les changements de la mer, Ça ne risque pas de vous arriver, La mère d'une tante, Une lectrice écrit; *La cinquième Colonne*.

308. [*For Whom the Bell Tolls*] *Pour qui sonne le glas*. London: Heinemann and Zsolnay, 1944. Tr. Denise V. Ayme.

309. ————. Paris: Heinemann et Zsolnay, 1948. Tr. Denise Van Moppès.

310. ————. Paris: Le Club Français du Livre, 1950. Tr. Denise Van Moppès.

311. [*Green Hills of Africa*] *Les vertes Collines d'Afrique*. Paris: Gallimard, 1937. Tr. Jeanine Delpech.

312. [*The Old Man and the Sea*] *Le vieil Homme et la Mer*. Paris: Gallimard, 1952. Tr. Jean Dutourd.

313. [*The Sun Also Rises*] *Le Soleil se lève aussi*. Paris: Gallimard, 1933. Tr. M. E. Coindreau. Préf. Jean Prévost.

314. [*To Have and Have Not*] *En avoir ou pas*. Paris: Gallimard, 1945. Tr. Marcel Duhamel.

OTHER TRANSLATIONS:

315. "Le batailleur." Tr. Jean George Auriol. *RE,* jan.-fév. 1928, 111-24.

316. "Une belle chasse." *NL,* 17 juillet 1937, 6. Excerpt from *Les vertes Collines d'Afrique.*

317. "C'est aujourd'hui vendredi." Tr. Marcel Duhamel. *Arb.* (see 38), 85-92.

318. "Chaud et froid." *Verve,* printemps 1938, 46.

319. "Cinquante mille dollars." Tr. Ott de Weymer. *NRF,* août 1927, 161-91.

320. *La cinquième Colonne.* Tr. Marcel Duhamel. *Arb.,* printemps 1945, 43-140.

321. "Une course poursuite." Tr. Marcel Duhamel. *Lab.,* 1 juin 1946, 5.

322. "Dans l'intimité d'Hemingway." *FUSA,* sept.-oct. 1952, 2. Reprint of the letter from Hemingway to Bernard Kalb. *SRL,* Sept. 6, 1952, 11.

323. "Dépêches d'Espagne." Tr. Georges Belmont. (See 18), 271-81.

324. "En Espagne, un endroit propre, bien éclairé." Tr. Jeanine Delpech. *NL,* 3 avril 1937, 9.

325. "L'heure triomphale de Francis Macomber." Tr. Marcel Duhamel. *Car.,* 9 fév. 1949, 4; 16 fév., 4; 23 fév., 4; 2 mars, 4; 9 mars, 4.

326. "Hommage à la Suisse." Tr. Marcel Duhamel. *TR* (cahier n° 1), Editions du Centre, 1944, 65-82.

327. "L'homme qui croyait à la chance." [*To Have and Have Not.*] Tr. Marcel Duhamel. *Paris-Matin,* 2 oct. 1945, 2; 3 oct., 2; 4 oct., 2; 5 oct., 2; 6 oct., 2; 7-8 oct., 2; 9 oct., 2; 10 oct., 2; 11 oct., 2; 12 oct., 2; 13 oct., 2; 14-15 oct., 2; 16 oct., 2; 17 oct., 2; 18 oct., 2; 19 oct., 2; 20 oct., 2; 21-22 oct., 2; 23 oct., 2; 24 oct., 2; 25 oct., 2; 26 oct., 2; 27 oct., 2; 28-29 oct., 2; 30 oct., 2; 31 oct., 2; 1 nov., 2; 2 nov., 2; 3 nov., 2; 4-5 nov., 2; 6 nov., 2; 7 nov., 2; 8 nov., 2; 9 nov., 2; 10 nov., 2; 11-12 nov., 2.

328. "L'invincible." Tr. Georges Duplaix. *NA* (see 49), 161-94. Short biographical sketch follows.

329. "Je vous salue Marie." Tr. Victor Llona. (See 22), 198-214.

330. "La lumière du monde." Tr. Marcel Duhamel. (See 28), 305-14.

331. "Montparnasse." Eugène Jolas (ed.), *Anthologie de la nou-*

velle Poésie américaine. Paris: Simon Kra, 1928, 102-3. Poem in French.

332. "Un pont dans la montagne." [Tr. Denise V. Ayme.] *LF,* 7 oct. 1944, 3, 8. Excerpt from *Pour qui sonne le glas.*

333. "Pour qui sonne le glas. Chapitre II." Tr. Robert Label. *Fon.* (see 45), 35-51.

334. "Préface." Tr. Paule de Beaumont. François Sommer, *Pourquoi ces bêtes sont-elles sauvages?* Paris: Nouvelles Editions de la Toison d'Or, 1951. Preface by Hemingway to a book on hunting in Africa.

335. "Propre et bien éclairé." Tr. Marcel Duhamel. *Sol.,* été 1946, 143-8.

336. "Trois jours de tourmente." [Tr. Marcel Duhamel.] *NL,* 25 juillet 1946, 1, 2.

337. "Vertes collines d'Afrique." [Tr. Jeanine Delpech.] *NL,* 17 juillet 1937, 6. Excerpt.

338. *Le vieil Homme et la Mer.* Tr. Jean Dutourd. *Paris-Presse-l'Intransigeant,* 2 déc. 1952, 2; 3 déc., 2; 4 déc., 2; 5 déc., 2; 6 déc., 2; 7-8 déc., 2; 9 déc., 2; 10 déc., 2; 11 déc., 2; 12 déc., 2; 13 déc., 2; 14-15 déc., 2.

339. "Le village indien." Tr. Ott de Weymer. *NRF,* juin 1928, 736-41.

CRITICAL ARTICLES:

340. Anon. "Depuis 20 ans la France a son Hemingway: Cendrars." *SS,* 16 fév. 1946, 2.

341. Anon. "Le dernier livre d'Hemingway encore inedit en français: 'Parmi les arbres, au delà de la Rivière' est le roman d'un homme qui va mourir, et d'une 'contessina' qui vivait peut-être à Venise." *SS,* 20 jan. 1951, 2.

342. Anon. "Hemingway a laissé à Venise un 'mystere Renata.' " *SS,* 20 jan. 1951, 1.

343. Anon. "Hemingway cherche les glas perdus." *Bat.,* 27 oct. 1948, 5. Brief account of a Hemingway visit to Paris.

344. Anon. "Hemingway fait un roman chaque fois qu'il risque sa vie." *SS,* 6 oct. 1945, 3. Biographical.

345. Anon. "Hemingway, l'Européen." *Réf.,* 11 oct. 1952, 7.

346. Anglès, Auguste. "Hemingway ou l'américain tel qu'on le parle." *TP,* 1 fév. 1946, 5.

347. Chadourne, Marc. "Rencontre avec Hemingway." *Car.,* 30 jan. 1947, 1, 2. Reminiscences.

348. Cowley, Malcolm. "Hemingway au coeur de la nuit." *RI,* juin-juillet 1946, 549-54.

349. de Fels, Marthe. "A la recherche d'Hemingway." *Bat.,* 16 juillet 1947, 6. Interview in Havana.

350. Delpech, Jeanine. "Ernest Hemingway, romancier de la vie dangereuse." *NL,* 3 avril 1937, 9.

351. ―――――. "Un musicien, un comédien, un écrivain, et un peintre nous parlent des livres de Hemingway et de Peyré sur la *'fiesta brava.'*" *NL,* 3 sept. 1938, 8. Louis Beydts, Alerme, Marcelle Auclair, and Roger Wild discuss the accuracy of the accounts of bullfighting in *The Sun Also Rises, Death in the Afternoon,* and *Sang et Lumière.*

352. de Montalet, R. H. "Le dernier roman de Hemingway et la critique anglo-saxonne." *Crit.,* avril 1951, 301-7.

353. Duesberg, J. "Grandeur et décadence d'Ernest Hemingway." *Syn.,* déc. 1951, 90-1.

354. Erval, François. "Transformations de Hemingway." *TM,* jan.-fév. 1953, 1248-53. Discussion of Hemingway's development; American criticism.

355. Forestier, Marie. "Un grand romantique: Ernest Hemingway." *RN,* 15 juin 1949, 570-9.

356. Las Vergnas, Raymond. "Deux romanciers de la liberté." *NL,* 18 oct. 1945, 1. Discussion and comparison of *For Whom the Bell Tolls* and Malraux, *L'Espoir.*

357. ―――――. "Ernest Hemingway." *CLM* (see 41), 165-81.

358. ―――――. "Ernest Hemingway," *NL,* 4 sept. 1947, 1, 2.

359. Maurois, André. "Ernest Hemingway." (See 22), 193-7.

360. Mohrt, Michel. "Hemingway, les héros et les dieux." *TR,* déc. 1952, 122-8.

361. Rousseaux, André. "Les nouveaux romans d'Hemingway." *Litt.,* 4 mai 1946, 2. Primarily a discussion of *For Whom the Bell Tolls* and *To Have and Have Not.*

362. Schneider, Marcel. "Ernest Hemingway." *Espace,* juin 1945, 98-105.

363. Sigaux, Gilbert. "Ernest Hemingway." *CLet.,* 16 mars 1946, 7.

364. Tavernier, René. "Ernest Hemingway ou la jeunesse du monde." *Con.*, mars 1945, 143-72.

REVIEWS:

[*Across the River and into the Trees*] Anon. *Roman*, jan. 1951, 91-3; Danchin, F. *LM*, juillet-août 1951, A71 (brief); Muller, H. *Car.*, 12 sept. 1950, 9; Vivet, J. *Ob.*, 19 oct. 1950, 20-1.

[*Death in the Afternoon*] Coindreau, M. *NRF*, nov. 1932, 778-81; Leiris, M. *NRF*, juin 1939, 1061-3.

[*A Farewell to Arms*] Buenzod, E. *GL*, 27 mars 1932, 1; Marion, D. *NRF*, oct. 1933, 632-3; Soupault, P. *Europe*, 15 sept. 1933, 140-1; V., L. *RAA*, fév. 1933, 287 (brief); Vignard, P. *Europe*, 15 oct. 1932, 279-80.

[*The Fifth Column and the First 49 Stories*] *Cinquante mille dollars*: Buenzod, E. *BURG*, nov. 1928, 1415-16; Buenzod, E. *GL*, 30 sept. 1928, 1; Celly, R. *RNou.* (see 51), 175-6; de Régnier, H. *Figaro*, 9 oct. 1928, 2 (brief); Finot, L. *RM*, 15 sept. 1928, 196 (brief); Les Treize, *Int.*, 22 août 1928, 2 (brief); Llona, V. *NRF*, jan. 1929, 123-4; Marin, E. *L'Avenir*, 5 sept. 1928, 2; Soupault, P. *Europe*, 15 sept. 1933, 140-1. *Dix Indiens*: Anon. *BCLF*, juillet-août 1946, 17 (brief); Anon. *SS*, 7 sept. 1946, 2 (brief); Bay, A. *GLet* (see 46), 13 (brief); Blanzat, J. *Litt.*, 10 août 1946, 4; Blanzat, J. *MonF.*, oct. 1946, 319; Laffay, A. *LM*, jan. 1946, 72-4; Lévy, Y. *Paru*, nov. 1946, 51-3; Magny, C. *Sem.*, 24 août 1946, 10; Nadeau, M. *Gav.*, 12 sept. 1946, 5; Sans, J. *Cli.*, 26 sept. 1946, 10 (brief); Sigaux, G. *Nef*, août-sept. 1950, 206-7; Thiébaut, M. *RP*, oct. 1946, 153-6. *Paradis perdu*: Anon. *SS*, 15 avril 1950, 2 (brief); Lalou, R. *NL*, 30 mars 1950, 3; Sigaux, G. *GLet.*, 27 mai 1950, 7-8.

[*For Whom the Bell Tolls*] Blanzat, J. *MonF.*, mars 1946, 471-3; Bory, J. *AL*, avril 1946, 194-6; Braspart, M. *Mondes*, 29 mai 1946, 6; Grenaud, P. *Europe*, sept. 1946, 107-8; Guilleminault, G. *Bat.*, 3 jan. 1946, 5; Jarlot, G. *Fon.*, mai 1946, 845-9; Laffay, A. *LM*, jan. 1946, 72-4; Lartigue, J. *CS*, n° 275, 1946, 160-2; Lévy, Y. *Paru*, avril 1946, 41-6; Magny, C. *Gav.*, 16 août 1945, 4; Mauriac, C. *Nef*, fév. 1946, 133-4; Molitor, A. *RN*, 15 fév. 1945, 134-43; Nadeau, M. *RI*, déc. 1945, 127-8; Sans, J. *Cli.*, 14 mars 1950, 8.

[*Green Hills of Africa*] Anon. *Mois*, juillet 1936, 161-2; Charensol, G. *NL*, 21 août 1937, 5 (brief); Hertz, H. *Europe*, 15 nov. 1937, 402-3 (brief); Pacteau, L. *EA*, oct.-déc. 1938, 441.

[*In Our Time*] Cestre, C. *RAA*, avril 1933, 372 (brief).

[*Men without Women*] Faÿ, B. *RE*, mars 1928, 322-3.

[*The Old Man and the Sea*] Blanzat, J. *FL*, 3 jan. 1953, 9; Cournot, M. *Nouvelle NRF*, fév. 1953, 351-3; Darnar, P. *SS*, 20 sept. 1952, 2; Dutourd, J. *Arts*, 17 oct. 1952, 5; Erval, F. *GLet.*, oct. 1952, 99-101; Gary, R. *NL*, 11 sept. 1952, 1; Guehenno, J. *Figaro*, 3 jan. 1953, 1; Lalou, R. *NL*, 18 déc. 1952, 3; Lebesque, M. *Cli.*, 1-7 jan. 1953, 9; Mohrt, M. *FUSA*, jan. 1953, 3; Muller, H. *Car.*, 24 sept. 1952, 7; Nadeau, M. *Ob.*, 8 jan. 1953, 17-18; Vallette, J. *MF*, jan. 1953, 151-6.

[*The Sun Also Rises*] Le Breton, M. *EA*, sept. 1937, 480; Sans, J. *Cli.*, 14 mars 1950, 8; Soupault, P. *Europe*, 15 sept. 1933, 140-1.

[*To Have and Have Not*] Blanzat, J. *MonF*, mars 1946, 468-74; Bory, J. *AL*, avril 1946, 197-8; Coindreau, M. *NRF*, mars 1938, 501-4; d'Aubarède, G. *NL*, 7 mars 1946, 3; de Fréminville, C. *Ren.*, mai 1946, 172-3; de Laprade, J. *Arts*, 22 mars 1946, 4; Fauchery, P. *Action*, 8 fév. 1946, 12; Hoog, A. *Car.*, 21 fév. 1946, 6; Lévy, Y. *Paru*, avril 1946, 41-6; Mauriac, C. *Nef*, mars 1946, 157-8; Mayoux, J. *EA*, avril-juin 1938, 194-5; Sans, J. *Cli.*, 14 mars 1950, 8.

[*The Torrents of Spring*] Cestre, C. *RAA*, août 1933, 574-5 (brief).

FAULKNER

BOOKS TRANSLATED:

364a. [*Absalom, Absalom!*] *Absalon! Absalon!* Paris: Gallimard, 1953. Tr. R. N. Raimbault avec le collaboration de Ch. P. Vorce.

365. [*As I Lay Dying*] *Tandis que j'agonise.* Paris: Gallimard, 1934. Tr. M. E. Coindreau. Préf. Valery Larbaud.

366. ————. Paris: J. Boisseau, 1946. Tr. M. E. Coindreau. Limited to 900 copies; illus. Burins de Courtin.

367. [*Doctor Martino and Other Stories*] *Le Docteur Martino*

et autres Histoires. Paris: Gallimard, 1948. Tr. R. N. Raimbault et Ch. P. Vorce.

368. [*Intruder in the Dust*] *L'Intrus.* Paris: Gallimard, 1952. Tr. R. N. Raimbault.

369. [*Knight's Gambit*] *Le Gambit du Cavalier.* Paris: Gallimard, 1951. Tr. André du Bouchet. Omits "Smoke."

370. [*Light in August*] *Lumière d'Août.* Paris: Gallimard, 1935. Tr. et préf. M. E. Coindreau.

371. [*Mosquitoes*] *Moustiques.* Paris: Les Editions de Minuit, 1948. [Tr. Pierre Desgroupes.] Préf. Raymond Queneau.

372. [*Pylon*] *Pylône.* Paris: Gallimard, 1946. Tr. R. N. Raimbault et Mme G. L. Rousselet.

373. [*Sanctuary*] *Sanctuaire.* Paris: Gallimard, 1933. Tr. R. N. Raimbault et Henri Delgove. Préf. André Malraux.

374. [*Sartoris*] *Sartoris.* Paris: Gallimard, 1937. Tr. R. N. Raimbault et Henri Delgove.

375. [*Soldiers' Pay*] *Monnaie de Singe.* Grenoble et Paris: B. Arthaud, 1948. Tr. et préf. Maxime Gaucher.

376. [*The Sound and the Fury*] *Le Bruit et la Fureur.* Paris: Gallimard, 1938. Tr. et préf. M. E. Coindreau.

377. [*These 13*] *Treize Histoires.* Paris: Gallimard, 1939. Tr. R. N. Raimbault et Ch. P. Vorce avec la collaboration de M. E. Coindreau. Préf. R. N. Raimbault.

378. [*The Unvanquished*] *L'Invaincu.* Paris: Gallimard, 1949. Tr. R. N. Raimbault et Ch. P. Vorce.

379. [*The Wild Palms*] *Les Palmiers sauvages.* Paris: Gallimard, 1952. Tr. et préf. M. E. Coindreau.

OTHER TRANSLATIONS:

380. "L'après-midi d'une vache." (Ernest V. Trueblood) Tr. et préf. M. E. Coindreau. *Fon.* (see 45), 67-81.

381. ————. Tr. M. E. Coindreau. *Poésie 43,* juillet-août-sept. 1943, 19-29.

382. "Au-delà." Tr. R. N. Raimbault. *Fon.,* mai 1946, 711-28.

383. "Chacun son tour." Tr. R. N. Raimbault. *SS,* 27 avril 1946, 6; 4 mai, 6; 11 mai, 6.

384. "Chasse au renard." Tr. R. N. Raimbault. (See 28), 141-64.

385. "Le chien." Tr. R. N. Raimbault. *TR* (cahier n° 2), Editions de la Table Ronde, 1945, 107-29.

386. "Deux soldats." Tr. R. N. Raimbault. (See 18), 227-45.

387. —————. Tr. R. N. Raimbault. *SS*, 27 déc. 1947, 8.

388. "Dewey Dell." Tr. M. E. Coindreau. (See 17), 22-3.

389. "Drôles de gens." Tr. Abel Léon. *Oeuvres Libres*, n.s., n° 20 (vol. 246), 1947, 51-64.

390. "Elly." Tr. Hèléne Bokanowski. *Fon.*, n° 36, 1944, 54-72.

391. "Feuilles rouges." Tr. R. N. Raimbault et Ch. P. Vorce. *Europe*, 15 avril 1936, 512-39.

392. "Il était une reine." Tr. M. E. Coindreau. *NRF*, août 1933, 213-33.

393. "L'incendiaire." Tr. R. N. Raimbault. *AN* (see 39), 12-31.

394. "Je me refuse à admettre la fin de l'homme." Tr. L. Jacoël. *Profils I*, oct. 1952, 239-40. Nobel Prize speech.

395. "Lumière d'août. Fragment. Chapitre VII." Tr. M. E. Coindreau. *CS*, fév. 1935, 83-101.

396. "Monnaie de singe." Tr. Maxime Gaucher. *GLet.*, 26 juin 1948, 13, 14. Excerpt.

397. "Les palmiers sauvages." Tr. M. E. Coindreau. *TM*, jan. 1951, 1153-92; fév., 1442-72; mars, 1623-53; avril, 1826-54; mai, 1990-2027. Only the title story.

398. "Point de nymphe aux seins tumescents pour troubler." "Un jour sur une montagne adolescente." Tr. R. N. Raimbault. *TR*, jan. 1951, 38-40. Two poems from *A Green Bough*; comments by translator.

399. "Une rose pour Emily." Tr. M. E. Coindreau. *Com.*, hiver 1932, 111-37.

400. "Septembre ardent." Tr. M. E. Coindreau. *NRF*, jan. 1932, 49-65.

401. "Soleil couchant." Tr. M. E. Coindreau. *Europe*, 15 jan. 1935, 37-60.

402. "Un toit pour le seigneur." Tr. Abel Léon. LF, 2 mai 1947, 3.

403. "Tous les hommes libres doivent un petit chose à la France." *Arts*, 5-11 juin 1952, 6. Faulkner's speech, May 30, 1952, at the festival *Oeuvres du XXe Siècle*.

404. "Trouble." Tr. R. N. Raimbault. *SS*, 10 nov. 1945, 6. Excerpt from *Pylône*.

405. "Victoire dans la montagne." Tr. R. N. Raimbault. *RP*, oct. 1948, 78-102.

406. "Voici le texte complet du discours de remerciement de William Faulkner à l'occasion de l'attribution du prix Nobel de littérature, traduit de la *Saturday Review* du 3 février 1951." *Etudes*, mai 1951, 253-4.

407. "La voix du poète." Tr. Daniel Apert. *LE*, mars 1951, 68. Nobel Prize speech.

408. "Wash." Tr. R. N. Raimbault. *Arb.* (see 38), 125-36.

CRITICAL ARTICLES:

409. Anon. "A propos d'une phrase de Faulkner." *Pre.*, juin 1952, 1-2. Comments on Faulkner's speech (see 403).

410. Anon. "Une discussion sur Faulkner chez les étudiants communistes américains." *NC*, juillet-août 1949, 87-96.

411. Anon. "Faulkner au cinéma." *GLet.*, 15 déc. 1950, 109. Brief account of movie, *Intruder in the Dust*.

412. Anon. "Faulkner ou le bon sens du romancier." *Roman*, mars 1951, 174-5.

413. Anon. "Portrait-Express: William Faulkner." *Car.*, 3 août 1949, 9. Caricature; biographical sketch.

414. Anon. "Qui est Faulkner?" *Réf.*, 16 fév. 1952, 7. Biographical sketch.

415. Anon. "Les romans horribles de M. William Faulkner." *Mois*, nov. 1931, 165-9.

416. Anon. "William Faulkner, prix Nobel de littérature." *AF*, 17 nov. 1950, 2.

417. Arban, Dominique. "Interview de William Faulkner." *FL*, 16 déc. 1950, 1.

418. Aymé, Marcel. "What French Readers Find in William Faulkner's Fiction." N. Y. *Times B. R.*, Dec. 17, 1950, 4.

419. Barbezat, Marc. "Les revues." *Con.*, nov. 1941, 678-9. Brief comparison of Audiberti to Faulkner.

420. Barrault, Jean Louis, et M. E. Coindreau. "Ce qu'ils pensent de Faulkner." *Car.*, 14 nov. 1950, 9.

421. Braspart, Michel. "Autant n'en emportera pas le vent." *Réf.*, 16 fév. 1952, 7.

422. Breit, Harvey. "Faulkner, que le prix Nobel n'a pas grisé, aime les parenthèses, les mules et Shakespeare." *SS*, 28 avril 1951, 2.

423. Brion, Marcel. "Les prix Nobel: Bertrand Russell et William Faulkner." *RDM*, 1 déc. 1950, 529-38.

424. Clément, Danielle. "Faulkner, priz Nobel." *TH*, fév. 1951, 122-7.

425. Clouard, Henri. "Faulkner, Dos Passos, Maupassant, Flaubert." (See 284.)

426. Coindreau, Maurice Edgar. "Préface aux 'Palmiers sauvages.'" *TM*, jan. 1952, 1187-96.

427. ————. "Le puritanisme de William Faulkner." *CS*, avril 1935, 259-67. Preface to *Lumière d'Août*.

428. ————. "William Faulkner." *NRF*, juin 1931, 926-30.

429. ————. "William Faulkner in France." *Yale Fr. Stu.*, no. 10 [1953], 85-91.

430. Cowley, Malcolm. "William Faulkner et la légende du Sud." *RI*, mars 1946, 263-73. Translation of Introduction to Viking *Portable Faulkner*.

431. Denoreaz, Michel. "William Faulkner ou le parti pris de la fausse réalité." *NC*, jan. 1951, 74-84. Communist point of view.

432. Doniol-Valcroze, J. "Faulkner et le cinéma." *Ob.*, 7 déc. 1950, 23. On the movie, *Intruder in the Dust*.

433. Duesberg, Jacques. "'Le bruit et le tumulte' de William Faulkner." *RG*, 15 déc. 1939, 834-41.

434. ————. "Un créateur de mythes: William Faulkner." *Syn.*, déc. 1948, 342-54.

435. Ehrenbourg, Ilya. "Les mains sales. Faulkner et Sartre vus par un écrivain soviétique." *LF*, 10 fév. 1949, 1, 6.

436. Elsen, Claude. "Faulkner et le roman noir." *Réf.*, 16 fév. 1952, 7.

437. F., J. "Faulkner parle pour la liberté." *FL*, 7 juin 1952, 1, 2. Comments on Faulkner's speech (see 403).

438. Fauchery, Pierre. "La mythologie faulknérienne dans Pylon." *Espace,* juin 1945, 106-12. Article first printed avril-mai, 93-9, reprinted because of "une regrettable erreur de mise en pages."

439. Fumet, Stanislas. "La saveur poétique du roman." *Con.* (see 42), 312-21. Faulkner considered *passim*.

440. Genova, Yvonne. "Elsa Triolet ou le nouveau réalisme français." *Fon.*, juin 1942, 214-18. Review of *Mille Regrets* with comparisons to Faulkner.

441. Greenburg, Al. "Letter to Editor." *NC*, oct. 1949, 120-1. On *New Foundations* articles and letters about Faulkner.

442. Guérard, Albert. "William Faulkner, chroniquer de l'apocalypse." *RN*, jan. 1951, 81-90.

443. Guyard, Marius François. "Faulkner le tragique." *Etudes*, fév. 1951, 172-83.

444. Hell, Henri. "Critique du roman." *Fon.*, mai 1942, 95-8. Opinions of Kléber Haedens and M. Caillois on the novel; Faulkner *passim*.

445. Julien, André. "Faulkner, l'homme du Sud." *GLet.*, 15 déc. 1950, 28-30.

446. La Ganipote. "Les prix Nobel." *LF*, 16 nov. 1950, 3. Faulkner and Russell.

447. Lalou, René. "Les gémeaux du Nobel." *NL*, 16 nov. 1950, 1. Faulkner and Russell.

448. Larbaud, Valery. "Un roman de William Faulkner. 'Tandis que j'agonise.'" *Ce Vice impuni, la Lecture. Domaine anglais.* Paris: Gallimard, 1936, 218-22. Reprint of preface to *Tandis que j'agonise*.

449. Las Vergnas, Raymond. "Faulkner." *NL*, 19 fév. 1946, 5.

450. Lebesque, Morvan. "William Faulkner, prix Nobel." *Cli.*, 23 nov. 1950, 8.

451. ————. "William Faulkner, prix Nobel de littérature." *Car.*, 14 nov. 1950, 9.

452. Le Breton, Maurice. "Technique et psychologie chez William Faulkner." *EA*, sept. 1937, 418-38.

453. ————. "Temps et personne chez William Faulkner." *Forms de l'Art; Forms de l'Esprit* (numéro spécial du *Journal de Psychologie*). Paris: Presses Universitaires de France, 1951, 344-54.

454. Liebowitz, René. "L'art tragique de William Faulkner." *CS*, nov. 1940, 502-8.

455. Malherbe, Henry. "L'avenir du roman." *Con.* (see 42), 394-7. Faulkner *passim*.

456. Malraux, André. "Préface à 'Sanctuaire' de W. Faulkner."
NRF, nov. 1933, 744-7. Reprinted in translation in *Yale Fr. Stu.*, no. 10 [1953], 92-4.

457. Mayoux, Jean Jacques. "La création du réel chez William Faulkner." *EA*, fév. 1952, 25-39.

458. ————. "Faulkner et le sens tragique." *Combat*, 6 mars 1952, 7.

459. ————. "Le temps et la destinée chez William Faulkner." Cahiers du Collége Philosophique, *La Profondeur et le Rythme*. Paris: B. Arthaud, 1948, 303-31.

460. Pouillon, Jean. "Le gambit du cavalier." *TM*, fév. 1952, 1490-6.

461. ————. "W. Faulkner, un témoin." *TM*, oct. 1946, 172-8. Point of view and time in *Pylon*.

462. Pozner, Vladimir. "Lettre à William Faulkner et à quelques autres." *LF*, 31 août 1950, 1, 6. An appeal to Faulkner to speak out and help the cause of the "Hollywood 10."

463. Rabi. "Faulkner et la génération de l'exil." *Esprit*, jan. 1951, 47-65. Reprinted in translation in Hoffman and Vickery (eds.), *William Faulkner: Two Decades of Criticism*. East Lansing, Mich.: Michigan State College Press, 1951, 118-38.

464. Raimbault, R. N. "Faulkner au naturel." *GLet*. (see 46), 15.

465. Ricard, Jean François. "Les romans: Faulkner en France." *Con.*, jan.-fév. 1945, 82-5.

466. Sartre, Jean Paul. "A propos de 'Le Bruit et la Fureur': la temporalité chez Faulkner." *NRF,* juin 1939, 1057-61; juillet, 146-51. Reprinted in *Situations I* (see 33); reprinted in translation in Hoffman and Vickery (see 463), 180-8.

467. ————. "Sartoris." *NRF*, fév. 1938, 323-8. Reprinted in *Situations I* (see 33); reprinted in translation in *Yale Fr. Stu.*, no. 10 [1953], 95-9.

468. Sigaux, Gilbert. "Sur Faulkner." *Nef*, fév. 1949, 117-20.

469. Soulac, Anne Marie. "William Faulkner." *CLM* (see 41), 239-49.

470. Trédant, Paul. "Faulkner à Paris." *NL*, 14 déc. 1950, 1.

471. Warren, Robert Penn. "Thèmes de William Faulkner."

RI, fév. 1947, 140-8. From review of Viking *Portable Faulkner* in *New Republic*.

472. Weidlé, Wladimir. "Notes." *CPl.*, printemps 1949, 52-3.

REVIEWS:

[*Absalom, Absalom!*] Coindreau, M. *NRF*, jan. 1937, 123-6.

[*As I Lay Dying*] Dabit, E. *Europe*, 15 oct. 1934, 294-6; Lassaigne, J. *RM*, 1 juillet 1934, 32; Le Breton, M. *RAA*, juin 1936, 471-2; Toesca, M. *GLet.*, 18 jan. 1947, 9.

[*Doctor Martino and Other Stories*] Blanzat, J. *FL*, 18 déc. 1948, 5; Lebesque, M. *Sem.*, 1 déc. 1948, 12; Le Breton, M. *RAA*, août 1935, 565-6 (brief); Vallette, J. *MF*, fév. 1949, 354 (brief).

[*Intruder in the Dust*] Blanzat, J. *FL*, 7 juin 1952, 11; Hamard, J. *LM*, sept.-oct. 1949, A96; Lalou, R. *NL*, 29 mai 1952, 3; Lauras, A. *Etudes*, nov. 1952, 278-9; Lebesque, M. *Cli.*, 11-17 juin 1952, 8; Magny, C. *SS*, 14 juin 1952, 2; Mohrt, M. *Car.*, 15 sept. 1949, 7.

[*Knight's Gambit*] Anon. *BCLF*, juillet-août 1952, 501 (brief); Lalou, R. *NL*, 10 jan. 1952, 3; Lebesque, M. *Car.*, 26 déc. 1951, 7; Lebesque, M. *Cli.*, 3-9 jan. 1952, 8; Mazars, P. *TR*, fév. 1952, 150-2; Schmidt, A. *Réf.*, 16 fév. 1952, 7 (brief).

[*Light in August*] Arland, M. *NRF*, oct. 1935, 584-6; Cestre, C. *RAA*, juin 1933, 466-7; Coindreau M. *NRF*, août 1933, 302-5; Emié, L. *CS*, oct. 1936, 770-3; Le Breton, M. *RAA*, juin 1936, 471-2; M., J. *Grin.*, 4 oct. 1935, 4 (brief); Sans, J. *Sem.*, 25 août 1948, 5.

[*Mosquitoes*] Anon. *BCLF*, nov. 1948, 788 (brief); Blanc-Dufour, A. *CS*, n° 290, 1948, 185 (brief); C., M. *LF*, 19 août 1948, 4 (brief); Forestier, M. *RN*, 15 jan. 1949, 110 (brief); Kemp, R. *NL*, 2 sept. 1948, 2; Paz, M. *Paru*, oct. 1948, 42-3; Séchan, O. *NL*, 8 juillet 1948, 3.

[Viking *Portable Faulkner*] Mossé, F. *LM*, mars-avril 1947, A59.

[*Pylon*] Anon. *BCLF*, juillet-août 1946, 17 (brief); Anon. *SS*, 28 sept. 1946, 2 (brief); Bay, A. *GLet.* (see 46), 13; Blanzat, J. *Litt.*, 24 août 1946, 4; Blanzat, J. *MonF*, oct. 1946, 316-21; Fauchery, P. *Action*, 25 oct. 1946, 15; Guilleminault, G. *Bat.*, 21 août 1946, 6; Guilloux, R. *GLet* (see 46), 12; Jarlot, G. *Fon.*, nov. 1946, 653-7; Le Breton, M. *RAA*, oct. 1935, 81-2 (brief); Magny, C. *Sem.*, 23 nov. 1946, 11; Nadeau, M. *Gav.*, 12 sept. 1946, 5; Rivallan, J. *Paru*, oct. 1946, 48-9; Rousseaux, A. *Litt.*, 19 oct. 1946, 2; Sans, J. *Cli.*, 17 oct. 1946, 10.

[*Requiem for a Nun*] Anon. *SS*, 29 sept. 1951, 2; Guérard, A. *Profils I*, oct. 1952, 215-18.

[*Sanctuary*] Cestre, C. *RAA*, avril 1933, 371-2; Dabit, E. *Europe*, 15 avril 1934, 599-600; Derycke, G. *CS*, oct. 1935, 697-8; Levinson, A. *NL*, 25 juin 1932, 6; Maxence, J. *Grin.*, 29 déc. 1933, 4; Trintzius, R. *Int.*, 8 jan. 1934, 6.

[*Sartoris*] Charensol, G. *NL*, 8 jan. 1938, 5; Jaloux, E. *NL*, 17 sept. 1938, 4; Le Breton, M. *EA*, oct.-déc. 1938, 441-2.

[*Soldiers' Pay*] Anon. *Car.*, 25 août 1948, 7 (brief); Anon. *Sem.*, 18 août 1948, 5 (brief); Blondel, J. *Réf.*, 21 août 1948, 7; C., M. *LF*, 19 août 1948, 4 (brief); d'Houville, G. *RDM*, 15 août 1948, 757-64; Douyan, J. *MNP*, n° 48, 1951, 58-9; Forestier, M. *RN*, 15 nov. 1949, 473 (brief); Kemp, R. *NL*, 2 sept. 1948, 2; Las Vergnas, R. *HM*, août 1948, 677-81; Sans, J. *Sem.*, 25 août 1948, 5; Sigaux, G. *TR*, déc. 1948, 2056-9.

[*The Sound and the Fury*] Chastel, A. *CS*, mars 1940, 196-7.

[*These 13*] Cestre, C. *RAA*, déc. 1933, 176 (brief); Maxence, J. *Grin.*, 27 juillet 1939, 4 (brief); Picon, G. *CS*, fév. 1940, 133-6.

[*The Unvanquished*] Anon. *LF*, 25 août 1949, 3; Blanzat, J. *FL*, 6 août 1949, 5; Boutang, P. *AF*, 21 juillet 1949, 3; Braspart, M. *Réf.*, 13 août 1949, 7; Carrouges, M. *Paru*, mars 1950, 43; Chauffeteau, J. *AL*, n° 16, 1949, 58-9; Lalou, R. *NL*, 1 sept. 1949, 3; Lebesque, M. *Cli.*, 5 août 1949, 8; Le Breton, M. *EA*, juillet-sept. 1939, 313-4; Sigaux, G. *GLet.*, 1 oct. 1949, 7; Vallette, J. *MF*, nov. 1949, 532 (brief).

[*The Wild Palms*] Anon. *BCLF*, juillet-août 1952, 501-2 (brief); Aury, D. *Arts*, 10-16 avril 1952, 5; Blanc-Dufour, A. *CS*, n° 311, 1952, 166 (brief); Blanzat, J. *FL*, 1 mars 1952, 9; Kanters, R. *AN*, mars 1952, 98-100; Lalou, R. *NL*, 20 mars 1952, 3 (brief); Las Vergnas, R. *HM*, mars 1952, 469-71; Le Breton, M. *EA*, juillet-sept. 1939, 313-14; Magny, C. *SS*, 6 oct. 1951, 2; Marceau, F. *TR*, juin 1952, 152-6; Mohrt, M. *TR*, nov. 1952, 160-5.

[Campbell and Foster, *William Faulkner, A Critical Appraisal*] Landré, L. *EA*, mai 1952, 183-4.

BOOKS TRANSLATED:

473. [*Episode in Palmetto*] *Episode à Palmetto.* Paris: Editions Mondiales, 1952. Tr. Jules Castier.

474. [*Georgia Boy*] *Un p'tit Gars de Géorgie.* Paris: Gallimard, 1949, Tr. et préf. L. M. Raymond.

475. [*God's Little Acre*] *Le petit Arpent du Bon Dieu.* Paris: Gallimard, 1936. Tr. M. E. Coindreau. Préf. André Maurois.

476. [*A House in the Uplands*] *Un Châtelain des Hautes-Terres.* Paris: Gallimard, 1948. Tr. Robert Vidal.

477. [*Journeyman*] *Les Voies du Seigneur.* Paris: Gallimard, 1950. Tr. et préf. Robert Merle.

478. [*Poor Fool*] *Un pauvre Type.* Paris: Gallimard, 1945. Tr. et préf. M. E. Coindreau.

479. [*Southways*] *Soleil du Sud.* Paris: Gallimard, 1952. Tr. Max Morise. Omits "Wild Flowers" and "Man and Woman."

480. [*The Sure Hand of God*] *Le Doigt de Dieu.* Paris: Gallimard, 1950. Tr. J. L. Bost et M. Duhamel.

481. [*This Very Earth*] *Toute la Vérité.* Paris: Gallimard, 1951. Tr. H. de Sarbois.

482. [*Tobacco Road*] *La Route au Tabac.* Paris: Gallimard, 1937. Tr. M. E. Coindreau.

483. ————. Paris: Editions du Pré aux Clercs, 1946. Tr. M. E. Coindreau. Limited to 900 copies; illus. Denyse de Bravura.

484. ————. *La Route au Tabac,* en 3 actes par Jack Kirkland, d'après la nouvelle d'Erskine Caldwell, adaptée par Marcel Duhamel. Paris: R. Laffont, 1947.

485. [*Tragic Ground*] *Terre tragique.* Paris: Gallimard, 1948. Tr. M. E. Coindreau.

486. [*Trouble in July*] *Bagarre de Juillet.* Paris: Gallimard, 1947. Tr. Jean Albert Bédé.

487. [*We Are the Living* and *Kneel to the Rising Sun*] *Nous les Vivants.* Paris: Gallimard, 1938. Tr. Ed. Michel-Tyl. Préf. M. E. Coindreau. Contents: La rivière chaude, Agnès, on te regarde! La voix populaire, La baignade, Rachel, Le

tonique indien, Dans un champ de coton, L'âne d'Amos, La photographie, La mulâtresse, Août, La petite fille à sa maman, Le premier automne, Après, Feu de cimes, La chambre vide, Le mariage en chemise, Feu d'herbes sèches, Une femme dans la maison, L'invasion des Suédois, La fille de Jim, Martha Jean, Candy Man, Mort lente, Les hommes, Prière au soleil levant.

OTHER TRANSLATIONS:

488. "Abe Latham, homme de couleur." Tr. Simone David. *Action*, 13 sept. 1946, 6, 12.

489. "L'automobile qui ne voulait pas marcher." Tr. Pascaline et Alain Gheerbrant. *QV*, n° III, 1945, 46-52.

490. "Beechum le beau." Tr. Annette David. *Action*, 17 mai 1946, 6.

491. "Dans la prairie." *AL*, n° 13-14, 1949, 1-4.

492. "Dorothy." Tr. Georges Belmont. (See 18), 349-55.

493. "Fichue journée." Tr. Suzanne et Jon Simon. *LF*, 25 août 1949, 1, 5.

494. "Fin d'été." Tr. Jean Rollin. *Fon.* (see 45), 137-48.

495. "L'homme de dieu." Tr. Georges Magnane. *Arb.* (see 38), 39-50. Excerpt from *Journeyman*.

496. "La mouche dans le cercueil." Tr. Max Morise. *FUSA*, mars 1953, 2.

497. "Le nègre dans le puits." Tr. Annette David. *Action*, 15 nov. 1946, 6.

498. "Prière au soleil levant." Tr. E. Michel-Tyl. *RP*, fév. 1938, 549-70.

499. "La route au tabac." Tr. M. E. Coindreau. (See 17), 27-8.

CRITICAL ARTICLES:

500. Anon. "L'Amérique à Paris." *GLet.*, 9 juillet 1949, 5. Note on Caldwell's passing through Paris.

501. Anon. "Fils d'un pasteur presbytérien ambulant: Erskine Caldwell scandalise les moralistes américains avec ses romans érotiques qui tirent à trois millions." *SS*, 23 août 1947, 2. Interview.

502. Arban, Dominique. "Erskine Caldwell a quitté la 'Route au

Tabac' pour l'avenue Montaigne." *FL*, 16 août 1947, 3. Interview.

503. Barbezat, Marc. "Caldwell et le mythe." *Con.* (see 42), 305-10.

504. Berger, Pierre. "Erskine Caldwell parmi nous." *Bat.*, 13 août 1947, 6. Interview.

505. Brest, René. "Erskine Caldwell à Paris." *NL*, 30 juin 1949, 1. Interview.

506. Chonez, Claudine. "Erskine Caldwell ou la violence sans pessimisme." *Sem.*, 16 août 1947, 6. Interview.

507. Coindreau, M. E. "Erskine Caldwell." *NRF*, nov. 1936, 908-12.

508. Delpech, Jeanine. "C'est à Paris que j'ai rencontré Faulkner nous dit Erskine Caldwell." *NL*, 10 mai 1951, 1. Interview.

509. ————. "Visite à Erskine Caldwell, le Céline américain." *NL*, 15 jan. 1938, 6.

510. [Dutourd, Camille]. "Je ne me sens pas d'affinité avec les écrivains français." *Car.*, 4 mars 1953, 9. Interview.

511. Pozner, Vladimir. "Erskine Caldwell." *NL*, 7 mai 1938, 6.

512. Sigaux, Gilbert. "Erskine Caldwell." *GLet.*, 23 août 1947, 3. Bibliography, biographical sketch, interview.

513. Thiébaut, Marcel. "Trois romanciers étrangers: Huxley, Morgan, Caldwell." *RP*, 1 déc. 1937, 685-700.

514. Vallette, Jacques. "Erskine Caldwell: plan de son oeuvre." *Nef*, août 1946, 130-2.

REVIEWS:

[*Episode in Palmetto*] Anon. *BCLF*, déc. 1952, 727-8 (brief); Anon. *FL*, 9 août 1952, 8 (brief); Brisville, J. *GLet.*, nov. 1952, 102 (brief); Las Vergnas, R. *HM*, nov. 1952, 466.

[*Georgia Boy*] Brest, R. *NL*, 11 août 1949, 3 (brief); Olivier, D. *Réf.*, 27 mai 1950, 7 (brief).

[*God's Little Acre*] de Rougemont, D. *Esprit*, nov. 1937, 355-6; Hertz, H. *Europe*, 15 nov. 1936, 406-7.

[*A House in the Uplands*] Anon. *Action*, 22-28 déc. 1948, 10 (brief); Brisville, J. *Nef*, jan. 1949, 129-30; d'Houville, G. *RDM*, 15 mars 1949, 356-63.

[*Journeyman*] Anon. *SS*, 15 avril 1950, 2 (brief); Blanzat, J. *FL*, 8 avril 1950, 7; Escoube, L. *GLet*., 27 mai 1950, 6 (brief); Grenaud, P. *RMed*., nov.-déc. 1950, 739-40; Lalou, R. *NL*, 13 avril 1950, 3; Rousselot, J. *Paru*, juin 1950, 40; Vallette, J. *MF,* juin 1950, 346.

[*Poor Fool*] Anon. *LF*, 19 mai 1945, 3 (brief); Astruc, C. *Paru*, juillet 1945, 54-6; Blanzat, J. *Bat*., 29 mars 1945, 3; Blanzat, J. *Poésie 45*, avril-mai 1945, 86-9; de Laprade, J. *Arts*, 13 avril 1945, 3; Jarlot, G. *Fon*., juin 1945, 426-7; Rode, H. *CS*, n° 271, 1945, 406-7.

[*The Sure Hand of God*] Lalou, R. *NL*, 13 août 1950, 3.

[*This Very Earth*] Las Vergnas, R. *HM*, oct. 1951, 154-6.

[*Tobacco Road*] Anon. *BCLF*, nov.-déc. 1947, 15 (brief); Bousquet, J. *CS*, oct. 1938, 731-2; C., J. *Paru*, fév. 1948, 45-6; Coindreau, M. *NRF*, juillet 1934, 125-7; Crémieux, F. *Europe*, juin 1947, 124-8; Deon, M. *AF*, 23 mars 1950, 4; Lelis, M. *Europe*, 15 déc. 1937, 561-2; Mignon, P. *Action*, 28 mars 1947, 10; Sartin, P. *CP*, n° 42, 1947, 78-80; Simiot, B. *HM*, juin 1950, 296-300; Toesca, M. *GLet*., 21 mai 1947, 9; Wessberge, E. *EA,* jan. 1938, 110 (brief).

[*Tragic Ground*] Fauchery, P. *Action*, 18 mai 1948, 10-11; Parrot, L. *LF*, 13 mai 1948, 3; Paz, M. *Paru*, juillet 1948, 38-9; Sigaux, G. *Livre,* juin 1948, 39 (brief).

[*Trouble in July*] Blanzat, J. *FL*, 6 déc. 1947, 5; Fauchery, P. *Action*, 6 jan. 1948, 8; Fouchet, M. *Car*., 3 déc. 1947, 6; Jouve, R. *Etudes*, juin 1948, 427; Minet, P. *Paru*, mars 1948, 39; Nadeau, M. *Gav*., 17 déc. 1947, 3; Sigaux, G. *GLet.,* 24 jan. 1948, 6 (brief); Sigaux, G. *Livre*, mai 1948, 40 (brief); Todrani, J. *CS*, n° 289, 1948, 529-30.

[*We Are the Living* and *Kneel to the Rising Sun*] Bousquet, J. *CS*, déc. 1938, 902-3.

STEINBECK

BOOKS TRANSLATED:

515. [*Bombs Away*] *Lâchez les Bombes! L'histoire d'une équipe de bombardment*. N. Y.: Overseas Editions, 1944. Préf. Steinbeck.

516 [*Burning Bright*] *La Flamme*. Paris: Del Duca, 1951. Tr. Henri Thies. Préf. Steinbeck.

517. [*Cannery Row*] *Rue de la Sardine.* Paris: Gallimard, 1947. Tr. Magdeleine Paz.

518. [*Cup of Gold*] *La Coupe d'Or.* Paris: Gallimard, 1952. Tr. Jacques Papy.

519. [*The Grapes of Wrath*] *Grappes d'Amertume.* Bruxelles: de Kogge, s.d. Tr. Karin Hatker. "Texte français définitif d'Albert Debaty."

520. ————. *Les Raisins de la Colère.* Paris: Gallimard, 1947. Tr. M. E. Coindreau et M. Duhamel.

521. [*In Dubious Battle*] *En un Combat douteux.* Paris: Gallimard, 1940. Tr. Ed. Michel-Tyl.

522. [*The Long Valley*] *La grande Vallée.* Paris: Gallimard, 1946. Tr. Marcel Duhamel et Max Morise.

523. [*The Moon Is Down*] *Nuits noires.* Paris: Editions de Minuit, 1944. [Tr. Y. Desvignes.] "Ce volume publié aux dépens de quelques lettrés patriotes a été achevé d'imprimer sous l'oppression à Paris le 29 février 1944."

524. ————. *Nuits sans Lune.* Lausanne: J. Marguerat, 1943. "Version française de Marvède Fischer." Slightly cut and altered because of the war situation.

525. [*Of Mice and Men*] *Des Souris et des Hommes.* Paris: Gallimard, 1939. Tr. et int. M. E. Coindreau. Préf. J. Kessel.

526. ————. Paris: Arts et Métiers Graphiques, 1948. Tr. M. E. Coindreau. Limited to 390 copies; illus. Reynold Arnould.

527. ————. *Des Souris et des Hommes,* en 4 [*sic*] actes. Paris: R. Laffont, 1946. Tr. Marcel Duhamel.

528. ————. *Des Souris et des Hommes,* en 3 actes. Paris: Le Club Français du Livre, 1949. Tr. Marcel Duhamel. Préf. Magdeleine Paz.

529. [*The Pastures of Heaven*] *Les Pâturages du Ciel.* Paris: Gallimard, 1948. Tr. Louis Guilloux.

530. [*The Pearl*] *La Perle.* Paris: Gallimard, 1950. Tr. Renée Vavasseur et Marcel Duhamel.

531. [*A Russian Journal*] *Journal Russe.* Paris: Gallimard, 1949. Tr. Marcel Duhamel.

532. [*To a God Unknown*] *Au Dieu inconnu.* Paris: Gallimard, 1950. Tr. Jeanne Witta-Montrobert.

533. [*Tortilla Flat*] *Tortilla Flat.* Lausanne: Marguerat, 1944. Tr. Brigitte V. Barbey.

534. ————. Paris: Marguerat, 1947. Tr. Brigitte V. Barbey.

535. ————. Paris: Le Club Français du Livre, 1949. Tr. Brigitte V. Barbey.

536. [*The Wayward Bus*] *Les Naufragés de l'Autocar.* Paris: Gallimard, 1949. Tr. Renée Vavasseur et Marcel Duhamel.

OTHER TRANSLATIONS:

537. "La caille blanche." Tr. M. Duhamel. *Lab.*, 15 déc. 1945, 4-5.

538. "Les chrysanthèmes." Tr. Max Morise. *RP*, jan. 1946, 77-85.

539. "Le cirque." Tr. Henri Thies. *NL*, 24 mai 1951, 7. Excerpt from *La Flamme*.

540. "Le coeur et les entrailles de la France." Tr. Claude Colin. *SS*, 13 sept. 1952, 8-9. Steinbeck's conversations with villagers in the Jura Mountains, summer 1952.

541. "Comment Edith McGillcuddy rencontra R. L. Stevenson." Tr. Léo Lack. (See 18), 359-72.

542. "Fuite." Tr. Roger l'Eleu. *Con.*, fév.-mars, 1944, 111-24.

543. "Le harnais." Tr. Max Morise. *SS*, 1 déc. 1945, 6; 8 déc., 6.

544. "Johnny l'ours." Tr. Sonia Mille. *QV*, n° 1, 1945, 62-83.

545. "Le meurtre." Tr. Simone Saint-Clair. *Grin.*, 8 juin 1939, 13. Brief biographical introduction.

546. ————. Tr. Georges Duthuit. *Fon.* (see 45), 52-66.

547. "Les pâturages du ciel." Tr. Louis Guilloux. *GLet.*, 17 avril 1948, 8, 9, 10. Excerpt.

548. "Petites histoires." Tr. Béatrix Gross-Morel. *Eto.*, 18 sept. 1945, 3.

549. "Le poney." Tr. Elisabeth Van Rysselberghe. *LF*, 11 nov. 1944, 4; 18 nov., 6; 25 nov., 6.

550. "Le poney rouge. Le cadeau." Tr. André Schaeffer. *Con.*, août 1944, 158-81. "Le poney rouge (fin)." Tr. Madeleine Schaeffer. *Con.*, nov. 1944, 150-69.

551. *Les Raisins de la Colère.* Tr. M. E. Coindreau et Marcel Duhamel. *LF*, 3 mai 1946, 1, 6; 10, 17, 24, 31 mai, 6; 6, 14, 21, 28 juin, 6; 5, 12, 19, 26 juillet, 6; 2, 9, 16, 23, 30 août,

6; 6, 13, 20, 27 sept., 6; 4, 11, 18, 25 oct., 6; 1, 8, 15, 22, 29 nov., 6; 6, 13 déc., 6; 20 déc., 9.

552. "Le requin." Tr. Louis Guilloux. *Arche,* mars 1947, 10-30.

553. "Rue de la sardine." [Tr. Magdeleine Paz.] *GLet.,* 24 jan. 1948, 10, 11, 12, 13. Excerpt.

554. *Des Souris et des Hommes* (play version). Tr. Marcel Duhamel. *MS,* juin 1946, 5-67; juillet, 91-124.

555. ————. *Paris Théâtre,* jan. 1949, 3-32.

556. "Vigile." Tr. Y. Desvignes. *Chroniques de Minuit,* avril 1945, 127-36.

CRITICAL ARTICLES:

557. Anon. "John Steinbeck, qui se défend d'être communiste, compte abreuver Moscou avec deux millions et demi de roubles de vodka." *SS,* 5 juillet 1947, 2. Interview.

558. Auger-Duvignaud, J. "Pour saluer Steinbeck." *LF,* 18 juillet 1947, 5. Account of a reception given Steinbeck by the Comité National des Ecrivains.

559. Barron, Marie Louise. "Steinbeck à Paris." *LF,* 11 juillet 1947, 1, 5. Interview.

560. Blanzat, J. "Les nouvelles de John Steinbeck et de William Saroyan." *Litt.,* 6 avril 1946, 4.

561. ————. "John Steinbeck, romancier de la fatalité." *Poésie 44,* nov.-déc. 1944, 101-6.

562. Brierre, Annie. "Steinbeck à Paris." *NL,* 24 juillet 1952, 4. Interview.

563. Chonez, Claudine. "John Steinbeck ou la vie contre le système." *Sem.,* 5 juillet 1947, 11. Interview.

564. Coindreau, M. E. "John Steinbeck." *LF,* 26 avril 1946, 1, 4.

565. Duché, Jean. "John Steinbeck visite l'Europe." *FL,* 5 juillet 1947, 3. Interview.

566. Forestier, Marie. "John Steinbeck le Californien." *RN,* 1 mars 1947, 253-61.

567. Gide, André. "Pages de Journal II." *Arche,* avril-mai 1944, 10-39. Journal from June 25 to Nov. 25, 1940. Entry for Sept. 27 discusses *In Dubious Battle.*

568. Guth, Paul. "L'interview de Paul Guth. Steinbeck." *GLet.,* 12 juillet 1947, 1, 2.

569. Lalou, René. "Le réalisme lyrique de John Steinbeck." *CLM* (see 41), 183-90.

570. Las Vergnas, Raymond. "Lettres anglo-américaines." *HM,* août 1951, 471-4. General article on Steinbeck's books.

571. ――――. "Visite à Steinbeck." *NL,* 10 juillet 1947, 1, 7. Interview.

572. Massin, Robert. "John Steinbeck nous dit: En Amérique, mes livres touchent le peuple." *Gav.,* 3 juillet 1947, 5. Interview.

573. Morphe, Jean Pierre. "Sur notre plateau: John Steinbeck." *Car.,* 25 avril 1946, 7.

574. Paley, Judith. "John Steinbeck: défenseur de la liberté des hommes." *Gav.,* 26 avril 1945, 2.

575. Remords, G. "Agrégation d'anglais. John Steinbeck." *BFLS,* avril 1950, 301-5. Bibliography.

576. Vallette, Jacques. "Lettres anglo-saxonnes: John Steinbeck et les petits." *MF,* 1 sept. 1947, 154-6.

577. ――――. "Steinbeck bifrons." *Nef,* avril 1946, 131-3.

578. Viel, Marie, Jeanne. "Steinbeck en Europe." *Bat.,* 23 juillet 1947, 6. Interview.

579. Viollis, Andrée. "John Steinbeck chez lui." *Eto.,* 2 avril 1946, 1, 7. Interview.

REVIEWS:

[*Bombs Away*] Aubier, D. *NL,* 27 sept. 1945, 3; M., H. *LF,* 8 sept. 1945, 3 (brief).

[*Burning Bright*] Anon. *BCLF,* oct. 1951, 669 (brief); Rousselot, J. *MNP,* n° 51-52, 1951, 86; Rousselot, J. *NL,* 21 juin 1951, 3.

[*Cannery Row*] Anon. *FicL,* avril 1948 (unpaged), presents several reviews of the book; Blanzat, J. *FL,* 14 fév. 1948, 5; Burucoa, C. *NL,* 15 juillet 1948, 3; Faure, M. *Gav.,* 18 fév. 1948, 5; Kanters, R. *GLet.,* 7 fév. 1948, 4, 5; Kanters, R. *Livre,* mai 1948, 41 (brief); Minet, P. *Paru,* avril 1948, 46-7; Parrot, L. *LF,* 13 mai 1948, 3; Roy, J. *TM,* mai 1948, 2105-8.

[*Cup of Gold*] Anon. *BCLF,* juillet-août 1952, 503 (brief); de Calan, M. *Etudes,* mai 1952, 284-5; Lalou, R. *NL,* 20 mars 1952, 3 (brief).

[*The Grapes of Wrath*] Anon. *FicL*, jan. 1948 (unpaged), presents several reviews of the book; Blanzat, J. *FL*, 13 sept. 1947, 5; C., M. *VI*, oct. 1947, 131 (brief); Delbech-Teissier, J. *TP*, 3 nov. 1944, 6; Fauchery, P. *Action*, 5 sept. 1947, 10-11; Guilleminault, G. *Bat.*, 10 sept. 1947, 6; Jouve, R. *Etudes*, oct. 1947, 121-2; Kanters, R. *GLet.*, 4 oct. 1947, 4-5; Lalou, R. *NL*, 25 sept. 1947, 3; Minet, P. *Paru*, déc. 1947, 40-1; Roux, M. *RI*, nov.-déc. 1947, 231 (brief).

[*In Dubious Battle*] Thomas, H. *NRF*, jan. 1941, 244-5.

[*The Long Valley*] Anon. *Mondes*, 2 avril 1946, 6; Bay, A. *GLet.*, 13 avril 1946, 11; Blanzat, J. *MonF*, mai 1946, 124-5; Fauchery, P. *Action*, 5 avril 1946, 12-13; Guilleminault, G. *Bat.*, 24 avril 1946, 6; Jouve, R. *Etudes*, avril 1947, 138-9; Lalou, R. *NL*, 4 avril 1946, 3; Magny, C. *Sem.*, 20 avril 1946, 8; Nadeau, M. *Gav.*, 25 avril 1946, 4; Thibault, H. *Paru*, juillet 1946, 42-3.

[*The Moon Is Down*] de Laprade, J. *Arts*, 4 mai 1945, 3; de Laprade, J. *Arts*, 4 avril 1947, 2; Gandrey-Rety, J. *Arts*, 25 avril 1947, 7; Kanters, R. *Let.*, jan. 1945, 68-72; Lalou, R. *Gav.*, 8 mai 1947, 8; Lalou, R. *Gav.*, 11 sept. 1947, 7; Miauray, J. *NL*, 22 nov. 1945, 3.

[*Of Mice and Men*] Anon. *BCLF*, avril 1947, 8 (brief); Anon. *LF*, 25 nov. 1948, 3 (brief); Arland, M. *NRF*, juillet 1939, 131-3; Beigbeder, M. *TP*, 1 fév. 1946, 5; Bernard, M. *MonF*, juin 1946, 324-6; Bouissounouse, J. *NL*, 24 juin 1939, 5; C., J. *Paru*, fév. 1948, 45-6; Catel, J. *MF*, 15 nov. 1937, 202-9; de Laprade, J. *Arts*, 4 avril 1947, 2; Frank, A. *GLet.*, 11 mai 1946, 13; Gandrey-Rety, J. *Arts*, 26 avril 1946, 5; Gignoux, H. *Etudes*, juin 1946, 386-92; Gogniat, R. *Arts*, 26 avril 1946, 5; Lalou, R. *Gav.*, 25 avril 1946, 7; Lalou, R. *Gav.*, 11 sept. 1947, 7; Mohrt, M. *MS*, juillet 1946, 133-6.

[*The Pastures of Heaven*] Blanzat, J. *FL*, 15 mai 1948, 5; Las Vergnas, R. *HM*, août 1948, 677-81; Parrot, L. *LF*, 13 mai 1948, 3; Paz, M. *Paru*, juillet 1948, 39-40; Sigaux, G. *Livre*, juin 1948, 40 (brief).

[*The Pearl*] Anon. *LF*, 20 juillet 1950, 3 (brief); de Laprade, J. *Arts*, 6 oct. 1950, 2; Jouve, R. *Etudes*, déc. 1950, 423; Lalou, R. *NL*, 10 sept. 1950, 3; Lange, M. *Ob.*, 6 juillet 1950, 20; Marchal, G. *RN*, 15 nov. 1950, 457-9.

[*A Russian Journal*] Anon. *BCLF*, oct. 1949, 615 (brief); Calle-waert, J. *RN*, 15 jan. 1950, 106 (brief); Olivier, D. *Réf.*, 22 oct. 1949, 7 (brief).

[*To a God Unknown*] Anon. *BCLF*, mai 1951, 359 (brief); Blanc-Dufour, A. *CS*, n° 305, 1951, 159; Blanzat, J. *FL*, 24 mars 1951, 283; Bosc, R. *Etudes*, mai 1951, 9; Lalou, R. *AC*, avril 1951, 13-17; Lalou, R. *NL*, 22 fév. 1951, 3; Sigaux, G. *GLet.*, avril 1951, 125, 127; Sigaux, G. *SS*, 24 fév. 1951, 2.

[*Tortilla Flat*] Blanzat, J. *FL*, 14 fév. 1948, 5; Delfosse, J. *RN*, 15 mars 1948, 325 (brief).

[*The Wayward Bus*] Anon. *BCLF*, juin 1949, 384-5 (brief); Anon. *SS*, 9 avril 1949, 2; B., A. *HM*, mai 1949, III (brief); Fouchet, M. *Car.*, 30 mars 1949, 9; Guilleminault, G. *Bat.*, 17 mars 1949, 9; Jouve, R. *Etudes*, nov. 1949, 278; Roy, J. *TM*, avril 1949, 752-4; Weidlé, W. *CPl.*, hiver 1948, 42 (brief).

INDEX

Absalom, Absalom!: review of American edition, 127; translation, 180

Académie Française, *see* French Academy

Acaste, article on Dos Passos, 94

Across the River and into the Trees: reviews of American edition, 115-17; not translated into French, 115; Italian background, 117

Action: article by Roy, 57; three short stories in 1946 by Caldwell, 154; review of *The Grapes of Wrath*, 170

Adam, George, discusses relationship between American life and literature, 187

Agrégation, questions on American writers, 184-85

Albatross Editions, publishes American books, 19

Alerme, contributes to a symposium on Hemingway and Peyré, 105

Algiers: wartime center of French publishing, 27; beginnings of postwar vogue of American novels, 29

Almanach des Lettres: quoted on vogue of American novel, 38-39; quoted on French writers influenced by Americans, 67-68; review of play version of *Of Mice and Men*, 166-67

American novels in France: in 1920's, 15-17; in 1930's, 17-22; read in English, 19; during World War II, 22-26; postwar vogue, 27-44; qualities inherent in, as reason for vogue, 43-44; reactions against vogue, 45-60; influence on French writers, 61-68, 182; present-day interest, 179-86

American Tragedy, An: need for translation, 17; reviewed, 20

American writers, contrasted with European, 22

Americans, French impressions of, 11-12, 190

Americans Abroad, anthology of expatriate writers, reviewed, 20

Anderson, Sherwood: translations in 1920's, 15, 16, 17; only American author in special issue of *La Revue Nouvelle*, 17; translations in 1930's, 18

Anglès, Auguste, comments on *For Whom the Bell Tolls*, 107

An premier du Siècle, L', see *1919*

Anthony Adverse, success in France in 1930's, 22

Aragon, Louis, works influenced by American writers, 66

Arbalète, L': special issue, 29, 69; short story by Hemingway, 108; short story by Faulkner, 130; excerpt from *Journeyman*, 150

Arban, Dominique, interview with Caldwell quoted, 155

Arche, L', comment by Gide on *In Dubious Battle*, 163

Arland, M., reviews *Of Mice and Men*, 162

Arts et Métiers Graphiques, publishes de luxe edition of *Of Mice and Men*, 173-74

Arts-Lettres, short story by Caldwell, 158

As I Lay Dying: translation, 18; de luxe edition, 30, 124; influence on *Les Mendiants*, 62; influence on *Gerbe Baude*, 62; preface by Valery Larbaud, 124; reviews, 125-26; theatrical adaptation, 125; excerpt published, 135

Astruc, Alexandre: quoted on excessive intellectualism in French novels, 41; comments on American style, 69; reviews *Poor Fool*, 153

Aubarède, Gabriel d', comments on French sources for American techniques, 46

Auclair, Marcelle, contributes to a symposium on Hemingway and Peyré, 105

Aymé, Marcel: reply in *NL enquête*,

42; *La Vouivre* compared to Caldwell, 65

Babbitt, translation and early sale, 17

Bailly, R., quoted on Steinbeck, 172

Baldensperger, Fernand, on French reading of American novels in 1920's, 16

Barbezat, Marc, article on Caldwell, 150-51

Barrault, Jean Louis, theatrical adaptation of *As I Lay Dying*, 125

Bataille, Mlle, radio adaptation of *Tortilla Flat*, 171

Bataille, review of *The Big Money*, 95

Baum, Vicki: books by, reviewed, 20; a best-selling author, 31

Bay, André, interviewed in *Combat enquête*, 50

Beauvoir, Simone de, *Le Sang des Autres* influenced by Faulkner, 62-63

Behavioristic psychology, popular in U. S., 78

Beigbeder, Marc, comments on Steinbeck, 168

Bernard, M., reviews play version of *Of Mice and Men*, 168

Best sellers in France: *Gone with the Wind* France's twentieth-century best seller, 22; for 1946, 30; American authors named, 31; for 1947, 34

Beyats, Louis, contributes to a symposium on Hemingway and Peyré, 105

Bibliography on America for Communist readers, 58-59

Bibliothèque Universelle et Revue de Genève, review of American edition of *Manhattan Transfer*, 89-90

Big Money, The: translation, 88; reviews, 95-96

Big Rock Candy Mountain, The, best seller in France, 31

Blanc-Dufour, A.: reasons for wanting fewer translations of American novels, 52; reviews *The Wayward Bus*, 175; reviews *To a God Unknown*, 176

Blanchot, Maurice, quoted on complaints against American novel, 45-46

Blancpain, Marc, reply in *NL enquête*, 42

Blanzat, Jean: suggests *Les Mendiants* influenced by Faulkner, 62; parallels Aymé's *La Vouivre* and Caldwell, 65; comments on Hemingway's popularity, 112; gives reasons for vogue of American novelists and suggests Caldwell most American of these writers, 153-54; comments on Caldwell, 157; article on Steinbeck, 165-66; compares *Cannery Row* and *Tortilla Flat*, 174; reviews *To a God Unknown*, 176

Bombs Away, translation, 25, 163

Book Club, French: sales of *For Whom the Bell Tolls*, 30; publishes *The 42nd Parallel*, 97-98; editions of *For Whom the Bell Tolls* in 1950 and 1952, 117; publishes the play version of *Of Mice and Men*, 174; publishes *Tortilla Flat*, 174; account of operations, 181-82

Bosc, R., reviews *To a God Unknown*, 176

Bost, Jacques Laurent: *Le Dernier des Métiers* influenced by American writers, 66; translation of *The Sure Hand of God*, 159

Boussinot, Roger, *Mal de Mer* influenced by American techniques, 61

Boyle, Kay: short stories published, 20; book by, reviewed, 20

Brion, Marcel, article on Faulkner, 141

Brodin, Pierre: *Le Roman régionaliste américain*, 20, 78, 148; *Les Ecrivains américains de l'entre-deux-guerres*, 32, 98, 134; evaluates American novel, 35; comments on Caldwell, 148, 154-55

Bromfield, Louis: on French reading of American novels, 16; translations in 1930's, 17; short story published, 20; book by, reviewed, 20; a best-selling author, 31

Brown, John, criticizes French readers for their ignorance of American scene, 36

Bruit et la Fureur, Le, see *The Sound and the Fury*

Buck, Pearl: translations in 1930's, 17; article on, 20; regarded as great novelist, 22; a best-selling author, 31

Buenzod, Emmanuel: reviews *Cinquante mille Dollars*, 100; reviews American edition of *A Farewell to Arms*, 100-101

Bulletin Critique du Livre Français, review of *The Wayward Bus*, 175

Burnett, W. H., published in *Série Noire*, 37

Burning Bright: translation, 177; reviews, 177-78

Cahen, Jacques Fernand, *La Littérature américaine*, 85

Cahiers de la Table Ronde, short story by Hemingway, 108

Cahiers de Paris, special issue on contemporary American novel, 20

Cahiers des Langues Modernes: special issue, 29, 168; article on Faulkner, 134; article on Steinbeck, 168-69

Cahiers du Collège Philosophique, article on Faulkner, 137-38

Cahiers du Sud: enquête on foreign literatures in France, 16-17; excerpt from *1919*, 92; review of *In All Countries*, 93; excerpt from *Light in August*, 126; preface to *Light in August*, 126; review of *Light in August*, 126; review of *These 13*, 129-30; article on Faulkner, 130

Caillé, Pierre François, interviewed in *Combat enquête*, 51

Caillois, Roger, interviewed in *Combat enquête*, 49-50

Cain, James M.: respect for, in France, 22; treated as Faulkner's equal, 33; bracketed with Steinbeck and Henry Miller, 33; published in *Série Noire*, 37

Caldwell, Erskine: interviewed, 12, 148-49, 155; *God's Little Acre*, 18, 53, 146, 147-48; *Tobacco Road*, 19, 30, 146, 148, 150, 154, 156; *We Are the Living*, 19, 149-50; commented on, by Gide, 21-22; reception in France during postwar years, 31, 151-60; pride of French avantgarde, 32; *Poor Fool*, 35, 45, 152-54; sales in Paris and New York of *Poor Fool*, 48; characters, 50; *Episode in Palmetto*, 55, 159 60; influence on French writers, 64-65; lyric quality, 73; social sense, 79;

reception during 1930's, 146-50; defended against charge of indecency, 147; reception during war years (from Algiers), 150-51; *Journeyman*, 150, 158-59; compared with Dostoevski, 151; *Tragic Ground*, 152, 157; *Trouble in July*, 155-56; *A House in the Uplands*, 157-58; *Georgia Boy*, 158; *The Sure Hand of God*, 159; *This Very Earth*, 159; *Southways*, 160; *Place Called Estherville*, 160; *Call It Experience*, 160; *A Lamp at Nightfall*, 160; future French publication prospects, 180

Call It Experience, soon to be published in French, 160, 180

Camus, Albert: *La Peste* leads best sellers in 1947, 34; interviewed in *Combat enquête*, 48-49; article in *Partisan Review*, 53; *L'Etranger* influenced by Hemingway, 65

Cannery Row: translation, 171; reviews, 173

Carisey, Maurice, quoted, 36

Carrefour: article on French best sellers of 1946, 30; on French best sellers of 1947, 34; review of *Aperçus de Littérature américaine*, 133; article on American reception of *Intruder in the Dust*, 139; articles on play version of *Of Mice and Men*, 167

Catel, Jean, article on Steinbeck, 161

Cather, Willa: translations of, in 1920's, 16; little known in France, 34

Celly, R., reviews *Cinquante mille Dollars*, 100

Cestre, Charles: reviews *Three Soldiers* and *Manhattan Transfer*, Tauchnitz editions, 92; reviews American edition of *In Our Time*, 103; reviews Crosby edition of *Torrents of Spring*, 103; reviews Crosby edition of *Sanctuary*, 124; reviews American edition of *Light in August*, 126; first holder of chair in American literature and civilization at the Sorbonne, 184

Chambrun, Comtesse de, efforts to keep American Library in Paris open during the war, 183

Chandler, Raymond, published in *Série Noire*, 37

Characters in American novels, found

to be typically simple people, 80-81

Charensol, Georges, interviewed in *Combat enquête*, 47-48

Chase, James Hadley, published in *Série Noire*, 37

Chêne, Editions du, *see* Editions du Chêne

Cheyney, Peter: published in *Série Noire*, 37; included in anthology of American stories, 69

Chrétien de Troyes, source of interior monologue, 46

Cinquante mille Dollars: publication and first reception, 16; reviews, 99-100

Climats: Caldwell interview, 12; Steinbeck interview, 12; review of *Aperçus de Littérature américaine*, 133

Club Français du Livre, *see* Book Club, French

Coindreau, Maurice E.: translation of *The Sound and the Fury*, 10, 128; translation of *As I Lay Dying*, 18, 124; translation of *The Grapes of Wrath*, 25, 169; *Aperçus de Littérature américaine*, 32, 36, 132-33; evaluates American novel, 35; criticizes French readers for ignorance of American scene, 36; called Gallimard's correspondent in America by Kanapa, 55; preface to *Le Roman régionaliste américain*, 78; preface to *Light in August*, 83, 126; comments on *Manhattan Transfer*, 89; reviews *Orient Express*, 89; reviews American edition of *1919*, 91; translation of *A Farewell to Arms*, 101; reviews American edition of *To Have and Have Not*, 105; is attacked for his criticism of Hemingway, 109; article in 1931 on Faulkner, 122; reviews American edition of *Light in August*, 126; reviews American edition of *Absalom, Absalom!*, 127; preface to *The Sound and the Fury*, 128; translation of *The Wild Palms*, 142; preface to *The Wild Palms*, 141-42; translation of *God's Little Acre*, 146; reviews American edition of *Tobacco Road*, 146; article on Caldwell, 147; preface to *We Are the Living*, 149-50; comments on Caldwell, 155; transla-tion of *Tragic Ground*, 157; translation of *Of Mice and Men*, 161; introduction to *Of Mice and Men*, 162; comments on *To a God Unknown*, 177

Combat, enquête on American litera-ture, 1947, 47-52

Commerce, short story by Faulkner, 123

Communist criticism of American novel, 54-60

Communist writers, French, influ-enced by American techniques, 61

Concreteness of American novels, 78

Confluences: article by Astruc on American style, 69; review of American edition of *Number One*, 95; comments on Faulkner in spe-cial issue on the novel, 131; short stories by Steinbeck, 164

Cormeau, Nelly, comments on Faulk-ner's influence on Luc Estang, 63

Cossery, Albert, *Les Hommes oubliés de Dieu* compared with Caldwell's world, 64

Courtade, Pierre, *Les Circonstances* influenced by American tech-niques, 61

Courtes Histoires américaines, short story by Faulkner, 135

Crosby Continental Editions: begun in 1932, 19; publishes *Torrents of Spring*, 103; publishes *Sanctuary*, 124

Cup of Gold, translation, 178

Curwood, James Oliver, read in France, 17

Dabit, Eugène: reviews *In All Coun-tries*, 93; reviews *As I Lay Dying*, 125

Daix, Pierre, attacks Hemingway for falsification of Spanish Civil War, 57

Danchin, F., reviews American edi-tion of *Across the River and into the Trees*, 116

Darkness at Noon, leading best seller of 1946, 30

Death in the Afternoon: translation, 18; reviews, 105; compared with book by Peyré, 105

Delfosse, J., reviews *Tortilla Flat*, 171

Delgove, Henri: translation of *Sanc-*

tuary, 18; translation of *Sartoris,* 127

Delpech, Jeanine: reply in *NL enquête,* 42; comments on symbolism in American novels, 45; article on Hemingway, 103-4; translation of *Green Hills of Africa,* 104; interviews Caldwell, 148-49

Delteil, Joseph, reply in *NL enquête,* 42-43

Démocratie Nouvelle, article by Sillen treats Spillane as typical American writer, 60

Denoreaz, Michel, attacks Faulkner, 60

Dépaysement, American novel source of, for French, 40, 81

Descartes, René, as French heritage, 7, 8

des Forêts, Louis René: interviewed in *Combat enquête,* 47; *Les Mendiants* influenced by Faulkner, 62

Des Souris et des Hommes, see *Of Mice and Men*

Desvignes, Y., translation of *The Moon Is Down,* 24

Dissertations, doctoral, on American literature at French universities, 185-86

Dix Indiens: publication, 109; first reception, 109; reviews, 113

Doctor Martino and Other Stories: translation, 135; reviews, 137

Doigt de Dieu, Le, see *The Sure Hand of God*

Dos Passos, John: *One Man's Initiation,* 15, 88-89; *Manhattan Transfer,* 15, 88, 89, 90, 91, 92, 94; *The 42nd Parallel,* 18, 87, 88, 92, 97-98; *In All Countries,* 18, 93; *1919,* 18, 20, 87, 88, 91, 93-94; articles on, 1937, 20; reception in France during postwar period, 31, 95-98; discussed by Pouillon, 32; a writer's writer for the French, 32, 98; *Three Soldiers,* 35, 89, 92, 94, 97; breaker of old traditions in American writing, 36; simultaneity, 41, 46, 49; novelty of technique, 51; compared with Balzac, 54, 96, 98; *U.S.A.,* 54, 87-88, 96; influence on French writers, 64; discussed by Magny, 74; treatment of time, 77; social sense, 79; not a popular writer in France, 87-88; *Tour of Duty,* 87, 96; *The Big Money,* 88, 95-96; few magazine publications in France, 88; first French publication, 88; compared with Duhamel and Barbusse, 89; *Orient Express,* 89; reception in 1920's, 88-90; reception in 1930's, 90-95; considered by Sartre greatest writer of our time, 94; *Number One,* 95, 180; *State of the Nation,* 96-97; future French publishing prospects, 180

Douze Hommes, see *Twelve Men*

Drama, American, influence on French, 13

Dreiser, Theodore: *Twelve Men,* 15, 17; *An American Tragedy,* 17, 20; translations in 1930's, 18; called true pioneer of American novel, 56

du Bouchet, André, translation of *Knight's Gambit,* 142

Duché, Jean, interviews Steinbeck, 172-73

Duesburg, Jacques: article on American edition of *Across the River and into the Trees,* 116; reviews *The Sound and the Fury,* 128; comments on Faulkner, 137

Duhamel, Marcel: translation of *The Grapes of Wrath,* 25, 169; conversation with Guérard, 36; director of *Série Noire,* 36-37; translation of story by Cheyney, 69; translation of *To Have and Have Not,* 108; translation of *The Sure Hand of God,* 159

Dujardin, Edmond, inventor of interior monologue, 46, 73

Dumas, Alexandre, and Maupassant most widely read French authors in America, 51

Dumoulin, G. M., novel by, published under an American pseudonym, 67

Duras, Marguerite: *La Vie tranquille* influenced by Faulkner, 63; *Un Barrage contre le Pacifique* influenced by Caldwell, 64; *La Vie tranquille* influenced by Caldwell, 65; *Le Marin de Gibralter* influenced by Hemingway, 65

d'Urfé, Honoré, source of interior monologue, 46

Dutourd, Jean: translation of *The Old Man and the Sea,* 118; preface to *The Old Man and the Sea,* 121; *Au bon Buerre* typical of French postwar novels, 182-83

Duvignaud, J., comments on Caldwell's omission from two anthologies of American writing, 158

East of Eden, to be published in French, 178
Eaubonne, Françoise d', reply in NL enquête, 42
Ecrit aux U.S.A., edited by Albert J. Guérard: short story by Faulkner, 134; short story by Caldwell, 155
Editions de Minuit: wartime publisher of Nuits noires, 24-25; publishes Mosquitoes, 136
Editions du Chêne, publisher of Henry Miller's books, 33
Editions du Pré au Clercs, publishes de luxe edition of Tobacco Road, 154
Editions Gallimard, see Gallimard
Editions Jean Marguerat (Lausanne): publishes Nuits sans Lune, 24; publishes Tortilla Flat, 171
Editions Mondiales, to publish East of Eden, 178
Editions Sociales Internationales: publishes 1919, 88; records confiscated, 88
Ehrenburg, Ilya: places American writers in high esteem, 54-55; criticizes Faulkner adversely, 57-58, 139
Elsen, Claude, comments on Caldwell's influence on Un Barrage contre le Pacifique, 64
En avoir ou pas, see To Have and Have Not
English literature compared with American, 70-71
English novel: influence on French, 13; influence compared with American, 48; contrasted with American, 165
En un Combat douteux, see In Dubious Battle
Epic stage, American literature in, 70
Episode in Palmetto: exotic appeal, 53; translation, 159-60
Erval, F., reviews The Old Man and the Sea, 120
Escape, factor in success of American novel, 39-40
Espace, article by Fauchery on Pylon, 132
Esprit: special issue, 29; article by

Magny on Pylon, 131; review of God's Little Acre, 148
Estang, Luc, Les Stigmates influenced by Light in August, 63
Etudes: review of The Big Money, 96; review of The Grapes of Wrath, 170
Etudes Anglaises: review of Green Hills of Africa, 104; review of American edition of To Have and Have Not, 105-6; article by Mayoux on Faulkner, 144; review of Tobacco Road, 150; present outlet for French scholarship in American literature, 185; article by Simon on American political events and French reactions, 189
Europe: article on Dos Passos, 54; article by de Jouvenel, 58-59; excerpt from One Man's Initiation, 88; article by Dos Passos, 91; article by Soupault on Dos Passos, 92; review of The Big Money, 95; review of A Farewell to Arms, 102; review of Green Hills of Africa, 104; article by Munson on Faulkner, 123; short story in 1935 by Faulkner, 126; short story in 1936 by Faulkner, 126; article on Caldwell and Faulkner, 146-47; review of God's Little Acre, 147-48; review of Tobacco Road, 148; review of play, Tobacco Road, 156
Existentialists: appeal of American novel for, 43-44; accused of literary snobbery, 46
Exoticism of American novel for the French, 53

Fabulet, Louis, on French reading of American books in 1920's, 16-17
Farewell to Arms, A: translation, 18; Gide comments on, 21; review of American edition, 100-101; account of translation, 101; preface by Drieu la Rochèlle, 101; reviews, 101-2; review of Tauchnitz edition, 101; reprinted 1944, 108
Farrell, James T., little known in France, 34
Fast, Howard: praised by Kanapa, 55; books by, reviewed in French Communist press, 59
Fate, role of, in American novels, 165
Fauchery, Pierre: article on Pylon,

132; reviews *The Grapes of Wrath*, 170

Faulkner, William: *The Sound and the Fury*, 10, 18; reception in France during 1930's, 17, 122-30; *As I Lay Dying*, 18, 30, 124-26, 135; *Sanctuary*, 18, 19, 85, 123, 124; *Light in August*, 18, 83, 126; *Sartoris*, 18, 127-28; *These 13*, 18; read by Gide, 21, 22; as a puritan, 22, 83-84, 126, 132; read during occupation, 23; reception during postwar period, 31, 130-45; discussed by Pouillon, 32; considered as best of Americans, 35; *Soldiers' Pay*, 35, 97, 135-36; *Mosquitoes*, 35, 136-37; equated with Balzac and Dostoevski, 38; use of time, 46, 77; compared with de Vigny, 50; dominating writer of present, 51; criticized by Ehrenburg, 57-58; discussed as a reactionary in exchange of student letters, 58; attacked in article in *LF*, 59; attacked by Denoreaz, 60; influence on French novelists, 61-63; lyric quality, 73; master of interior monologue, 74; named as practitioner of *littérature noire*, 85; compared with Greek tragedians, 86; sales of books in France, 122; as a moralist, 122; *Absalom, Absalom!*, 127; not a postwar phenomenon, 129; tragic sense, 129; *Pylon*, 131-32; *Doctor Martino and Other Stories*, 135, 137; *The Unvanquished*, 138-39; *Intruder in the Dust*, 139, 144; Nobel Prize, 140-41; *The Green Bough*, 140-41; *The Wild Palms*, 141, 142-43; *Requiem for a Nun*, 142; *Knight's Gambit*, 142; compared with Kafka, 144; reception, May, 1952, at Salle Gaveau in Paris, 144-45; article by Soupault on Faulkner and Caldwell, 146-47; future French publication prospects, 180

Faÿ, Bernard: reviews American edition of *Men without Women*, 99; article on Faulkner, 126-27

Fifth Column, The: printed in *L'Arbalète*, 108; included in *Paradis perdu*, 115

Figaro Littéraire, Le: review of American edition of *Requiem for a Nun*, 142; article on Caldwell by Blanzat, 157

Fitzgerald, F. Scott, translations in 1920's, 16

Flaubert, Gustave, source for American novelists' attacks on puritanism, 46

Fontaine: special issue on American literature in 1943, 29; article by Henry Miller, 34; article by Genova, 63; article by de Rougement, 72; excerpt from *For Whom the Bell Tolls*, 108; short story in 1943 by Faulkner, 130; short story in 1944 by Faulkner, 131; short story in 1946 by Faulkner, 134; short story by Caldwell, 150

Forestier, Marie: article on Hemingway, 114-15; discusses wartime circulation of *The Grapes of Wrath*, 169; article on Steinbeck, 172

Forever Amber, by Kathleen Winsor: on best seller list for 1946, 30; sales, 31

42nd Parallel, The: translation, 18, 87, 92; French Book Club edition, 97-98

For Whom the Bell Tolls: translation, 30; sales, 30; compared to Stendhal's *The Red and the Black*, 47-48, 51; compared to Malraux's *L'Espoir*, 49, 50, 51, 106; attacked for its falsification of Spanish Civil War, 57; reviews, 106-8; excerpt in *Fontaine*, 108; quality of translation criticized, 111; French Book Club edition, 117

Fouchet, Max Pol: comments on Faulkner, 133; reviews *The Wayward Bus*, 175

France: comparison with America, 3-7; publishing in, 5-6, 27-28

France-U.S.A., enquête on best books from America in 1952, 180

Freeman, Marc, translation of *One Man's Initiation*, 15

French Academy: attempts to standardize language, 8; accepts American words into French language, 10

Fulbright teaching and research awards, 186

Gadoffre, Gilbert, directs discussions on American novel at Royaumont, 38

Gallimard (Editions): refuses to publish *The Grapes of Wrath* during war, 23; publisher of Henry Miller, 33; publisher of *Série Noire*, 36; accused of pro-American policy by Kanapa, 55; publishes Dos Passos trilogy, 88; publishes *A Farewell to Arms*, 101; publishes *Death in the Afternoon*, 105; publishes *To Have and Have Not*, 109; publishes *Dix Indiens*, 109; reason for not yet publishing *Across the River and into the Trees*, 115; publishes *The Old Man and the Sea*, 118-19; publishes *Aperçus de Littérature américaine*, 132; publishes *Intruder in the Dust*, 144; publishes *Tobacco Road* and *We Are the Living*, 146; publishes *Poor Fool*, 152; publishes *Trouble in July*, 156-57; publishes *Of Mice and Men*, 162; publishes *The Long Valley*, 166; publishes *Cannery Row*, 171; publishes *The Pastures of Heaven*, 173; publishes *A Russian Journal* and *The Wayward Bus*, 174; publishes *The Pearl* and *To a God Unknown*, 175

Gambit du Cavalier, Le, see *Knight's Gambit*

Gary, R., reviews American edition of *The Old Man and the Sea*, 120

Gautier, Jean Jacques, reply in *NL enquête*, 42

Gazette des Lettres: review of *The Old Man and the Sea*, 120; article on Faulkner, 134; excerpt from *Soldiers' Pay*, 135; review of *The Grapes of Wrath*, 169-70

Genova, Yvonne, comments on Faulkner's influence on Elsa Triolet, 63

Gentlemen Prefer Blondes, best seller in 1930's, 19

Georgia Boy: translation, 158; reviews, 158

German use of American books for propaganda, 23

Gide, André: quoted on Faulkner, Steinbeck, Dos Passos, Hemingway, Caldwell, 21-22; return from Algiers after war, 27; satirizes infatuation for psychoanalysis, 168

Glasgow, Ellen, ignored in France, 34

God's Little Acre: translation, 18; exotic appeal, 53; influence on *Un Barrage contre le Pacifique*, 65; preface by Maurois, 146, 147; reviews, 147-48

Gone with the Wind: success in France in 1930's, 22; sales, 22-23; reasons for black market success, 23; on best-seller list for 1946, 30; movie version, 31; success of, in America, 51

Good Earth, The, success in France in 1930's, 22

Grapes of Wrath, The: Gide discusses, 21; permission to print offered to Gallimard during occupation, 23; published during war in Belgium, 23-24; wartime circulation of English and American editions, 24; sixth on list of best sellers for 1947, 34; compared with *Uncle Tom's Cabin*, 79; wartime circulation of Brussels edition, 169; serialized in *Les Lettres Françaises*, 169; sales, 169; reviews, 169-71; movie version, 173

Grappes d'Amertume, see *The Grapes of Wrath*

Grasset, Bernard, publishes *The 42nd Parallel*, 87, 92

Green Bough, The, two poems from, published, 140-41

Green Hills of Africa, The: translation, 18; excerpts published, 20, 104; reviews, 104; quality of translation criticized, 111

Green, Julien, *Moira* a true picture of American life, 84

Grenaud, P., reviews *For Whom the Bell Tolls*, 107-8

Gringoire: short story by Steinbeck, 162; editor on stature of Steinbeck, 162

Guehenno, Jean, reviews *The Old Man and the Sea*, 53

Guérard, Albert J.: *Ecrit aux U.S.A.*, preface, sales, 35; conversation with Marcel Duhamel, 36; comments on postwar years in Paris, 37-38; quoted on Hemingway, 110, 111; compares French and American reception of Faulkner, 135; article on Faulkner, 141; comments on Caldwell, 155-56

Guilleminault, G., reviews *The Grapes of Wrath*, 170

Guterman, N., translation of *The 42nd Parallel*, 87, 88

Guyard, Marius, article on Faulkner, 141

Guyot, Charly: evaluates American novel, 35; comments on Heming-

way, 114; comments on Faulkner,
138; comments on Caldwell, 158

Hammett, Dashiell: treated as Faulk-
ner's equal, 33; published in *Série
Noire*, 37
Hauger, Raymond, quoted on American style, 36
Heine, Maurice, defines *littérature
noire*, 85
Heinemann and Zsolnay, publishes
For Whom the Bell Tolls, 30
Hemingway, Ernest: *Three Stories
and Ten Poems*, 15; *in our time*,
15, 65, 102; *Cinquante mille Dollars*, 16, 99-100; *A Farewell to Arms*,
18, 21, 100-101, 102, 108; *The Sun
Also Rises*, 18; *The Green Hills of
Africa*, 18, 20, 104, 111; *Death in
the Afternoon*, 18, 105; *In Our
Time*, 19; short story published 1937,
20; Gide discusses, 21; *For Whom
the Bell Tolls*, 30, 47, 49, 50, 51,
57, 106-8, 111, 117; reception in
France during postwar period, 31,
106-21; loss of snob appeal, 32;
Paradis perdu, 35, 113, 115; for-
mulator of American style, 36;
Mauriac admires, 50; *The Old
Man and the Sea*, 53, 118-21; influence on French writers, 65; first
French publication, 99; reception
in 1920's, 99-100; *Men without
Women*, 99; reception during
1930's, 100-106; compared with
Proust, 100; compared with Maupassant, 101; *To Have and Have
Not*, 105, 108, 111, 112; compared
with Stendhal, 106; lyricism, 108;
The Fifth Column, 108, 115; *Dix
Indiens*, 109, 113; reasons for popularity, 111-12; *Across the River and
into the Trees*, 115-17; preface
to *Pourquoi ces bêtes sont-elles
sauvages?*, 118; future French publication prospects, 180
Henriot, Emile, interviewed in *Combat enquête*, 50-51
Hertz, H., reviews *God's Little Acre*,
147-48
Homme qui croyait à la chance, L',
see *To Have and Have Not*
Hommes et Mondes, review-article by
Las Vergnas on *This Very Earth*,
159
Hoog, Armand: comments on Henry
Miller, 33; quoted on *To Have and*

Have Not and American optimism,
113
Hoosier Holiday, A, reviewed, 20
Horses and Men, translation, 15
House in the Uplands, A: transla-
tion, 157; reviews, 158
Houville, Gérard d', reviews *A House
in the Uplands*, 158
Humanité, L', article attacking
American literature, 55
Human quality of American novels,
79

Immaturity, American, as seen by
French, 70, 192
Immediacy of American novels, 78
In All Countries: translation, 18;
reviews, 93
In Dubious Battle: translation, 19;
Gide discusses, 21, 163; sales per-
mitted by Germans, 23; review,
162-63
Initiation d'un Homme, L', see *One
Man's Initiation*
in our time, published in Paris, 15
In Our Time, reviewed, 19
Intellectuality lacking in American
novels, 70
Intercultural relationships, 190-91
In the American Grain, by William
Carlos Williams, needing transla-
tion in 1927, 17
Intruder in the Dust: article on
American reception, 139; film ver-
sion shown at Biarritz, 140; trans-
lation, 144; reviews, 144
Intrus, L', see *Intruder in the Dust*

James, Henry, Proust as source for,
50
Jansenism, a factor in French in-
tellectual history, 82
Jarlot, G., reviews *For Whom the
Bell Tolls*, 107
Jausion, Jean, *Un Homme marche
dans la Ville* influenced by Hem-
ingway, 65
Jazz music, influence of, on Ameri-
can novel techniques, 75
J'irai cracher sur vos Tombes, see
Vian, Boris
Jolas, Eugene, on French reading of
American books in 1920's, 17
Journal de Psychologie, article by Le
Breton on Faulkner, 141-42
Journalism, influence on American
writing, 71-72

Journeyman: excerpt published, 150; translation, 158-59; preface by Robert Merle, 159; reviews, 159

Jouve, R.: reviews *The Big Money*, 96; reviews *The Grapes of Wrath*, 170; reviews *The Wayward Bus*, 175

Jouvenel, Renaud de, criticizes American writings of 1930's, 58

Joyce, James: influence on French novel, 13; developed interior monologue, 74

Kanapa, Jean: attacks American literature, 55-57; *Comme si la Lutte entière* influenced by American techniques, 61

Kanters, Robert: quoted on end of vogue for American novels, 52; complains that because of Americans unintelligibility is a virtue, 63; reviews *The Grapes of Wrath*, 169-70; reviews *Cannery Row*, 173

Kessel, Joseph, preface to *Of Mice and Men*, 161-62

Knight's Gambit: translation, 142; reviews, 142

Kreymborg, Alfred, article on, in 1933, 20

Kromer, Tom, short story published, 20

Labyrinthe, short story by Hemingway, 109

Lâchez les Bombes!, see *Bombs Away*

Laffont, Robert: publishes *Ecrit aux U.S.A.*, 35; publishes play version of *Tobacco Road*, 156; publishes play version of *Of Mice and Men*, 168

Lalou, René: attacks literary snobbism, 46; reviews *The Old Man and the Sea*, 120; reviews *Intruder in the Dust*, 144; reviews play version of *Of Mice and Men*, 167; article on Steinbeck, 168-69; reviews *The Grapes of Wrath*, 169; reviews *To a God Unknown*, 177

Lamp at Nightfall, A, soon to be published in French, 160

Language: American, 9, 10, 75-76; French, 9, 10, 41, 75-76; comparisons, 9, 10, 75-76

Lanux, Pierre de, quoted on cultural lag between France and America, 11

Laporte, René, reviews play version of *Of Mice and Men,* 166-67

Laprade, J. de: reviews *Poor Fool,* 153; comments on Steinbeck's plays, 172

Larbaud, Valery, preface to *As I Lay Dying,* 18, 74, 124

la Rochèlle, Drieu: wartime editor of *NRF,* 27, 162; preface to *A Farewell to Arms,* 101

Lartigue, J., reviews *For Whom the Bell Tolls,* 107

Las Vergnas, Raymond: criticizes French readers for their ignorance of the American scene, 36; comments on *For Whom the Bell Tolls,* 108; quoted on Hemingway, 109; comments on Hemingway's prose, 110-11; calls Hemingway the Clark Gable of American literature, 112; comments on reasons for Faulkner's prestige, 137; review-article on *This Very Earth,* 159; article on Steinbeck, 177-78

Lawrence, D. H., puritanism compared to Faulkner's 83-84

Lebesque, Morvan, reviews *Knight's Gambit,* 142

Le Breton, Maurice: article in 1937 on Faulkner, 127; reviews American edition of *Pylon,* 131; article in 1951 on Faulkner, 141-42; present holder of chair in American literature and civilization at the Sorbonne, 184

Leiris, M., reviews *Death in the Afternoon,* 105

Lelis, M., reviews *Tobacco Road,* 148

Lemarchand, Jacques, interviewed in *Combat enquête,* 48

Lemonnier, Léon, quoted on stature of American literature, 20

Lettres Françaises, Les: serializes *The Grapes of Wrath,* 25, 169; article by Kanapa, 55-57; article by Daix, 57; article by Ehrenburg, 57-58; article on Faulkner, 59; short story by Hemingway, 108; short story by Faulkner, 134; short story by Caldwell, 158; short story by Steinbeck, 164

Levinson, A., reviews English edition of *Sanctuary,* 123

Lévy, Y., quoted on Hemingway and morality, 110

Lewis, Sinclair: translation problems in *World So Wide*, 9; translations in 1920's, 16; *Babbitt*, 17; translations in 1930's, 17; regarded as great novelist, 22

Lewisohn, Ludwig, *Expression in America* reviewed, 20

Library, American, in Paris, 183-84

Liebowitz, René, article on Faulkner, 130

Light in August: translation, 18; influenced *Les Stigmates*, 63; preface, 83, 126; excerpt published, 126; American edition reviewed, 126; reviews, 126

Literature, American: nineteenth-century, compared with twentieth, 49; constituted by Whitman, London, Sinclair, and Dos Passos, 52; in French higher education, 184-86

Littéraire, Le, review of *Aperçus de Littérature américaine*, 133-34

Littérature noire: defined, 85; American practice of, 85

Littérature prolétarienne aux Etats-Unis, excerpt from *As I Lay Dying*, 135

Llona, Victor: reviews *Cinquante mille Dollars*, 100; editor of *Les Romanciers américains*, 100

London, Jack: translations between 1918 and 1929, 15; translations in 1930's, 17

Long Valley, The: Gide discusses, 21; reviewed by Lalou, 46; translation, 166; reviews, 166

Lucet, Charles, compares life in Caldwell's books with that in William Byrd's, 151

MacCoy, Horace, published in *Série Noire*, 37

Magasin du Spectacle, prints play version of *Of Mice and Men*, 168

Magazines: influence in American writings, 49; widely read in America, 72

Magnane, Georges, *Gerbe Baude* influenced by *As I Lay Dying*, 62

Magny, Claude Edmonde: *L'Age du Roman américain*, 31, 74, 78, 98, 138; active in defense of Henry Miller, 33; evaluates American novel, 35; interviewed in *Combat enquête*, 51; comments on extent of influence of American writers,

61; parallels techniques of movies and American novels, 74-75; points out popularity of behavioristic psychology in U. S., 78; deplores neglect of Dos Passos, 95; preface to Book Club edition of *The 42nd Parallel*, 97-98; comments on Hemingway, 114; comments on *Pylon*, 131-32; compares Balzac's *Human Comedy* and Yoknapatawpha Saga, 138

Malartic, Yves: *New-York, Ville farouche* influenced by American writers, 66; translation of *Tour of Duty*, 87; translation of *1919*, 87

Malraux, André: preface to *Sanctuary*, 18, 45, 85, 124; *L'Espoir* compared to *For Whom the Bell Tolls*, 49, 50, 106; quoted on American myths, 68; quoted on lack on intellectuality in American novels, 70, 79

Maltz, Albert, books by, reviewed in Communist press, 59

Manhattan Transfer: translation, 15, 90; influence on Jules Romains, 64; excerpts published, 89; American edition reviewed, 89-90; reviews, 90; sales, 90; praised, 91; Tauchnitz edition reviewed, 92; Simon discusses, 94

Marchal, G., reviews *The Pearl*, 176

Marguerat, Editions Jean, *see* Editions Jean Marguerat

Materialism, American: constant in concept of America by French, 189-90; compared with Russian power materialism, 189; novels of *les cinq grands* as force against, 190

Maulnier, Thierry: quoted on status of American novel in France before 1939, 20; interviewed in *Combat enquête*, 52; quoted on decrease of influence of American novel, 52

Maupassant, Guy de: as source for American novelists' attacks on puritanism, 46; influence for American novelists, 50; and Dumas most widely read French writer in America, 51

Mauriac, Claude, comments on Russian reception of movie version of *The Grapes of Wrath*, 179

Mauriac, François: interviewed in

Combat enquête, 50; a modern Jansenist, 82

Maurois, André: comments on Hemingway short story, 100; quoted on Hemingway, 110; preface to *God's Little Acre,* 146, 147; comments on American edition of *Tragic Ground,* 151-52; comments on optimism of American life and pessimism of American literature, 187

Mayoux, Jean Jacques: speech on time in American novel, 38; reviews American edition of *To Have and Have Not,* 105-6; article on time and fate in Faulkner, 137-38; article in 1952 on Faulkner, 144

Meckert, Jean, novel by, signed with American pseudonym, 67

Melville, Herman: book by, reviewed, 20; compared with Steinbeck, 48-49; recent interest in, 73

Men without Women, American edition reviewed, 99

Mercure de France: review of American edition of *Number One,* 95; article by Catel on Steinbeck, 161

Merle, Robert: *Week-end à Zuydcoote* influenced by American writers, 66; preface to *Journeyman,* 159

Michel-Tyl, Ed, translation of *We Are the Living,* 149

Miller, Henry: as part of postwar enthusiasm, 31; Hoog praises, 33; case of, 33-34; adverse comment, 48; compared with Céline, 52; attacked by Kanapa, 55-56; practitioner of *littérature noire,* 85

Minet, P.: reviews *The Grapes of Wrath,* 170; reviews *Cannery Row,* 173

Minuit, Editions de, *see* Editions de Minuit

Moby Dick: untranslated in 1927, 17; recent interest in, 73

Mohrt, Michel: article on American edition of *Across the River and into the Trees,* 116; article on *The Old Man and the Sea,* 119, 120-21; quoted on *The Wild Palms,* 143

Mois, Le: article on Dos Passos, 91-92; article by Acaste on Dos Passos, 94; review of American edition of *Green Hills of Africa,* 104; article on Faulkner, 123

Molitor, André: quoted on new American writers appearing in 1930's, 18; reviews *For Whom the Bell Tolls,* 107

Mondiales, Editions, *see* Editions Mondiales

Monnaie de Singe: explanation of title, 135-36; see *Soldiers' Pay*

Monnerot, Jules, *On meurt les Yeux ouverts* influenced by American writers, 66

Monologue, interior: source in French writings, 46; characteristic of American novels, 73-74

Montalet, R. H. de, article on American reviews of *Across the River and into the Trees,* 116-17

Moon Is Down, The: wartime publications, 24; postwar sales, 24-25; Swiss publication, 28; reviews, 164-65; play version produced, 171

Moral tradition: in French literature, 40, 80-81; lacking in American writing, 51; found in certain American writers, 82

Morel, Robert, reply in *NL enquête,* 42

Mosquitoes: translation, 35; preface, 135; reviews, 136-37

Mouloudji: influenced by Americans, 63; plays role of Dude Lester, 63

Moussinac, Léon, estimates prewar printing of *1919,* 88

Movies, American: French concept of America based on, 16, 188; related to American novel, 65, 74-75

Muller, Henry: translation of article on Dos Passos, 91; translation of poem by Dos Passos, 91; reviews American edition of *Across the River and into the Trees,* 115-16; reviews *The Old Man and the Sea,* 119

Munson, Gorham, article on Faulkner, 123

Nadeau, Maurice: active in defense of Henry Miller, 33; quoted on decline of French novel, 41; reviews *The Old Man and the Sea,* 119-20

Navire d'Argent, short story by Hemingway, 99

Nef, La: article by Lucet on Caldwell, 151; article by Vallette on Caldwell, 154

1919: translation, 18; excerpt pub-

lished, 20; American edition reviewed, 91; reviews, 93-94
Nomadism, called a theme in American literature, 167
Northwest Passage: success in France in 1930's, 22; success in America an indication of search for a past, 51
Notebook, 1926, translation, 15
Nous les Vivants, see *We Are the Living*
Nouvel Age: article by Upton Sinclair on Dos Passos, 91; poem by Dos Passos, 91
Nouvelle Critique: exchange of student letters about Faulkner, 58; attack on Faulkner by Denoreaz, 60
Nouvelle Revue Française: wartime collaboration, 27; reappearance 1953, 27; review of *In All Countries,* 93; short story by Hemingway, 99; advertisement for *Cinquante mille Dollars,* 100; review of *A Farewell to Arms,* 101; review of *Death in the Afternoon,* 105; review of American edition of *To Have and Have Not,* 105; article on Faulkner, 122; short story in 1932 by Faulkner, 123; short story in 1933 by Faulkner, 124; Malraux's preface to *Sanctuary,* 124; article on *Sartoris,* 128; review of American edition of *Tobacco Road,* 146; article on Caldwell, 147; review of *Of Mice and Men,* 162; review of *In Dubious Battle,* 162-63
Nouvelles Littéraires, Les: publications on American literature in 1930's, 19 and *enquête* on *origin* in French novel, 41-43; prize for best French novel, 46-47; review of *1919,* 93; article on Hemingway by Delpech, 104; article compares books on bullfighting by Hemingway and Peyré, 105; short story by Hemingway, 109; article on Hemingway by Las Vergnas, 112; review of American edition of *The Old Man and the Sea,* 120; review of English edition of *Sanctuary,* 123; article on Faulkner, 134; review of *Mosquitoes,* 136; interview with Caldwell, 148-49; review of *Of Mice and Men,* 162
Novels, American, and American life,

relationship as conceived by the French, 186-87
NRF, see *Nouvelle Revue Française*
Nuits Noires, see *The Moon Is Down*
Nuits sans Lune, see *The Moon Is Down*
Number One: reviews of American edition, 95; translation, 180

Obey, André, *Maria* influenced by a Faulkner short story, 63
Objectivity in American novels, 78
Oeuvres Libres, Les, short story by Faulkner, 134
Of Mice and Men: translation, 19; preface by Kessel, 161-62; introduction by Coindreau, 162; reviews, 162; play version produced, 166; reviews of play version, 166-68; play version published and sales, 168; a work of pure classicism, 172-73; de luxe edition, 173-74; play version published in *Paris Théâtre,* 174; published by French Book Club, 174
O'Hara, John, short stories published, 20
O. Henry, short story published in 1933, 20
Old Man and the Sea, The: review by Guehenno, 53; not printed in continental edition of *Life,* 118; account of publication by Gallimard, 118-19; serialized in *Paris-Presse-L'Intransigeant,* 118-19; reviews, 119-21; called one of two best books from America in 1952, 180
One Man's Initiation: translation and sales, 15; excerpt published, 88; reviews, 88-89
Orient Express: reviewed by Coindreau, 89; excerpts published, 89
Overseas Editions, publishes *Bombs Away,* 25

Palmiers sauvages, Les, see *The Wild Palms*
Paradis perdu: published, 35; reviews, 115
Paris-Matin, opening issues serialize *To Have and Have Not,* 108
Parisot, Henri, interviewed in *Combat enquête,* 50
Paris-Presse-L'Intransigeant, serializes *The Old Man and the Sea,* 118-19
Paris Théâtre, publishes play version of *Of Mice and Men,* 174

Parker, Daniel, attacks Henry Miller, 33

Paru: review of American edition of *Number One*, 95; review of play, *Tobacco Road*, 156

Past: absence of, with Americans, 22, 50, 51; burden of, with French, 22, 50

Pastures of Heaven, The: translation, 35; reviews, 174

Pauwels, Louis, *Saint Quelqu'un* influenced by American writers, 66

Paz, Madeleine, preface to French Book Club edition of *Tortilla Flat*, 174

Pazos, José R., article on Dos Passos, 89

Pearl, The: translation, 175; reviews, 175-76

Pessimism: factor in success of American novel, 44; reason for American writers being pessimistic, 52; characteristic of puritan morality, 83; opposed to optimism of American life, 187-88

Petit Arpent du Bon Dieu, Le, see *God's Little Acre*

Petit, G., reviews *One Man's Initiation*, 88-89

Peyre, Henri, comments on importance in French criticism of Benjy's soliloquy in *The Sound and the Fury*, 128

Peyret-Chappuis, Charles de, quoted on decline of the French novel, 40-41

Place Called Estherville, soon to be published, 160

Pocket-books in France, 181

Poe, Edgar Allan: called French, 69; victim of American materialism, 189

Poésie: article by Blanzat comparing Caldwell and Aymé, 65; articles by Magny comparing techniques of movies and American novels, 74-75; short story by Faulkner, 130

Poetic quality in American novel, 73

Poetry, American, influence on French, 13

Poor Fool: translation, 35; adverse reviews, 45; preface by Coindreau, 152; reviews, 152-54

Pouillon, Jean: *Temps et Roman,* 32, 77; discusses Dos Passos, 98; discusses Faulkner, 134; article on *Knight's Gambit,* 142

Poulaille, Henry, interviewed in *Combat enquête,* 52

Pour qui sonne le glas, see *For Whom the Bell Tolls*

Pourquoi ces bêtes sont-elles sauvages?, by Summer, preface by Hemingway, 118

Pré au Clercs, see Editions du Pré au Clercs

Prévost, Jean, preface to *The Sun Also Rises,* 102

Primitivism in American novel: source of exoticism for French, 80; of little importance in French criticism of American novels, 80

Profils, Nobel Prize acceptance speech of Faulkner, 140

Prokosch, Frederick: books by, occasionally reviewed in Communist press, 59; called French, 69

Proust, Marcel: source for Faulkner's use of time, 46; source for Henry James, 50; subjective use of time, 77

Psychoanalysis: popularity in America evidence of immaturity, 84; over-soul of Emerson equated with the unconscious, 161; satirized by Gide in 1920's, 168; all American novelists except Hemingway infatuated with, 168

Psychological analysis, novel of: dominant in France, 12; decline a reason for vogue of American novels, 40-43, 190-91; defined, 70

Puritanism in America: in attacks against, American writers influenced by French, 46; only tradition in America, 50; cause for American desire to hurry, 51; prevalence of, 82-84; present in all American writers except Steinbeck, 114-15; a theme in American literature, 132

Pylon: translation, 131; review of American edition, 131; reviews, 131-32; excerpt published, 131

Queneau, Raymond: *Lion de Rueil* influenced by American writers, 66; preface to *Soldiers' Pay,* 136

Rabi, article on Faulkner, 141

Raimbault, R. N.: translation of *Sanctuary,* 18, 124; translation of *Three Soldiers,* 97; article on publication of *As I Lay Dying,* 124-25;

translation of *Sartoris*, 127; translation of *Pylon*, 131; translation of *The Unvanquished*, 138

Raisins de la Colère, Les, see *The Grapes of Wrath*

Rapin, R., reviews American edition of *Manhattan Transfer*, 89-90

Reasons for success of American novels in France: early success, 25-26; postwar success, 39-44

Réforme: articles on Faulkner, 144; article by Roux on books a French student should read, 179-80

Regionalism: in American and Russian literature, 71; almost ignored by French critics in American writings, 78; American critics attacked for regarding Faulkner as a regionalist, 141

Regnier, Henri de, reviews *Cinquante mille Dollars*, 100

Rémon, Maurice, translation of *1919*, 88

Renaissances, special issue, 29

Reportage: factor in American novel, 51, 70; derived from American novelists' training in journalism, 71-72; Dos Passos as writer of, 96

Requiem for a Nun, reviews of American edition, 142

Revue Anglo-Américaine: reviews of Tauchnitz editions of *Three Soldiers* and *Manhattan Transfer*, 92; review of Tauchnitz edition of *A Farewell to Arms*, 101; review of American edition of *In Our Time*, 103; review of Crosby edition of *Torrents of Spring*, 103; review of Crosby edition of *Sanctuary*, 124; review of American edition of *Light in August*, 126; former outlet for French scholarship in American literature, 185

Revue de Paris: short story by Faulkner, 135; article on Caldwell, 148

Revue Générale, review of *The Sound and the Fury*, 128

Revue Internationale: article by Malcolm Cowley on Faulkner, 134; article by Robert Penn Warren on Faulkner, 134

Revue Nouvelle, La: special issue on "contemporary foreign literatures," 17; review of *One Man's Initiation*, 88-89; biographical sketch of Dos Passos, 89; excerpts from *Manhattan Transfer*, 89; review of and excerpts from *Orient Express*, 89

Revue Nouvelle, La (Brussels), article on Hemingway, 114-15

Rhetoric, American, defined by de Rougement, 72

Richter, Charles de, translation of *The Big Money*, 88

Rieder, F., publishes *One Man's Initiation*, 88

Romains, Jules: source of Dos Passos' simultaneity, 46, 95; influenced by Dos Passos, 64

Romanciers américains, Les, contains articles by and on Dos Passos, 90-91

Romanticism in American novel, 77-78

Roosevelt, Franklin Delano, symbol of greatness of America, 39

Rosmer, Alfred, interviewed in *Combat enquête*, 48

Rougement, Denis de: article on American rhetoric, 72; introduces Faulkner at Salle Gaveau, 145

Rousseaux, André, comments on vogue for Faulkner in France, 133-34

Rousselet, G. L., translation of *Pylon*, 131

Rousset, David, *Les Jours de notre Mort* influenced by Dos Passos, 64

Route au Tabac, La, see *Tobacco Road*

Roux, Michel: reviews *The Grapes of Wrath*, 170; article on books a French student should read, 179-80

Roy, Claude: comments on Dos Passos, 54; criticizes decadent American novels, 57; comments on influence of American writers on French Communists, 61; deplores neglect of Dos Passos, 95

Roy, J.: reviews *Cannery Row*, 173; reviews *The Wayward Bus*, 175

Russian Journal, A: translation, 174; reviews, 174

Russian novel: influence on French, 13; compared with American, 71

Samedi-Soir: article about *J'irai cracher sur vos Tombes*, 67; article about Italian background of *Across the River and into the Trees*, 117; excerpt from *Pylon*, 131; review of *Pylon*, 132; short story in 1946 by Faulkner, 134;

short story in 1947 by Faulkner, 134; review of American edition of *Requiem for a Nun*, 142

Sanctuary: translation, 18; review of Crosby edition, 19; called chef-d'-oeuvre of *littérature noire*, 85; review of English edition, 123; reviews, 124

Sans, Julien: interviews Caldwell, 12; comments on Hemingway, 109-10; comments on Faulkner's greatness, 133; comments on comparative sales of *Poor Fool* in France and U. S., 154; article on *The Grapes of Wrath*, 170-71

Saroyan, William: short story published, 20; part of postwar enthusiasm, 31

Sartoris: translation, 18; reviews, 127-28

Sarte, Jean Paul: quoted on vogue of American novel, 20-21; associated with intellectual postwar vogue of American novels, 32; quoted on reasons for success of American novels, 41, 43; interviewed in *Combat enquête*, 47, comments on influence of American writers, 61, 62; comments on Mouloudji and Americans, 63; influenced by Dos Passos, 64; comments on Hemingway and Jausion, 65; states theme of *The Sound and the Fury*, 77, 128-29; article on Dos Passos, 93-94; considers Dos Passos the greatest writer of our time, 94; article on *Sartoris*, 128

Savitzky, Ludmila, article on Dos Passos, 90-91

Schneider, Marcel, quoted on Hemingway, 110

Schoell, Frank, on French reading of American novels in 1920's, 17

Scholarship, French, on American literature, 185-86

School of writing, American, believed by French to exist, 36, 69

Semaine dans le Monde, Une, review of *The Big Money*, 95

Série Noire: account, 36-37; acceptance of hard-boiled formula, 53; one of sources for French concept of America, 188

Short story: characteristic of American literature, 72-73; an American monopoly since O. Henry, 166

Show Boat, best seller in 1930's, 19

Sigaux, Gilbert, criticizes French readers for their ignorance of American scene, 36

Silence de la Mer, Le, sixth on best seller list for 1946, 30

Sillen, Samuel, treats Mickey Spillane as typical American writer, 60

Simenon, Georges, comments on stature of American novelists, 29

Simon, Jean: quoted on 1930's, 19; comments on vogue of *Gone with the Wind*, 22; *Le Roman américain au XXᵉ Siècle*, 38; comments on Dos Passos and Romains, 64; article on Dos Passos, 94; comments on Hemingway, 114; comments on Faulkner, 139-40; comments on play, *Tobacco Road*, 156; comments on Caldwell, 159; comments on Steinbeck, 177; article on relationship between American political events and reactions of the French writers, 189

Simultaneity of Dos Passos: called valuable for French, 41; allegedly invented by Jules Romains, 46; dissatisfaction with technique, 49

Sinclair, Upton, translations in 1920's, 15; translations in 1930's, 17; article on, in 1933, 20; article on Dos Passos, 91

Slaughter, Frank G., a best-selling author in France, 31

Snobbism, literary: a factor in success of American novels, 32; enthusiasts for American novels accused of, 46

Sociales Internationales, Editions, *see* Editions Sociales Internationales

Social sense in American writers, 79

Solstice, short story by Hemingway, 109

Soldiers' Pay: translation, 35; compared to *Three Soldiers*, 97; excerpt published, 135; reviews, 136

Soleil du Sud, see *Southways*

Sound and the Fury, The: translation problems, 10; theme stated by Sartre, 77; preface by Coindreau, 128; reviews, 128-29

Soupault, Philippe: article on Dos Passos, 92-93; article on Hemingway, 102-3; article on Caldwell and Faulkner, 146-47

Southways, translation, 160

Spillane, Mickey, treated as typical American writer, 60

State of the Nation: translation, 96; reviews, 96-97; compared with travel book by Samuel Butler, 97

Stein, Gertrude, two books by, reviewed, 20

Steinbeck, John: interviewed, 12, 171, 172-73; *Of Mice and Men,* 19, 24, 161-62, 166-68, 173; *In Dubious Battle,* 19, 21, 23, 24, 162-63; Gide discusses, 21; *The Long Valley,* 21, 46, 166; *The Grapes of Wrath,* 21, 23-24, 79, 163, 169-71; wartime enthusiasm of French for, 24-25, 163-64; *The Moon Is Down,* 24-25, 28, 163, 164-65, 171; *Bombs Away,* 25, 163; *Tortilla Flat,* 25, 29, 163, 171; reception during postwar period, 31, 164-78; loss of snob appeal, 32; bracketed with Henry Miller and Cain, 33; *The Pastures of Heaven,* 35, 173, 174; labeled a father of existentialism, 43; compared with Tolstoi, 71; lyric quality, 73; reception during late 1930's, 161-63; compared with D. H. Lawrence and Jean Giono, 162; *Cannery Row,* 171, 173; *A Russian Journal,* 174; *The Wayward Bus,* 174-75; *The Pearl,* 175-76; *To a God Unknown,* 175, 176-77; *Burning Bright,* 177-78; *Cup of Gold,* 178; *East of Eden,* 178; future French publication prospects, 180

Story Teller's Story, The, translation, 15

Stream of consciousness, *see* Monologue, interior

Style, American: formed by Hemingway and Dos Passos in 1920's, 36; conceived by the French, 69-00

Sullivan, Vernon, *see* Vian, Boris

Sun Also Rises, The: translation, 18; influence on *L'Etranger,* 65; preface by Prévost, 102

Sure Hand of God, The, translation, 159

Sur toute la Terre, see *In All Countries*

Symbolism in American novel, existence of, questioned, 45

Table Ronde, La: article on Caldwell's influence, 64; article on *The Old Man and the Sea,* 119, 120-21; two of Faulkner's poems, 140-41; review of *The Wild Palms,* 143

Tandis que j'agonise, see *As I Lay Dying*

Tauchnitz Edition: publishes American books, 19; publishes *Three Soldiers* and *Manhattan Transfer,* 92; publishes *A Farewell to Arms,* 101

Tavernier, René, quoted on Hemingway and America, 109

Taylor, Bayard, origin of interior monologue found in his ballads, 74

Techniques of the American novel: French literature as ultimate source for, 46; similarity to techniques of movies, 74-75; influenced by jazz music, 75; narrative problems, 76

Temps Modernes, Les: special issue, 29; article on Faulkner, 134; article on aesthetics of Faulkner, 139; serializes title story of *The Wild Palms,* 141; preface to *The Wild Palms,* 142

These 13: translation, 18; reviews, 129-30

Thiébaut, Marcel, discusses *God's Little Acre* and *Tobacco Road,* 148

This Very Earth, translation, 159

Thomas, Henri, reviews *In Dubious Battle,* 162-63

Three Soldiers: translation, 35; comment on American edition, 89; review of Tauchnitz edition, 92; comment by Simon, 94; reviews, 97; sales, 97; compared to *Soldiers' Pay,* 97

Three Stories and Ten Poems, published in Paris in 1923, 15

Time in novels: speech by Mayoux on, in American novels, 38; Faulkner, Proust, and, 46; in American novel, 76-77

To a God Unknown: translation, 175, reviews, 176-77

Tobacco Road: translation, 19; de luxe edition, 30, 154; review of American edition, 146; reviews, 148, 150; play version a success in Paris, 156; play version published, 156; sales of play version, 156

To Have and Have Not: reviews of American edition, 105-6; serialized in *Paris-Matin,* 108; quality of translation criticized, 111; reviews, 112-13

Tortilla Flat: translation, 25; published in Switzerland, 29; reviews, 171; radio adaptation, 171

Tour of Duty: translation, 87; almost ignored on publication, 96

Tracy, Don, published in *Série Noire*, 37

Tragedy, Greek: similarities to contemporary American novel, 43, 85-86; Faulkner's tragic sense and, 130; American novelists as the heirs of, 165

Tragic Ground: American edition discussed by Maurois, 152; translation, 157

Translation: problem of, 8-10; lag in, 10

Treize Histoires, see *These 13*

Triolet, Elsa: short stories influenced by Faulkner, 63; works influenced by American writers, 66

Triumph of the Egg, The, translation, 15

Trouble in July: translation, 155-56; reviews, 156; compared with Wright's books, 156

Twelve Men, translation, 15; only translation of Dreiser by 1927, 17

Uncle Tom's Cabin: most popular American book in Europe in nineteenth century, 31; compared with *The Grapes of Wrath,* 79

United States: political and economic position a factor in success of American novel, 39; French concept of, as affected by American novels, 186; sources for French concept of, 188; political events affecting French concept of, 188-89

Universities, French, work in American literature, 184-86

Unvanquished, The: translation, 138; reviews, 138-39

U.S.A.: praised, 54; publishing history, 87-88; called most important novelist enterprise in America, 96

Vagne, Jean, criticizes adversely *Poor Fool* and vogue of American novels, 45, 152

Vallette, Jacques: article on Caldwell, 154; article on Steinbeck, 172

Vian, Boris, *J'irai cracher sur vos Tombes,* 66-67

Vidal, Robert, translation of *A House in the Uplands,* 157

Vieil Homme et la Mer, Le, see *The Old Man and the Sea*

Vivet, J., reviews American edition of *Across the River and into the Trees,* 115

Vorce, Ch. P., translation of *The Unvanquished,* 138

Warren, Robert Penn: article on Faulkner, 134; treated as heir to Faulkner, 180

Wayward Bus, The: translation, 174; reviews of American edition, 174-75; reviews, 175

We Are the Living: translation, 19; preface by Coindreau, 149-50

Weidlé, W., reviews American edition of *The Wayward Bus,* 174-75

Wessberge, E., reviews *Tobacco Road,* 150

Wharton, Edith, translations in 1920's, 16

White, Stewart Edward, read in France, 17

Whitfield, Raoul, published in *Série Noire,* 37

Wild, Roger, contributes to a symposium on Hemingway and Peyré, 105

Wilder, Thornton, called French, 69

Wild Palms, The: title story serialized, 141; translation, 142; preface by Coindreau, 141-42; reviews, 142; called one of two best novels from America in 1952, 180

Williams, William Carlos, *In the American Grain,* 17

Winesburg, Ohio, translation, 15

Wolfe, Thomas; ignored in France, 34; Dostoevski and Joyce as sources, 50

Wolfson, P. J., published in *Série Noire,* 37

Woolf, Virginia, influence on French novel, 13

Wright, Richard: part of postwar enthusiasm, 31; attacked by Kanapa, 56

Yerby, Frank, a best-selling author in France, 31

Zola, Emile: source for American novelists' attacks on puritanism, 46; Americans criticized for their admiration for, 48; source for Frank Norris, 50